Scenarios

1. Accommodation

is there an inexpensive hotel you can recommend?
▶ ¿puede recomendarme un hotel económico?
[pwedeh rekomendarmeh oon otel ekonomiko]

---

desgraciadamente parece que todos están llenos ◀
[desgras-yada-menteh pareseh keh todos estan yenos]
I'm sorry, they all seem to be fully booked

---

can you give me the name of a good middle-range hotel?
▶ ¿me puede dar el nombre de un buen hotel que no sea caro?
[meh pwedeh dar el nombreh deh un bwen otel keh no seh-a karo]

---

déjeme ver ¿prefiere estar en el centro? ◀
[deHemeh ber pref-yereh estar en el sentro]
let me have a look; do you want to be in the centre?

---

if possible
▶ si es posible
[see es poseebleh]

¿le importa estar un poco lejos del centro? ◀
[leh eemporta estar oon poko leHos del sentro]
do you mind being a little way out of town?

---

not too far out
▶ no demasiado lejos
[no demas-yado leHos]

---

where is it on the map?
▶ ¿dónde está en el mapa?
[dondeh esta en el mapa]

---

can you write the name and address down?
▶ ¿puede anotar el nombre y la dirección?
[pwedeh anotar el nombreh ee la deereks-yon]

I'm looking for a room in a private house
▶ busco un cuarto en una casa particular
[boosko oon kwarto en oona kasa parteekoolar]

2. Banks

bank account	la cuenta bancaria	[kwenta bankar-ya]
to change money	cambiar dinero	[kamb-yar deenairo]
cheque	el cheque	[chekeh]
to deposit	depositar	[deposeetar]
dollar	el dólar	[dolar]
peso	el peso	[peso]
pin number	el pin	[peen]
pound	la libra	[leebra]
to withdraw	retirar	[reteerar]

can you change this into pesos?
▶ ¿puede cambiarme esto por pesos?
[pwedeh kamb-yarmeh esto por pesos]

¿cómo quiere el dinero? ◀
[komo k-yaireh el deenairo]
how would you like the money?

small notes
▶ en billetes pequeños
[en bee-yetes peken-yos]

big notes
▶ en billetes grandes
[en bee-yetes grandes]

do you have information in English about opening an account?
▶ ¿tiene información en inglés sobre cómo abrir una cuenta?
[t-yeneh eenformas-yon en eengles sobreh komo abreer oona kwenta]

sí ¿qué tipo de cuenta quiere? ◀
[see keh teepo deh kwenta k-yereh]
yes, what sort of account do you want?

I'd like a checking account
▶ quisiera una cuenta corriente
[kees-yaira oona kwenta korr-yenteh]

permítame su pasaporte, por favor ◀
[pairmeetameh soo pasaporteh por fabor]
your passport, please

can I use this card to draw some cash?
▶ ¿puedo sacar dinero con esta tarjeta?
[pwedo sakar deenairo kon esta tarHeta]

tiene que pasar a la caja ◀
[t-yeneh keh pasar ala kaHa]
you have to go to the cashier's desk

I want to transfer this to my account at the Banco de Comercio
▶ quisiera hacer una transferencia a mi cuenta en el Banco de Comercio
[kees-yaira asair oona transferens-ya a mee kwenta en el banko deh komers-yo]

con todo gusto, pero tendremos que cobrarle la llamada ◀
[kon todo goosto pero tendremos keh kobrarleh la yamada]
OK, but we'll have to charge you for the phonecall

3. Booking a room

shower	la regadera	[regadera]
telephone in the room	teléfono en el cuarto	[telefono en el kwarto]
payphone in the lobby	teléfono público en el vestíbulo	[telefono poobleeko en el besteeboolo]

do you have any rooms?
▶ ¿tiene cuartos libres?
[t-yeneh kwartos leebres]

▶ ¿para cuántas personas?　　　**for one/for two**
[para kwantas pairsonas]　　　　▶ para una/para dos
for how many people?　　　　[para oona/para dos]

　　　　　　　　　　　sí, tenemos cuartos libres ◀
　　　　　　　　　　　[see tenemos kwartos leebres]
　　　　　　　　　　　　　　yes, we have rooms

▶ ¿para cuántas noches?　　　**just for one night**
[para kwantas noches]　　　　▶ sólo para una noche
for how many nights?　　　　[solo para oona nocheh]

how much is it?
▶ ¿cuánto es?
[kwanto es]

　　　　　90 pesos con baño y 70 sin baño ◀
　　　　[nobenta pesos kon ban-yo ee setenta seen ban-yo]
　　90 pesos with bathroom and 70 without bathroom

does that include breakfast?
▶ ¿está incluido el desayuno?
[esta eenkloo-eedo el desa-yoono]

can I see a room with bathroom?
▶ ¿puedo ver un cuarto con baño?
[pwedo bair oon kwarto kon ban-yo]

ok, I'll take it
▶ está bien, lo voy a tomar
[esta b-yen lo boy a tomar]

when do I have to check out?
▶ ¿a qué hora hay que desocupar?
[a keh ora ī keh desokoopar]

is there anywhere I can leave luggage?
▶ ¿tiene dónde dejar el equipaje?
[t-yeneh dondeh deHar el ekeepaHeh]

4. Car hire

automatic	automático	[owtomateeko]
full tank	depósito lleno	[deposeeto yeno]
manual	manual	[manwal]
rented car	el coche alquilado	[kocheh alkeelado]

I'd like to rent a car
▶ quisiera alquilar un auto
[kees-yaira alkeelar oon owto]

▶ ¿por cuánto tiempo?
[por kwanto t-yempo]
for how long?

two days
▶ dos días
[dos dee-as]

I'll take the ...
▶ me llevo el ...
[meh yebo el ...]

is that with unlimited mileage?
▶ ¿es sin límite de kilómetros?
[es seen leemeeteh deh keelometros]

sí ◀
[see]
yes

¿me permite su licencia por favor? ◀
[meh pairmeeteh soo leesens-ya por fabor]
can I see your driving licence, please?

y su pasaporte ◀
[ee soo pasaporteh]
and your passport

is insurance included?
▶ ¿está incluido el seguro?
[esta eenkl-ooeedo el segooro]

sí, pero usted tendría que pagar los primeros cien pesos ◀
[see pairo oosteh tendreea keh pagar los preemairos s-yen pesos]
yes, but you have to pay the first 100 pesos

¿puede dejar una fianza de cien pesos? ◀
[pwedeh deHar oona fee-ansa deh s-yen pesos]
can you leave a deposit of 100 pesos?

and if this office is closed, where do I leave the keys?
▶ y si esta oficina está cerrada ¿dónde dejo las llaves?
[ee see esta ofeeseena esta serrada dondeh deHo las yabes]

las pone en esa caja ◀
[las poneh en esa kaHa]
you drop them in that box

5. Communications

ADSL modem	el módem ADSL	[modem a-deh-eseh-eleh]
at	arroba	[arroba]
dial-up modem	el módem de discado	[modem deh deeskado]
dot	punto	[poonto]
Internet	internet	[eentairnet]
mobile (phone)	el celular	[seloolar]
password	la contraseña	[kontrasen-ya]
telephone socket adaptor	el adaptador para el teléfono	[adaptador para el teléfono]
wireless hotspot	el punto de acceso inalámbrico	[poonto deh akseso eenalambreeko]

is there an Internet café around here?
▶ ¿hay por aquí un cibercafé?
[ī por akee oon seebairkafeh]

can I send email from here?
▶ ¿puedo mandar emails desde aquí?
[pwedo mandar eemayls desdeh akee]

where's the at sign on the keyboard?
▶ ¿dónde está la arroba en el teclado?
[dondeh esta la arroba en el teklado]

can you switch this to a UK keyboard?
▶ ¿se puede cambiar a teclado británico?
[seh pwedeh kamb-yar a teklado breetaneeko]

can you help me log on?
▶ ¿me puede ayudar a conectarme?
[meh pwedeh a-yoodar a konektarmeh]

I'm not getting a connection, can you help?
▶ no está conectando ¿puede ayudarme?
[no esta konektando pwedeh a-yoodarmeh]

where can I get a top-up card for my mobile?
▶ ¿dónde puedo comprar una tarjeta para el celular?
[dondeh pwedo komprar oona tarHeta para el seloolar]

can you put me through to ...?
▶ ¿puede ponerme con ...?
[pwedeh ponairmeh kon ...]

zero	five
cero	cinco
[sero]	[seenko]
one	six
uno	seis
[oono]	[says]
two	seven
dos	siete
[dos]	[s-yeteh]
three	eight
tres	ocho
[tres]	[ocho]
four	nine
cuatro	nueve
[kwatro]	[nwebeh]

6. Directions

hi, I'm looking for Calle Real
▶ hola, estoy buscando la Calle Real
[**o**la est**oy** boosk**a**ndo la k**a**-yeh reh-**al**]

disculpe, no la conozco ◀
[deesk**oo**lpeh no la kon**o**sko]
sorry, never heard of it

hi, can you tell me where Calle Real is?
▶ hola, ¿me puede decir dónde queda la
Calle Real?
[**o**la meh pw**e**deh des**ee**r d**o**ndeh k**e**da la k**a**-yeh reh-**al**]

yo tampoco soy de aquí ◀
[yo tamp**o**ko soy deh ak**ee**]
I'm a stranger here too

hi, Calle
Real, do
you know
where it is?
hola, ¿sabe
dónde
queda la
Calle Real?
[**o**la s**a**beh
d**o**ndeh k**e**da
la k**a**-yeh
reh-**al**]

where?
¿dónde?
[d**o**ndeh]

which direction?
¿por dónde?
[por d**o**ndeh]

▶ a la vuelta de la esquina
[a la bw**e**lta deh la esk**ee**na]
around the corner

▶ entonces es la primera calle a la derecha
[ent**o**nses es la preem**ai**ra ka-yeh a la der**e**cha]
then it's the first street on the right

▶ a la izquierda en el segundo semáforo
[a la eesk-y**ai**rda en el seg**oo**ndo sem**a**foro]
left at the second traffic lights

a la derecha [a la der**e**cha] **on the right**	calle [k**a**-yeh] **street**	justo después [H**oo**sto despw**e**s] **just after**	todo derecho [t**o**do der**e**cho] **straight ahead**
a la izquierda [a la eesk-y**ai**rda] **on the left**	cerca [s**ai**rka] **near**	más allá [mas a-y**a**] **further**	voltee [bolt**eh**-eh] **turn off**
allí [a-y**ee**] **over there**	delante de [del**a**nteh deh] **in front of**	pasado el... [pas**a**do el...] **past the ...**	
atrás [atr**a**s] **back**	en frente de [en fr**e**nteh deh] **opposite**	siguiente [seeg-y**e**nteh] **next**	

download these scenarios as MP3s from:

7. Emergencies

accident	el accidente	[akseed**e**nteh]
ambulance	la ambulancia	[amboolans-ya]
consul	el cónsul	[k**o**nsool]
embassy	la embajada	[embaH**a**da]
fire brigade	los bomberos	[bomb**ai**ros]
police	la policía	[poleess**ee**-a]

help!
▶ ¡socorro!
[sok**o**rro]

can you help me?
▶ ¿puede ayudarme?
[pw**e**deh a-yood**a**rmeh]

please come with me! it's really very urgent
▶ ¡por favor, venga conmigo! es muy urgente
[por fab**o**r b**e**nga konm**ee**go es mwee oorH**e**nteh]

I've lost (my keys)
▶ perdí (las llaves)
[pairdee (las y**a**bes)]

(my car) is not working
▶ (mi auto) no funciona
[(mee **ow**to) no foons-y**o**na]

(my purse) has been stolen
▶ me robaron (el monedero)
[meh rob**a**ron (el moned**ai**ro)]

I've been mugged
▶ me asaltaron
[meh asalt**a**ron]

¿cómo se llama? ◀
[k**o**mo seh y**a**ma]
what's your name?

¿me permite su pasaporte? ◀
[meh pairm**ee**teh soo pasap**o**rteh]
I need to see your passport

I'm sorry, all my papers have been stolen
▶ disculpe, me robaron todos los documentos
[deesk**oo**lpeh meh rob**a**ron t**o**dos los dokoom**e**ntos]

8. Friends

hi, how're you doing?
▶ hola ¿cómo estás?
[**o**la **ko**mo est**a**s]

muy bien ¿y tú? ◀
[mwee b-yen ee too]
OK, and you?

yeah, fine   not bad
▶ bien   ▶ aquí ando
[b-yen]   [ak**ee a**ndo]

d'you know Antonio?
▶ ¿conoces a Antonio?
[kon**o**ses a ant**o**n-yo]

and this is Marta   sí, ya nos conocíamos ◀
▶ y ésta es Marta   [see ya nos konos**ee**-amos]
[ee **e**sta es m**a**rta]   yeah, we know each other

where do you know each other from?
▶ ¿cómo se conocieron?
[**ko**mo seh konos-y**e**ron]

nos conocimos en casa de Gonzalo ◀
[nos konos**ee**mos en **ka**sa deh gons**a**lo]
we met at Gonzalo's place

that was some party, eh?   ▶ fabulosa
▶ la fiesta estuvo buenísima, ¿no?   [fabool**o**sa]
[la f-y**e**sta est**oo**bo bwen**ee**seema no]   the best

are you guys coming for a beer?
▶ ¿vienen a tomar una cerveza?
[b-y**e**nen a tom**a**r **oo**na sairb**e**sa]

▶ genial, vamos   ▶ no, quedé con Carolina
[Hen-yal b**a**mos]   [no ked**eh** kon karol**ee**na]
cool, let's go   no, I'm meeting Carolina

see you at Gonzalo's place tonight   hasta luego ◀
▶ nos vemos esta noche en casa de Gonzalo   [**a**sta lw**e**go]
[nos b**e**mos **e**sta n**o**cheh en **ka**sa deh gons**a**lo]   see you

            download these scenarios as MP3s from:

9. Health

I'm not feeling very well
▶ no me siento bien
[no meh s-yento b-yen]

can you get a doctor?
▶ ¿puede llamar a un médico?
[pwedeh yamar a oon medeeko]

¿dónde le duele? ◀
[dondeh leh dweleh]
where does it hurt?

it hurts here
▶ me duele aquí
[meh dweleh akee]

▶ ¿es un dolor constante?
[es oon dolor konstanteh]
is the pain constant?

it's not a constant pain
▶ no es un dolor constante
[no es oon dolor konstanteh]

can I make an appointment?
▶ ¿puedo hacer una cita?
[pwedo asair oona seeta]

can you give me something for ...?
▶ ¿puede darme algo para ...?
[pwedeh darmeh algo para]

yes, I have insurance
▶ sí, tengo seguro
[see tengo segooro]

antibiotics	el antibiótico	[anteeb-yoteeko]
antiseptic ointment	la pomada antiséptica	[pomada anteesepteeka]
cystitis	la cistitis	[seesteetees]
dentist	el dentista	[denteesta]
diarrhoea	la diarrea	[d-yarreh-a]
doctor	el médico	[medeeko]
hospital	el hospital	[ospeetal]
ill	enfermo	[enfairmo]
medicine	la medicina	[medeeseena]
painkillers	analgésicos	[analHeseekos]
pharmacy	la farmacia	[farmas-ya]
to prescribe	recetar	[resetar]
thrush	las aftas	[aftas]

10. Language difficulties

a few words	unas palabras	[**oo**nas pal**a**bras]
interpreter	el intérprete	[eent**ai**rpreteh]
to translate	traducir	[tradoos**ee**r]

le rechazaron la tarjeta de crédito ◀
[leh recha**sa**ron la tarнeta deh kr**e**deeto]
your credit card has been refused

---

what, I don't understand; do you speak English?
▶ ¿cómo? no entiendo; ¿habla usted inglés?
[**ko**mo no ent-**ye**ndo **a**bla oost**eh e**engl**e**s]

esto no es válido ◀
[**e**sto no es b**a**leedo]
this isn't valid

---

could you say that again?
▶ ¿puede repetir?
[pw**e**deh repet**ee**r]

slowly
▶ despacio
[desp**a**s-yo]

I understand very little Spanish
▶ entiendo muy poco español
[ent-**ye**ndo mwee p**o**ko espan-y**o**l]

I speak Spanish very badly
▶ hablo español muy mal
[**a**blo espan-y**o**l mwee mal]

no puede pagar con esta tarjeta ◀
[no pw**e**deh pag**a**r kon **e**sta tarнeta]
you can't use this card to pay

▶ ¿entiende?
[ent-**ye**ndeh]
do you understand?

sorry, no
▶ me temo que no
[meh **te**mo keh no]

---

is there someone who speaks English?
▶ ¿hay alguien que hable inglés?
[ī **a**lgen keh **a**bleh **e**engles]

oh, now I understand
▶ ah, ahora entiendo
[ah a-**o**ra ent-**ye**ndo]

is that ok now?
▶ ¿ya está bien?
[ya est**a** b-yen]

download these scenarios as MP3s from:

11. Meeting people

hello
▶ hola
[**o**la]

---

hola, me llamo Blanca ◀
[**o**la meh **y**amo bl**a**nka]
hello, my name's Blanca

Graham, from England, Thirsk
▶ soy Graham, de Thirsk, Inglaterra
[soy graham deh thirsk eenglat**ai**rra]

---

no lo conozco ¿dónde está? ◀
[no lo kon**o**sko d**o**ndeh est**a**]
don't know it, where is it?

---

not far from York, in the North; and where are you from?
▶ cerca de York, en el norte ¿de dónde es usted?
[s**e**rka deh york en el n**o**rteh deh d**o**ndeh es **oo**steh]

---

soy de Lima; ¿está aquí solo? ◀
[soy deh l**ee**ma; est**a** ak**ee** s**o**lo]
I'm from Lima; here by yourself?

---

no, I'm with my wife and two kids
▶ no, vengo con mi mujer y mis dos hijos
[no b**e**ngo kon mee moo**H**air ee mees dos **ee**Hos]

---

what do you do?
▶ ¿a qué se dedica?
[a keh seh ded**ee**ka]

a la informática ◀
[a la eenform**a**teeka]
I'm in computers

---

me too
▶ yo también
[yo tamb-**ye**n]

---

here's my wife now
▶ aquí viene mi mujer
[ak**ee** b-**ye**neh mee moo**H**air]

---

encantada de conocerla ◀
[enkant**a**da deh konos**ai**rla]
nice to meet you

---

12. Post offices

airmail	correo aéreo	[korreh-o a-airay-o]
post card	la postal	[postal]
post office	Correos	[korreh-os]
stamp	la estampilla	[estampeeya]

---

what time does the post office close?
▶ ¿a qué hora cierra el correo?
[a keh ora s-yairra el korreh-o]

a las cinco entre semana ◀
[a las seenko entreh semana]
five o'clock weekdays

---

is the post office open on Saturdays?
▶ ¿el correo abre los sábados?
[el korreh-o abreh los sabados]

hasta mediodía ◀
[asta med-yodee-a]
till midday

I'd like to send this registered to England
▶ quisiera mandar esto certificado a Inglaterra
[kees-yaira mandar esto sairteefeekado a eenglatairra]

---

sí, claro, son 10 pesos ◀
[see klaro son d-yes pesos]
certainly, that will cost 10 pesos

---

and also two stamps for England, please
▶ y también dos estampillas para Inglaterra, por favor
[ee tamb-yen dos estampee-yas para eenglatairra por fabor]

---

do you have some airmail stickers?
▶ ¿tiene adhesivos de correo aéreo?
[t-yeneh adeseebos deh korreh-o a-airay-o]

---

do you have any mail for me?
▶ ¿tiene correo para mí?
[t-yeneh korreh-o para mee]

---

cartas	letters
lista de correos	poste restante
paquetes	parcels

13. Restaurants

bill	la cuenta	[kw**e**nta]
menu	la carta	[k**a**rta]
table	la mesa	[m**e**sa]

can we have a non-smoking table?
▶ ¿nos da una mesa para no fumadores?
[nos da **oo**na m**e**sa para no foomad**o**res]

there are two of us
▶ somos dos
[s**o**mos dos]

there are four of us
▶ somos cuatro
[s**o**mos kw**a**tro]

what's this?
▶ ¿qué es esto?
[keh es **e**sto]

es pescado ◀
[es pesk**a**do]
it's fish

es una especialidad de la zona ◀
[es **oo**na espes-yale**e**da deh la s**o**na]
it's a local speciality

pase y se lo enseño ◀
[p**a**seh ee seh lo ens**e**n-yo]
come inside and I'll show you

we would like two of these, one of these, and one of those
▶ queremos dos de éstos, uno de éstos y uno de aquéllos
[ker**e**mos dos deh **e**stos **oo**no deh **e**stos ee **oo**no deh ak**eh**-yos]

▶ ¿y para beber?
[ee p**a**ra beb**ai**r]
and to drink?

red wine
▶ vino tinto
[b**ee**no t**ee**nto]

white wine
▶ vino blanco
[b**ee**no bl**a**nko]

a beer and two orange juices
▶ una cerveza y dos jugos de naranja
[**oo**na sairb**e**sa ee dos H**oo**gos deh naran**H**a]

some more bread please
▶ más pan, por favor
[mas pan por fab**o**r]

▶ ¿cómo estuvo la comida?
[k**o**mo est**oo**bo la kom**ee**da]
how was your meal?

excellent!, very nice!
▶ ¡ estupenda! ¡muy buena!
[estoop**e**nda mwee bw**e**na]

▶ ¿algo más?
[**a**lgo mas]
anything else?

just the bill thanks
▶ sólo la cuenta, por favor
[s**o**lo la kw**e**nta por fab**o**r]

14. Shopping

¿en qué puedo servirle? ◀
[en keh **pwe**do sair**beer**leh]
can I help you?

can I just have a look around?
▶ quiero mirar nada más
[k-**yai**ro meerar **n**ada mas]

yes, I'm looking for ...
▶ sí, estoy buscando ...
[see es**toy** boos**k**ando]

how much is this?
▶ ¿cuánto vale esto?
[**k**wanto **b**aleh **e**sto]

treinta y dos pesos ◀
[**tray**nta ee dos **pe**sos]
thirty-two pesos

OK, I think I'll have to leave it; it's a little too expensive for me
▶ está bien, no me lo llevo; es demasiado caro para mí
[es**ta** b-yen no meh lo **ye**bo es demas-**ya**do **k**aro **p**ara mee]

¿y esto? ◀
[ee **e**sto]
how about this?

can I pay by credit card?
▶ ¿puedo pagar con tarjeta de crédito?
[**pwe**do pa**ga**r kon tar**н**eta deh kre**dee**to]

it's too big
▶ es demasiado grande
[es demas-**ya**do **gra**ndeh]

it's too small
▶ es demasiado pequeño
[es demas-**ya**do pe**ken**-yo]

it's for my son – he's about this high
▶ es para mi hijo – es más o menos así de alto
[es **p**ara mee **ee**нo es mas o **me**nos a**se**e deh **a**lto]

▶ ¿va a querer algo más?
[ba a ker**air a**lgo mas]
will there be anything else?

that's all thanks
▶ eso es todo, gracias
[**e**so es **to**do gras-yas]

make it twenty pesos and I'll take it
▶ si me lo deja en veinte pesos me lo llevo
[see meh lo **de**нa en **ba**ynteh **pe**sos meh lo **ye**bo]

fine, I'll take it
▶ bien, me lo llevo
[b-yen meh lo **ye**bo]

abierto	caja	cambiar	cerrado	rebajas
open	**cash desk**	**to exchange**	**closed**	**sale**

download these scenarios as MP3s from:

15. Sightseeing

art gallery	la galería de arte	[galairee-a deh arteh]
bus tour	el tour en camión	[toor en kam-yon]
city centre	el centro	[sentro]
closed	cerrado	[serrado]
guide	la guía	[gee-a]
museum	el museo	[mooseh-o]
open	abierto	[ab-yairto]

I'm interested in seeing the old town
▶ quisiera ver el casco antiguo
[kees-yaira bair el kasko anteegwo]

are there guided tours?
▶ ¿hay visitas guiadas?
[ī beeseetas gee-adas]

disculpe, está completo ◀
[deekoolpeh esta kompleto]
I'm sorry, it's fully booked

how much would you charge to drive us around for four hours?
▶ ¿cuánto nos cobra por un paseo en auto de cuatro horas?
[kwanto nos kobra por oon paseh-o en owto deh kwatro oras]

can we book tickets for the concert here?
▶ ¿podemos reservar aquí los boletos para el concierto?
[podemos resairbar akee los boletos para el kons-yairto]

▶ sí ¿a qué nombre?   ▶ ¿qué tarjeta de crédito?
[see a keh nombreh]   [keh tarHeta deh kredeeto]
yes, in what name?   which credit card?

where do we get the tickets?   recójanlos en la entrada ◀
▶ ¿dónde nos dan los boletos?   [rekoHanlos en la entrada]
[dondeh nos dan los boletos]   just pick them up at the entrance

is it open on Sundays?   how much is it to get in?
▶ ¿abren los domingos?   ▶ ¿cuánto cuesta la entrada?
[abren los domeengos]   [kwanto kwesta la entrada]

are there reductions for groups of 6?
▶ ¿hay rebaja para grupos de 6?
[ī rebaHa para groopos deh says]

that was really impressive!
▶ ¡estuvo impresionante!
[estoobo eempres-yonanteh]

16. Trains

to change trains	hacer correspondencia	[asair korrespondensee-ya]
platform	el andén	[andén]
return	el boleto de ida y vuelta	[boleto deh eeda ee bwelta]
single	el boleto de ida	[boleto deh eeda]
station	la estación	[estas-yon]
stop	la parada	[parada]
ticket	el boleto	[boleto]

how much is ...?
▶ ¿cuánto es ...?
[kwanto es]

a single, second class to ...
▶ un boleto de ida, en clase turista a ...
[oon boleto deh eeda en klaseh tooreesta a]

two returns, second class to ...
▶ dos boletos de ida y vuelta, en clase turista a ...
[dos boletos deh eeda ee bwelta en klaseh tooreesta a]

for today	**for tomorrow**	**for next Tuesday**
▶ para hoy	▶ para mañana	▶ para el próximo martes
[para oy]	[para man-yana]	[para el prokseemo martes]

¿quiere reservar el asiento? ◀
[k-yaireh resairbar el as-yento]
do you want to make a seat reservation?

tiene que hacer correspondencia en Córdoba ◀
[t-yeneh keh asair korrespondens-ya en kordoba]
you have to change at Córdoba

what time is the last train to Santiago?
▶ ¿a qué hora es el último tren para Santiago?
[a keh ora es el oolteemo tren para santee-ago]

is this seat free?
▶ ¿está libre este asiento?
[esta leebreh esteh as-yento]

excuse me, which station are we at?
▶ disculpe, ¿en qué estación estamos?
[deeskoolpeh en keh estas-yon estamos]

is this where I change for Santa Fe?
▶ ¿es aquí donde tengo que hacer correspondencia para Santa Fe?
[es akee dondeh tengo keh asair korrespondens-ya para santa feh]

English → Spanish

(For words with *, see **How the Language Works**, p. 271 onwards)

A
—

a, an* un [oon], una [oona]

about: about 20 unos veinte

  it's about 5 o'clock son aproximadamente las cinco [aprokseemadamenteh]

  a film about Mexico una película sobre México [sobreh]

above ... arriba de ... [arreeba deh]

abroad en el extranjero [estranHairo]

absolutely! (I agree) ¡claro!

accelerator el acelerador [aselairador]

accept aceptar [aseptar]

accident el accidente [akseedenteh]

  there's been an accident hubo un accidente [oobo]

accommodation alojamiento [aloHam-yento]

accurate exacto

ache el dolor

  my back aches me duele la espalda [meh dweleh]

across: across the road al otro lado de la calle [ka-yeh]

adapter el adaptador

address la dirección [deereks-yon]

  what's your address? ¿cuál es su dirección? [kwal]

address book la libreta de direcciones [deh deereks-yon-es]

admission charge la entrada

adult el adulto [adoolto], la adulta

advance: in advance por adelantado

aeroplane el avión [ab-yon]

after después (de) [despwes (deh)]

  after you pase usted [paseh oosteh]

  after lunch después de comer

afternoon la tarde [tardeh]

  in the afternoon por la tarde

  this afternoon esta tarde

aftershave el aftershave

aftersun cream la crema para después del sol [despwes]

afterwards luego [lwego]

again otra vez [bes]

against contra

age la edad [eda]

ago: a week ago hace una semana [aseh]

agree: I agree de acuerdo [deh akwairdo]

AIDS el sida [seeda]

air el aire [Ireh]

  by air en avión [ab-yon]

air-conditioned climatizado [kleemateesado]

air-conditioning el aire acondicionado [Ireh akondees-yonado]

airmail: by airmail por avión [ab-yon]

airmail envelope el sobre aéreo [sobreh a-aireh-o]

airplane el avión [ab-yon]

airport el aeropuerto [a-airopwairto]

  to the airport, please al aeropuerto, por favor [fabor]

airport bus el autobús del aeropuerto [owtoboos]

aisle seat el asiento al lado de pasillo [as-yento – deh pasee-yo]

alarm clock el despertador

alcohol el alcohol [alkol]

alcoholic alcohólico

all: all the boys todos los chicos

all the girls todas las chicas

all of it/them todo/todos

that's all eso es todo

allergic: I'm allergic to ... tengo alergia a ... [alairHee-a]

alligator el caimán [kiman]

allowed: is it allowed? ¿se permite? [seh pairmeeteh]

all right! ¡bueno! [bweno]

I'm all right estoy bien [b-yen]

are you all right? (fam) ¿estás bien?

(pol) ¿se encuentra bien? [seh enkwentra]

almond la almendra

almost casi

alone solo

alphabet el alfabeto

a a	n eneh
b beh larga	ñ en-yeh
c seh	o o
ch cheh	p peh
d deh	q koo
e eh	r airreh
f efeh	s eseh
g Heh	t teh
h acheh	u oo
i ee	v beh cheeka
j Hota	w dobleh-oobeh
k ka	x ekees
l eleh	y ee gr-yega
m emeh	z seta

already ya

also también [tamb-yen]

although aunque [ownkeh]

altogether del todo

always siempre [s-yempreh]

am*: I am soy; estoy

a.m.: at seven a.m. a las siete de la mañana [deh la man-yana]

amazing (surprising) increíble [eenkreh-eebleh]

(very good) extraordinario [estra-ordeenar-yo]

ambulance la ambulancia [amboolans-ya]

call an ambulance! ¡llame a una ambulancia! [yameh]

America Estados Unidos

American el norteamericano [norteh-amaireekano]

(woman) la norteamericana, el/la estadounidense [estado-ooneedenseh],

(Arg) el/la yanqui [yankee]

(adj) norteamericano, estadounidense,

(Arg) yanqui

I'm American (man/woman) soy norteamericano/norteamericana

among entre [entreh]

amount la cantidad [kanteeda]

(money) la suma

amp: a 13-amp fuse el fusible de trece amperios [fooseebleh deh – ampairee-os]

and y [ee]

Andes los Andes [and-es]

angry enojado [enoHado]

animal el animal

ankle el tobillo [tobee-yo]

anniversary (wedding) el
aniversario de boda
[aneebairsar-yo deh]

annoy: this man's annoying
me este hombre me está
molestando [esteh ombreh
meh]

annoying molesto,
(Col, Ven) cansón

another otro

can we have another room?
¿puede darnos otro cuarto?
[pwedeh – kwarto]

another beer, please otra
cerveza, por favor [fabor]

antibiotics los antibióticos
[anteeb-yoteekos]

antifreeze el anticongelante
[anteekonHelanteh]

antihistamines los
antihistamínicos [antee-
eestameeneekos]

antique: is it an antique? ¿es
antiguo? [anteegwo]

antique shop la tienda de
antigüedades [t-yenda deh
anteegwedad-es]

antiseptic el antiséptico

any: have you got any
bread/tomatoes? ¿tiene
pan/tomates? [t-yeneh]

do you have any? ¿tiene?

sorry, I don't have any lo
siento, no tengo [s-yento]

anybody cualquiera [kwalk-
yaira]

does anybody speak English?
¿alguien habla inglés? [algen
abla eeng-les]

there wasn't anybody there
(allí) no había nadie
[(a-yee) no abee-a nad-yeh]

anything algo
(negative) nada

dialogues

anything else? ¿algo
más?
nothing else, thanks nada
más, gracias [gras-yas]

would you like anything
to drink? ¿quiere algo de
beber? [k-yaireh – deh
bebair]
I don't want anything,
thanks no quiero nada,
gracias [k-yairo]

apart from aparte de [aparteh
deh]

apartment el departamento

appendicitis la apendicitis
[apendeeseetees]

appetizer aperitivo,
(Mex) la botana

aperitif el aperitivo
[apereeteebo]

apologize: I apologize
disculpe [deeskoolpeh]

apology la disculpa

apple la manzana [mansana]

appointment la cita [seeta]

dialogue

good afternoon, sir, how can I help you? buenas tardes, señor, ¿en qué puedo servirle? [bwenas tard-es sen-yor, en keh pwedo sairbeerleh]

I'd like to make an appointment quisiera hacer una cita [kees-yaira asair oona seeta]

what time would you like? ¿a qué hora le conviene? [keh ora leh konb-yeneh]

three o'clock a las tres

I'm afraid that's not possible, is four o'clock all right? me temo que no será posible, ¿está bien a las cuatro? [keh no saira poseebleh – b-yen]

yes, that's fine sí, está bien

the name was ...? ¿su nombre ...? [nombreh]

---

apricot el albaricoque, (Mex) el chabacano, (CSur) el damasco

April abril

are*: we are somos; estamos
  you are (fam) eres [air-es], sos; estás
  (pol) es; está
  they are son; están

area la zona [sona]

area code el prefijo [prefeeHo]

Argentina Argentina [arHenteena]

Argentine (adj) argentino [arHenteeno]
  (man) el argentino
  (woman) la argentina

arm el brazo [braso]

arrange: will you arrange it for us? ¿nos lo organiza usted? [organeesa oosteh]

arrival la llegada [yegada]

arrive llegar [yegar]
  when do we arrive? ¿cuándo llegamos? [kwando yegamos]
  has my fax arrived yet? ¿llegó ya mi fax? [yego]
  we arrived today llegamos hoy [yegamos oy]

art el arte [arteh]

art gallery la galería de arte [galeree-a deh]

artist (man/woman) el pintor, la pintora

as: as big as tan grande como
  as soon as possible lo más pronto posible [poseebleh]

ashtray el cenicero [seneesairo]

ask preguntar
  to ask for pedir
  I didn't ask for this no pedí esto
  could you ask him to ...? ¿puede decirle que ...? [pwedeh deseerleh keh]

asleep: she's asleep está dormida

aspirin la aspirina

asthma el asma

astonishing increíble [eenkreh-eebleh]

at: at the hotel en el hotel

at the station en la estación
at six o'clock a las seis
at Pedro's en casa de Pedro
(Rpl) en lo de Pedro
athletics el atletismo
Atlantic Ocean el Océano
Atlántico [oseh-ano]
attractive atractivo [atrakteebo]
aubergine la berenjena
[berenHena]
August agosto
aunt la tía
Australia Australia [owstral-ya]
Australian (adj) australiano
I'm Australian (man/woman) soy
australiano/australiana
automatic automático
[owtomateeko]
automatic teller el cajero
automático [kaHairo]
autumn el otoño [oton-yo]
in the autumn en otoño
avenue la avenida [abeneeda]
average (ordinary) normal
[nor-mal]
(not good) regular [regoolar]
on average por término
medio [tairmeeno med-yo]
avocado el aguacate
[agwakateh],
(Bol, CSur, Pe) palta
awake: is he awake? ¿está
despierto? [desp-yairto]
away: go away! ¡lárguese!
[largeseh]
he's gone away se fue [seh
fweh]
is it far away? ¿está lejos?
[leHos]

awful horrible [oreebleh]
axle el eje [eHeh]
Aztec (adj) azteca [asteka]

B

baby el bebé [beh-beh]
baby food la comida de bebé
[deh]
baby's bottle el biberón
[beebairon],
(CSur, Pe) la mamadera,
(Col) el tetero,
(Mex) la mamila
baby-sitter la niñera [neen-
yaira]
back (of body) la espalda
(back part) la parte de atrás
[parteh deh]
at the back en la parte de
atrás
can I have my money back?
¿me devuelve el dinero? [meh
debwelbeh el deenairo]
to come/go back regresar
backache el dolor de espalda
[deh]
bacon el tocino [toseeno],
(Rpl) la panceta
bad malo
a bad headache un fuerte
dolor de cabeza [fwairteh – deh
kabesa]
badly mal
(injured) gravemente
[grabementeh]
bag la bolsa
(handbag) la cartera,

(Col) el bolso
(suitcase) la maleta,
(Mex) la petaca,
(Rpl) la valija [baleeHa]
baggage el equipaje
[ekeepaHeh]
baggage check la consigna
[konseegna], la paquetería
[paketairee-a]
baggage claim la recogida
de equipajes [rekoHeeda deh
ekeepaH-es]
bakery la panadería
[panadairee-a]
balcony el balcón
  a room with a balcony un
  cuarto con balcón [kwarto]
bald calvo [kalbo]
ball (large) la pelota, el balón
(small) la bola
ballet el ballet
banana el plátano,
(C.Am) el banano,
(Per, Rpl) la banana,
(Ven) el cambur [kamboor]
band (musical) la orquesta
[orkesta]
bandage la venda [benda]
Bandaid® la curita [koorita]
bandit el bandido
bank (money) el banco
bank account la cuenta
bancaria [kwenta]
bar el bar
  a bar of chocolate una barra
  de chocolate[deh chokolateh]
barber's la peluquería
[pelookairee-a]
bargain regatear [regateh-ar]

dialogue

> **how much is this?** ¿a cómo
> está?
> **100 pesos** a cien pesos
> **that's too expensive, how
> about 50?** es muy caro,
> ¿me lo deja en cincuenta?
> [mwee – deHa]
> **I'll let you have it for 80** se
> lo dejo en ochenta [seh
> lo deHo]
> **can't you reduce it a bit
> more, to 70?** ¿me lo rebaja
> un poco más? ¿a setenta?
> [rebaha]
> **that's the lowest I'll go** es
> lo último
> **OK** de acuerdo [deh
> akwairdo]

baseball el béisbol [baysbol]
basement el sótano
basket la canasta
(in shop) la cesta [sesta]
bath el baño [ban-yo], la tina,
(Arg) la bañadera [ban-yadaira]
  can I have a bath? ¿puedo
  bañarme? [pwedo ban-yarmeh]
bathroom el (cuarto de) baño
[kwarto]
  with a private bathroom con
  baño privado [preebado]
bath towel la toalla de baño
[to-a-ya deh]
battery la pila
(car) la batería [batairee-a]
bay la bahía [ba-ee-a]
be* ser [sair]; estar

beach la playa [pla-ya]
 on the beach en la playa
beach umbrella la sombrilla
 [sombree-ya]
beans los frijoles [freeHol-es],
 (CSur) los porotos
 runner beans las habichuelas
 [abeechoo-elas],
 (Chi) los porotos verdes
 [bairdes],
 (Mex) los ejotes [eHot-es],
 (Rpl) las chauchas [chowchas],
 (Ven) las vainitas [bīneetas]
 broad beans las habas [abas]
beard la barba
beautiful lindo
because porque [porkeh]
 because of ... debido a ...
bed la cama
 I'm going to bed now me voy
 a acostar ahora [meh boy – a-
 ora]
bed and breakfast cuarto y
 desayuno [kwarto ee desa-yoono]
bedroom el cuarto,
 (Mex) la recámara
beef la carne de res [karneh
 deh]
beer la cerveza [sairbesa]
 two beers, please dos
 cervezas, por favor [fabor]
before antes
begin empezar [empesar]
 when does it begin? ¿cuándo
 empieza? [kwando emp-yesa]
beginner el/la principiante
 [preenseep-yanteh]
beginning: at the beginning al
 principio [preenseep-yo]

behind atrás
 behind me detrás de mí [deh]
beige beige [baysh]
believe creer [kreh-air]
Belize Belice [beleeseh]
below abajo [abaHo]
belt el cinturón [seentooron]
bend (in road) la curva [koorba]
berth (on ship) el camarote
 [kamaroteh]
beside: beside the ... al lado
 de la ... [deh]
best el mejor [meHor]
better mejor
 are you feeling better? ¿se
 siente mejor? [seh s-yenteh]
between entre [entreh]
beyond más allá [a-ya]
bicycle la bicicleta [beeseekleta]
big grande [grandeh]
 too big demasiado grande
 [demas-yado]
 it's not big enough no es
 lo suficientemente grande
 [soofees-yentementeh]
 big game fishing la pesca
 mayor [ma-yor]
bike la bicicleta [beeseekleta]
 (motorbike) la moto
bikini el bikini
bill la cuenta [kwenta]
 (US: banknote) el billete [bee-
 yeteh]
 could I have the bill, please?
 ¿me pasa la cuenta, por
 favor? [meh – fabor]
bin el cubo de la basura,
 (Ch) el tarro de la basura,
 (Col) la caneca de la basura,

(Csur, Per) el tacho de la basura,

(Mex) el bote de la basura [boteh],

(Ven) el tobo de la basura

bin liners las bolsas de basura

binding (ski) la atadura

bird el pájaro [paHaro]

biro® el bolígrafo,

(Ch) el lápiz de pasta [lapees deh],

(Col) el esfero,

(Mex) la pluma atómica,

(Rpl) el birome [beeromeh]

birthday el cumpleaños [koompleh-an-yos]

happy birthday! ¡feliz cumpleaños! [felees]

biscuit la galleta [ga-yeta]

bit: a little bit un poquito [pokeeto]

a big bit un pedazo grande [pedaso grandeh]

a bit of ... un pedazo de ... [deh]

a bit expensive un poco caro

bite (by insect) la picadura

(by dog) la mordedura

bitter (taste etc) amargo

black negro [neh-gro]

black coffee el café americano [kafeh]

(strong) el café solo

blanket la cobija [kobeeHa], la frazada [frasada]

bleach (for toilet) la lejía [leHee-a],

(Arg) la lavandina,

(Ch) el agua de cuba [agwa deh kooba],

(Col, Mex) el blanqueador [blankeh-ador]

(Urug) el agua Jane® [Haneh]

bless you! ¡salud! [saloo]

blind ciego [s-yego]

blinds las persianas [pers-yanas]

blister la ampolla [ampo-ya]

blocked (road, pipe) bloqueado [blokeh-ado]

(sink) atascado

block (city) la cuadra [kwadra]

block of flats el edificio de departamentos [edeefees-yo deh]

blond rubio,

(Col) mono,

(Mex) güero [gwairo],

(Ven) catire [kateereh]

blood la sangre [sangreh]

high blood pressure la tensión alta [tens-yon]

blouse la blusa

blow-dry (verb) secar a mano

I'd like a cut and blow-dry quisiera un corte y un marcado [kees-yaira oon korteh ee]

blue azul [asool]

blusher el colorete [koloreteh],

(Mex, Rpl) el rubor

boarding house la pensión [pens-yon], la hostería [ostairee-a]

boarding pass la tarjeta de embarque [tarHeta deh embarkeh]

boat el barco

body el cuerpo [kwairpo]

boiled egg el huevo pasado (por agua) [webo pasado por agwa]

boiler la caldera [kaldaira]

Bolivia Bolivia [boleebya]

Bolivian (adj) boliviano [boleebyano]
(man) el boliviano
(woman) la boliviana

bone el hueso [weso]

bonnet (of car) el capó,
(Mex) el cofre [kofreh]

book el libro
(verb) reservar [resairbar]
can I book a seat? ¿puedo reservar un asiento? [pwedo – as-yento]

dialogue

I'd like to book a table for two quisiera reservar una mesa para dos personas [kees-yaira]
what time would you like it booked for? ¿para qué hora la quiere? [keh ora la k-yaireh]
half past seven las siete y media
that's fine de acuerdo [deh akwairdo]
and your name? ¿me da su nombre ...? [meh da soo nombreh]

bookshop, bookstore la librería [leebrairee-a]

boot (footwear) la bota

(of car) el maletero [maletairo], (Ch, Pe) la maleta, (Col, Rpl) el baúl [ba-ool], (Mex) la cajuela [kaHwela]

border (of country) la frontera [frontaira]

bored: I'm bored (said by man/woman) estoy aburrido/ aburrida

boring aburrido, pesado

born: I was born in Manchester nací en Manchester [nasee]
I was born in 1960 nací en mil novecientos sesenta

borrow pedir prestado
may I borrow ...? ¿puede prestarme ...? [pwedeh prestarmeh]

both los dos
both... and... tanto ... como ...

bother: sorry to bother you siento molestarlo [s-yento]

bottle la botella [boteh-ya], el frasco
a bottle of house red una botella de tinto de la casa [deh]

bottle-opener el destapador [destapador]

bottom (of person) el trasero [trasairo], el culo, (CSur) el traste [trasteh]
at the bottom of the ... (hill/ road) al pie del/de la ... [p-yeh del/deh]
(sea) al fondo de ...

box la caja [kaHa]

box office la taquilla [takee-ya], la boletería [boletairee-a]
boy el chico, el joven [Hoven], (Mex, Ven) el chavo [chabo]
boyfriend el novio [nob-yo]
bra el sostén, (Col, Mex) el brasier [bras-yair], (Rpl) el corpiño [korpeen-yo], (Urug) el soutien [sootyen]
bracelet la pulsera [poolsaira]
brake el freno
brandy el coñac [kon-yak]
Brazil Brasil
Brazilian (adj) brasilero [braseel-airo]
(man) el brasilero
(woman) la brasilera
bread el pan
white bread el pan blanco
brown bread el pan de centeno [deh senteno]
wholemeal bread el pan integral [eentegral]
break (verb) romper [rompair]
I've broken the ... rompí el ...
I think I've broken my ... creo que me he roto el ... [kreh-o keh meh eh]
break down descomponerse [deskomponairseh]
I've broken down se me ha descompuso el auto [seh meh deskompooso el owto]
breakdown (mechanical) la avería [abairee-a]
breakdown service el servicio de grúa [serbees-yo deh groo-a]
breakfast el desayuno [desa-yoono]

break-in: I've had a break-in entraron en mi casa a robar
breast el pecho
breathe respirar
breeze la brisa
bribe el soborno, (Csur, Per) la coima [koyma], (Mex) la mordida
bridge (over river) el puente [pwenteh]
brief breve [brebeh]
briefcase la cartera [kartaira], el portafolios
bright (light etc) brillante [bree-yanteh]
bright red rojo vivo [roHo beebo]
brilliant (idea, person) brillante [bree-yanteh]
bring traer [tra-air]
I'll bring it back later lo devolveré luego [debolbaireh lwego]
Britain Gran Bretaña [bretan-ya]
British británico
I'm British (man/woman) soy británico/británica
brochure el folleto [fo-yeto]
broken roto
bronchitis la bronquitis [bronkeetees]
brooch el broche [brocheh]
broom la escoba
brother el hermano [airmano]
brother-in-law el cuñado [koon-yado]
brown color café [kafeh]
brown hair el pelo castaño [kastan-yo]

brown eyes los ojos castaños
[oHos]
bruise el moretón,
(Ven) el morado
brush (for hair, cleaning) el
cepillo [sepee-yo]
(artist's) el pincel [peensel]
bucket el balde [baldeh],
(Mex) la cubeta [koobeta],
(Ven) el tobo
buffet car el vagón restaurante
[bagon restowranteh]
buggy (for child) el carrito
de niño [deh neen-yo], el
cochecito [kocheseeto]
building el edificio [edeefees-
yo]
bulb (light bulb) la bombilla,
(Ch) la ampolleta [ampo-yeta],
(Col, Ven) el bombillo [bombee-
yo],
(Mex) el foco,
(Rpl) la bombita
bull el toro
bullfight la corrida
bullring la plaza de toros [plasa
deh]
bumper la defensa
bunk la litera [leetaira]
bureau de change el cambio
[kamb-yo], la casa de cambio
[deh]
burglary el robo (con
allanamiento de morada)
[a-yanam-yento]
burn la quemadura [kemadoora]
(verb) quemar [kemar]
burnt: this is burnt está
quemado [kemado]

burst: a burst pipe la cañería
rota [kan-yairee-a]
bus el autobús, el bus,
(Arg, Ven) el colectivo,
(C.Am, Mex) el camión [kam-
yon],
(Ch) el micro,
(Cu) la guagua [gwagwa],
(Per, Urug) el ómnibus
  what number bus is it to ...?
  ¿qué número tomo para ...?
  [keh noomairo]
  when is the next bus to ...?
  ¿cuándo sale el próximo
  autobús para ...? [kwando
  saleh]
  what time is the last bus?
  ¿a qué hora sale el último
  autobús? [keh ora – oolteemo]
  could you let me know
  when we get there? ¿puede
  avisarme cuando lleguemos?
  [pwedeh abeesarmeh kwando
  yegemos]

dialogue

does this bus go to ...?
¿este autobús va a ...?
[esteh ...ba]
no, you need a number ...
no, tiene que tomar el ...
[t-yeneh keh]

business el negocio [negos-yo]
bus station la estación de
autobuses [estas-yon deh
owtoboos-es],
(Col) la terminal de

transportes [tairmeenal deh transport-es],
(Mex) la central camionera [sentral kam-yonaira]
bus stop la parada de autobús
bust el pecho, el busto
busy (restaurant etc) concurrido
I'm busy tomorrow (said by man/woman) estoy ocupado/ocupada mañana [man-yana]
but pero [pairo]
butcher's la carnicería [karneesairee-a]
butter la mantequilla [mantekee-ya]
button el botón
buy (verb) comprar
where can I buy ...? ¿dónde puedo comprar ...? [dondeh pwedo]
buzzard el buitre [bweetreh], (CAm, Mex) el zopilote [sopeeloteh]
(Ven) el zamuro
by: by bus/car en camión/carro
written by ... escrito por ...
by the window junto a la ventana [Hoonto]
by the sea a orillas del mar [oree-yas]
by Thursday para el jueves
bye! ¡hasta luego! [asta lwego]

C

cabbage el repollo [repo-yo]
cabin (on ship) el camarote [kamaroteh]

cable car el teleférico [telefaireeko], el funicular [fooneekoolar]
cactus el cactus
café la cafetería [kafetairee-a]
cagoule el chubasquero [choobaskairo]
cake el pastel
cake shop la pastelería [pastelairee-a]
call (verb) llamar [yamar]
(to phone) llamar (por teléfono)
what's it called? ¿cómo se llama ? [seh yama]
he/she is called ... se llama ...
please call the doctor llame al médico, por favor [yameh – fabor]
please give me a call at 7.30 a.m. tomorrow por favor, llámeme mañana a las siete y media de la mañana [yamemeh man-yana]
please ask him to call me por favor, dígale que me llame [deegaleh keh meh yameh]
call back: I'll call back later regresaré más tarde [regresareh mas tardeh]
(phone back) volveré a llamar [bolbaireh a yamar]
call round: I'll call round tomorrow mañana paso
camcorder la videocámara [beedeh-o-kamara]
camera la cámara
camera shop la tienda fotográfica [t-yenda]
camp (verb) acampar

can we camp here? ¿se puede acampar aquí? [seh pwedeh – akee]
camping gas canister la bomba de butano [deh bootano]
campsite el camping
can la lata
a can of beer una lata de cerveza [deh sairbesa]
can*: can you ...? ¿puede ...? [pwedeh]
can I have ...? ¿me da ...? [meh]
I can't ... no puedo ... [pwedo]
Canada el Canadá
Canadian (adj) canadiense [kanad-yenseh]
I'm Canadian soy canadiense
canal el canal
cancel cancelar [kanselar]
candies los dulces [dool-ses]
candle la vela [bela]
canoe la canoa
canoeing el piragüismo [peeragweesmo], (SAm) el canotaje [kanotaheh]
can-opener el abrelatas
canyon el cañón [kan-yon], la cañada [kan-yada]
cap (hat) la gorra
(of bottle) el tapón
car el auto [owto], el carro, el automóvil
by car en auto
caravan la caravana [karabana]
caravan site el camping
carburettor el carburador
card (birthday etc) la tarjeta

[tarHeta]
here's my (business) card aquí tiene mi tarjeta (de visita) [akee t-yeneh – deh beeseeta]
cardigan
(Ch) la chaleca,
(Mex) la chamarra,
(Rpl) el saco tejido [teheedo]
cardphone el teléfono de tarjeta [deh tarHeta]
careful cuidadoso [kweedadoso]
be careful! ¡cuidado! [kweedado]
caretaker el portero [portairo]
car ferry el ferry, el transbordador de autos [deh]
car hire el alquiler de autos [alkeelair deh]
car park el estacionamiento [estas-yonam-yento]
carpet la alfombra, el tapete [tapeteh]
car rental el alquiler de autos [alkeelair deh]
carriage (of train) el vagón [bagon]
carrier bag la bolsa de plástico [deh]
carrot la zanahoria [sana-or-ya]
carry llevar [yebar]
carry-cot el capazo [kapaso]
carton el cartón
carwash el lavado de autos [labado deh]
case (suitcase) la maleta
cash el dinero [deenairo], la plata
to pay (in) cash pagar en

efectivo [efekteebo], pagar al contado

will you cash this for me? ¿podría hacerme efectivo un cheque? [asairmeh – chekeh]

cash desk la caja [kaHa]

cash dispenser el cajero automático [kaHairo owtomateeko]

cassette la cassette [kaset]

cassette recorder la grabadora

castle el castillo [kastee-yo]

casualty department urgencias [oorHens-yas]

cat el gato

catch (verb) agarrar

where do we catch the bus to ...? ¿dónde se toma el autobús para ...? [dondeh seh]

cathedral la catedral

Catholic (adj) católico

cauliflower el coliflor

cave la cueva [kweba]

ceiling el techo

celery el apio [ap-yo]

cellar (for wine) la bodega

cellular phone el teléfono celular [seloolar]

cemetery el cementerio [sementair-yo], el panteón [panteh-on]

centigrade* centígrado [senteegrado]

centimetre* el centímetro [senteemetro]

central central [sentral]

Central America Centroamérica [sentro-amaireeka]

Central American (adj) centroamericano

central heating la calefacción central [kalefaks-yon sentral]

centre el centro [sentro]

how do we get to the city centre? ¿cómo se llega al centro? [seh yega]

cereals los cereales [sereh-al-es]

certainly por supuesto [soopwesto]

certainly not de ninguna manera [deh neengoona manaira]

chair la silla [see-ya]

champagne el champán

change (loose) el suelto [swelto] (after payment) el vuelto [bwelto] (verb) cambiar [kamb-yar]

can I change this for ...? ¿puedo cambiar esto por ...? [pwedo]

I don't have any change no tengo suelto

can you give me change for a 1,000 peso note? ¿puede cambiarme un billete de mil? [pwedeh kamb-yarmeh oon bee-yeteh deh meel]

dialogue

do we have to change (trains)? ¿tenemos que hacer correspondencia? [keh aser korrespondens-ya]

yes, change at Cordoba/no it's a direct train sí, haga

trasbordo en Córdoba/no, es directo [aga]

changed: to get changed cambiarse [kamb-yarseh]
chapel la capilla [kapee-ya]
charge (verb) cobrar
cheap barato
do you have anything cheaper? ¿tiene algo más barato? [t-yeneh]
check (US) el cheque [chekeh] (US: bill) la cuenta [kwenta]
check (verb) revisar [rebeesar]
could you check the ..., please? ¿puede revisar el ..., por favor? [pwedeh – fabor]
check book la chequera [chekaira]
check-in la facturación [faktooras-yon]
check in facturar
where do we have to check in? ¿dónde se factura? [dondeh seh]
cheek la mejilla [meHee-ya]
cheerio! ¡hasta luego! [asta lwego]
cheers! (toast) ¡salud! [saloo]
cheese el queso [keso]
cheesecake
(Arg) el pastel de queso [deh keso],
(Mex) el pay de queso [pī]
chemist's la farmacia [farmas-ya]
cheque el cheque [chekeh]
do you take cheques? ¿aceptan cheques? [aseptan chek-es]
cheque book la chequera [chekaira]
cheque card la tarjeta de banco [tarHeta deh]
cherry la cereza [sairesa] (black) la guinda [geenda]
chess el ajedrez [aHed-res]
chest el pecho
chewing gum el chicle [cheekleh]
chicken el pollo [po-yo], la gallina [ga-yeena]
chickenpox la varicela [bareesela]
child (male/female) el niño [neen-yo], la niña
child minder la niñera [neen-yaira]
children los niños
children's pool la piscina infantil [peeseena eenfanteel], (Mex) la alberca infantil [albairka], (Rpl) la pileta infantil [peeleta]
children's portion la ración pequeña (para niños) [ras-yon peken-ya – neen-yos]
Chile Chile [cheeleh]
Chilean (adj) chileno [cheeleno] (man) el chileno (woman) la chilena
chilli el chile [cheeleh]
chin la barbilla [barbee-ya]
china la porcelana [porselana]
Chinese (adj) chino [cheeno]
chips las papas fritas
chocolate el chocolate [chokolateh]

milk chocolate el chocolate con leche [lecheh]
plain chocolate el chocolate negro [neh-gro]
a hot chocolate una taza de chocolate [tasa deh]
choose elegir [eleHeer], escoger [eskoHair]
Christian name el nombre de pila [nombreh deh]
Christmas Navidad [nabeeda]
Christmas Eve Nochebuena [nocheh-bwena]
merry Christmas! ¡Feliz Navidad! [felees]
church la iglesia [eegles-ya]
cider la sidra
cigar el puro [pooro]
cigarette el cigarrillo [seegarree-yo]
cigarette lighter el mechero [mechairo]
cinema el cine [seeneh]
circle el círculo [seerkoolo]
(in theatre) el anfiteatro [anfeeteh-atro]
city la ciudad [s-yooda]
city centre el centro de la ciudad [sentro deh]
clean (adj) limpio [leemp-yo]
can you clean these for me? ¿puede limpiarme estos? [pwedeh leemp-yarmeh]
cleaning solution (for contact lenses) el líquido limpiador para los lentes [leekeedo leemp-yador]
cleansing lotion la crema limpiadora

clear claro
clever listo
cliff el acantilado
cliff-diving el clavado de acantilado [deh]
climbing el montañismo [montan-yeesmo]
cling film el plástico de envolver [deh embolbair]
clinic la clínica
cloakroom el guardarropa [gwardarropa]
clock el reloj [reloH]
close (verb) cerrar [serrar]

dialogue

what time do you close? ¿a qué hora cierran? [keh ora s-yairran]
we close at 8 p.m. on weekdays and 1.30 p.m. on Saturdays cerramos a las ocho de la noche entre semana y a la una y media los sábados [serramos – deh la nocheh entreh]
do you close for lunch? ¿cierra a mediodía? [s-yairra]
yes, between 1 and 3.30 p.m. sí, desde la una hasta las tres y media de la tarde [desdeh – asta]

closed cerrado [sairrado]
cloth (fabric) la tela
(for cleaning etc) el trapo
clothes la ropa

clothes line la cuerda para tender [kwairda para tendair]

clothes peg la pinza de la ropa [peensa deh]

cloud la nube [noobeh]

cloudy nublado

clutch el embrague [embrageh]

coach (bus) el autobús [owtoboos]
(on train) el vagón [bagon]

coach station la estación de autobuses [estas-yon deh owtoboos-es],
(Col) la terminal de transportes [tairmeenal],
(Mex) la estación de camiones [estas-yon deh kam-yon-es]

coach trip la excursión (en autobús) [eskoors-yon]

coast la costa
on the coast en la costa

coat (long coat) el abrigo
(jacket) el saco

coathanger la percha [pairpcha]

cockroach la cucaracha [kookaracha]

cocoa el cacao [kaka-o]

coconut el coco

code (for phoning) el prefijo [prefeeHo], el código
what's the (dialling) code for Managua? ¿cuál es el prefijo de Managua? [kwal – deh managwa]

coffee el café [kafeh]
two coffees, please dos cafés, por favor [fabor]

coin la moneda

Coke® la Coca-Cola

cold frío
I'm cold tengo frío
I have a cold tengo un resfriado [resfr-yado]

collapse: he's collapsed se desmayó [seh desma-yo]

collar el cuello [kweh-yo]

collect recoger [rekoHair]
I've come to collect ... vine a recoger ... [beeneh]

collect call la llamada por cobrar [yamada]

college la universidad [ooneebairseeda]

Colombia Colombia [kolomb-ya]

Colombian (adj) colombiano [kolomb-yano]
(man) el colombiano
(woman) la colombiana

colour el color
do you have this in other colours? ¿tiene otros colores? [t-yeneh – kolor-es]

colour film la película en color

comb el peine [payneh],
(Ch) la peineta

come venir [beneer]

dialogue

where do you come from? ¿de dónde es? [deh dondeh]
I come from Edinburgh soy de Edimburgo

come back regresar
I'll come back tomorrow regreso mañana

come in entrar
come in! ¡pase! [paseh]
comfortable cómodo
compact disc el compact disc
company (business) la
  compañía [kompan-yee-a]
compartment (on train) el
  compartimento
compass la brújula [brooHoola]
complain quejarse [keh-Harseh]
complaint la queja [keHa]
  I have a complaint tengo una
  queja
completely completamente
  [kompletamenteh]
computer la computadora
concert el concierto [kons-
  yairto]
concussion la conmoción
  cerebral [konmos-yon sairebral]
conditioner (for hair) el
  acondicionador de pelo
  [akondees-yonador deh]
condom el condón
condor el cóndor
conference el congreso
confirm confirmar
congratulations! ¡felicidades!
  [feleeseedad-es]
connecting flight el vuelo de
  conexión [bwelo deh koneks-
  yon]
connection el enlace [enlaseh]
conscious consciente [kons-
  yenteh]
constipation el estreñimiento
  [estren-yeem-yento]
consulate el consulado
contact (verb) ponerse en

contacto con [ponairseh]
contact lenses los lentes de
  contacto
contraceptive el
  anticonceptivo
  [anteekonsepteebo]
convenient a mano
  that's not convenient no
  conviene [konb-yeneh]
cook (verb) cocinar [koseenar]
  not cooked poco hecho
  [echo]
cooker la cocina [koseena]
cookie la galleta [ga-yeta]
cooking utensils los utensilios
  de cocina [ootenseel-yos deh
  koseena]
cool fresco
cork el corcho
corkscrew el sacacorchos
corner: on the corner en la
  esquina [eskeena]
  in the corner en el rincón
cornflakes los cornflakes
correct (right) correcto
corridor el pasillo [pasee-yo]
cosmetics los cosméticos
cost (verb) costar, valer [balair]
  how much does it cost?
  ¿cuánto vale? [kwanto baleh]
Costa Rica Costa Rica
Costa Rican costarricense
  [kostarreesenseh]
  (person) el/la costarricense
cot la cuna
cotton el algodón
cotton wool el algodón
couch (sofa) el sofá
couchette la litera [leetaira]

cough la tos
cough medicine la medicina para la tos [medeseena]
could: could you ...? ¿podría ...?
could I have ...? ¿quisiera ...? [kees-yaira]
I couldn't ... no podría ...
country (nation) el país [pa-ees]
(countryside) el campo
countryside el campo
couple (two people) la pareja [pareHa]
a couple of ... un par de ... [deh]
courgette la calabacita [kalabaseeta], el calabacín [kalabaseen]
courier (male/female) el guía turístico [gee-a], la guía turística
course (main course etc) el plato
of course por supuesto [soopwesto]
of course not! ¡claro que no! [keh]
cousin (male/female) el primo, la prima
cow la vaca [baka]
crab el cangrejo [kangreHo], la jaiba [Hība]
cracker (biscuit) la galleta salada [ga-yeta]
craft shop la tienda de artesanías [t-yenda deh]
crash el accidente [akseedenteh]
(verb) chocar
I've had a crash tuve un accidente [toobeh]

crazy loco
cream la crema
(colour) color crema
creche la guardería infantil [gwardairee-a]
credit card la tarjeta de crédito [tarHeta deh kredeeto]

dialogue

can I pay by credit card? ¿puedo pagar con tarjeta? [pwedo – kon tarHeta]
which card do you want to use? ¿qué tarjeta quiere usar? [keh – k-yaireh oosar]
yes, sir sí, señor [sen-yor]
what's the number? ¿qué número tiene? [noomairo t-yeneh]
and the expiry date? ¿y la fecha de caducidad? [deh kadooseeda]

crisps las papas fritas (de bolsa),
(Urug) las papas chips
crockery la loza [losa]
crocodile el cocodrilo [kokodreelo]
crossing (by sea) la travesía [trabesee-a]
crossroads el cruce [krooseh]
crowd la muchedumbre [moocheh-doombreh]
crowded atestado
crown (on tooth) la corona,
(Mex) la funda [foonda]

cruise el crucero [kroosairo]

crutches las muletas

cry (verb) llorar [yorar]

Cuba Cuba [kooba]

Cuban (adj) cubano

(man) el cubano

(woman) la cubana

cucumber el pepino

cup la taza [tasa]

a cup of ..., please una taza de ..., por favor [deh – fabor]

cupboard el armario [armar-yo]

cure la cura [koora]

curly rizado [reesado],

(CSur) crespo,

(Mex) chino

current la corriente [korr-yenteh]

curtains las cortinas

cushion el cojín [koHeen]

custom la costumbre [kostoombreh]

Customs la aduana [adwana]

cut el corte [korteh]

(verb) cortar

I've cut myself me corté [meh korteh]

cutlery los cubiertos [koob-yairtos]

cycling el ciclismo [seekleesmo]

cyclist el/la ciclista [seekleesta]

D

dad el papá

daily cada día [dee-a], todos los días

(adj) diario [d-yar-yo], de cada

día [deh]

damage: damaged dañado [dan-yado]

damn! ¡caramba!

damp (adj) húmedo [oomedo]

dance el baile [bīleh]

(verb) bailar [bīlar]

would you like to dance? ¿quiere bailar? [k-yaireh]

dangerous peligroso

Danish danés [dan-es]

dark (adj: colour) oscuro [oskooro]

(hair) moreno, oscuro

it's getting dark está oscureciendo [oskoores-yendo]

date* la fecha

what's the date today? ¿qué fecha es hoy? [keh – oy]

let's make a date for next Monday quedamos para el próximo lunes [kedamos – prokseemo]

dates (fruit) los dátiles

daughter la hija [eeHa]

daughter-in-law la nuera [nwaira]

dawn el amanecer [amanesair]

at dawn al amanecer

day el día

the day after el día siguiente [seeg-yenteh]

the day after tomorrow pasado mañana [man-yana]

the day before el día anterior [antair-yor]

the day before yesterday anteayer [anteh-a-yair]

every day todos los días

all day todo el día
in two days' time dentro de
dos días [deh]
have a nice day! ¡que pase
buen día! [keh paseh bwen]
day trip la excursión [ekskoors-
yon]
dead muerto [mwairto]
deaf sordo
deal (business) el negocio
[negos-yo]
it's a deal trato hecho [echo]
death la muerte [mwairteh]
decaffeinated coffee el
café descafeinado [kafeh
deskafaynado]
December diciembre [dees-
yembreh]
decide decidir [deseedeer]
we haven't decided yet
todavía no hemos decidido
[todabee-a no emos deseedeedo]
decision la decisión [desees-
yon]
deck (on ship) la cubierta [koob-
yairta]
deckchair la tumbona,
(Col, Per) la perezosa,
(Rpl) la reposera,
(Urug) el perezoso
deduct descontar
deep profundo
definitely (certainly) sin duda
definitely not ni hablar [ablar]
degree (qualification) el título
delay la demora
the train was delayed se
demoró el tren [seh]
deliberately a propósito

delicatessen la charcutería
[charkootairee-a],
(CSur) la fiambrería,
(Col) la salsamentaria,
(Mex) la salchichonería
delicious delicioso [delees-
yoso]
deliver entregar
delivery (of mail) el reparto
Denmark Dinamarca
dental floss el hilo dental
[eelo]
dentist el/la dentista

dialogue

it's this one here es ésta de
aquí [deh akee]
this one? ¿ésta?
no, that one no, aquélla
[akeh-ya]
here? ¿aquí?
yes sí

dentures la dentadura postiza
[posteesa],
(Col) la caja de dientes [d-
yentes],
(Ch) la placa de dientes
deodorant el desodorante
[desodoranteh]
department el departamento
department store la tienda de
departamentos [t-yenda deh]
departure la salida
departure lounge la sala de
embarque [deh embarkeh]
depend: it depends depende
[dependeh]

it depends when según cuándo [kwando]

it depends on ... depende de ... [deh]

deposit (as security) la fianza [fee-ansa]

(as part payment) la entrega inicial [eenees-yal]

description la descripción [deskreeps-yon]

desert el desierto [des-yairto]

dessert el postre [postreh]

destination el destino

develop (photos) revelar [rebelar]

dialogue

could you develop these films? ¿puede revelar estos carretes? [pwedeh – karret-es]

when will they be ready? ¿cuándo estarán listos? [kwando]

tomorrow afternoon mañana por la tarde [man-yana – tardeh]

how much is the four-hour service? ¿cuánto es el servicio de cuatro horas? [kwanto – sairbees-yo deh kwatro oras]

diabetic (man/woman) el diabético [dee-abeteeko], la diabética

diabetic foods la comida para diabéticos

dial (verb) marcar

dialling code el prefijo

[prefeeHo], el código

diamond el diamante [d-yamanteh]

diaper el pañal [pan-yal]

diarrhoea la diarrea [d-yarreh-a]

diary (business etc) la agenda [aHenda]

(for personal experiences) el diario [d-yar-yo]

dictionary el diccionario [deeks-yonar-yo]

didn't see not

die morir

diesel el gasoil, el diesel [deesel],

(Col) el ACPM [asepeh-emeh]

diet la dieta [d-yeta]

I'm on a diet estoy a régimen [reHeemen]

I have to follow a special diet tengo que seguir una dieta especial [keh segeer – espes-yal]

difference la diferencia [deefairens-ya]

what's the difference? ¿cuál es la diferencia? [kwal]

different distinto

this one is different éste es distinto [esteh]

a different table otra mesa

difficult difícil [deefeeseel]

difficulty la dificultad [deefeekoolta]

dinghy el bote [boteh]

dining room el comedor

dinner (evening) la cena [sena]

to have dinner cenar [senar]

direct (adj) directo

is there a direct train? ¿hay

un tren directo? [i]

direction la dirección [deereks-yon], el sentido

which direction is it? ¿en qué dirección está? [keh]

is it in this direction? ¿es por aquí? [akee]

directory enquiries información [eenformas-yon]

dirt la suciedad [soos-yeda], la mugre [moogreh]

dirty sucio [soos-yo]

disabled minusválido [meenoosbaleedo]

is there access for the disabled? ¿hay acceso para minusválidos? [i akseso]

disappear desaparecer [desaparesair]

it's disappeared desapareció [desapares-yo]

disappointed decepcionado [deseps-yonado]

disappointing decepcionante [deseps-yonanteh]

disaster el desastre [desastreh]

disco la discoteca

discount el descuento [deskwento]

is there a discount? ¿hay descuento? [i]

disease la enfermedad [enfairmeda]

disgusting repugnante [repoognanteh]

dish (meal) el plato

dishcloth el trapo de cocina [deh koseena],
(Col) el limpión,

(Rpl) el repasador

disinfectant el desinfectante [deseenfektanteh]

disk (for computer) el disco, el disquete [deesketeh]

disposable diapers/nappies los pañales desechables [pan-yal-es desechab-les]

distance la distancia [deestans-ya]

in the distance a lo lejos [leHos]

distilled water el agua destilada [agwa]

district el barrio

disturb molestar, estorbar

diversion (detour) el desvío [desbee-o]

diving board el trampolín

divorced divorciado [deebors-yado]

dizzy: I feel dizzy (said by man/woman) estoy mareado/mareada [mareh-ado]

do hacer [asair]

what shall we do? ¿qué hacemos? [keh asemos]

how do you do it? ¿cómo se hace? [seh aseh]

will you do it for me? ¿me lo puede hacer usted? [meh lo pwedeh asair oosteh]

Do

dialogues

how do you do? ¿cómo está? [komo]
nice to meet you encantado de conocerlo [deh konosairlo]

what do you do? (work) ¿a qué se dedica? [keh seh]

I'm a teacher, and you? soy profesor, ¿y usted? [ee oosteh]

I'm a student soy estudiante [estood-yanteh]

what are you doing this evening? ¿qué hace esta noche? [aseh – nocheh]

we're going out for a drink; do you want to join us? salimos a tomar una copa, ¿nos acompaña? [akompan-ya]

do you want cream? ¿quiere crema? [k-yaireh]

I do, but she doesn't yo sí, pero ella no [pairo eh-ya]

doctor el médico (woman) la médica

we need a doctor necesitamos un médico [neseseetamos]

please call a doctor por favor, llame a un médico [fabor yameh]

dialogue

where does it hurt? ¿dónde le duele? [dondeh leh dweleh]

right here justo aquí [Hoosto akee]

does that hurt now? ¿le duele ahora? [leh dweleh a-ora]

yes sí

take this to the chemist's lleve esto a la farmacia [yebeh – farmas-ya]

document el documento [dokoomento]

dog el perro [pairro]

doll la muñeca [moon-yeka]

domestic flight el vuelo nacional [bwelo nas-yonal]

donkey el burro [boorro]

don't! ¡no lo haga! [aga]

don't do that! ¡no haga eso! see not

door la puerta [pwairta]

doorman el portero [portairo]

double doble [dobleh]

double bed la cama matrimonial [matreemon-yal]

double room el cuarto doble [kwarto dobleh]

doughnut la dona

down: down here aquí abajo [akee abaHo]

downwards hacia abajo [as-ya]

put it down over there déjelo ahí [deh-Helo a-ee]

it's down there on the right está ahí a la derecha [dairecha]

it's further down the road está bajando la calle [baHando la ka-yeh]

downhill skiing el esquí alpino [eskee alpeeno]

downmarket (restaurant etc) popular [popoolar]

downstairs abajo [abaHo]
dozen la docena [dosena]
  half a dozen media docena [med-ya]
drain (in sink, road) el desagüe [desagweh]
draught beer la cerveza de barril [sairbesa deh]
draughty: it's draughty hay corriente [i korr-yenteh]
drawer el cajón [kaHon]
drawing el dibujo [deebooHo]
dreadful horrible [orreebleh]
dream el sueño [swen-yo]
dress el vestido [besteedo]
dressed: to get dressed vestirse [besteerseh]
dressing (for cut) el vendaje [bendaHeh]
  salad dressing el aliño [aleen-yo]
dressing gown la bata
drink la bebida
  (verb) beber [bebair]
  a cold drink una bebida fría
  can I get you a drink? ¿quiere beber algo? [k-yaireh]
  what would you like (to drink)? ¿qué le apetece beber? [keh leh apeteseh]
  no thanks, I don't drink no gracias, no bebo alcohol [gras-yas – alkol]
  I'll just have a drink of water sólo agua [agwa]
drinking water agua potable [agwa potableh]
  is this drinking water? ¿esto es agua potable?

drive (verb) manejar [maneHar]
  we drove here vinimos en auto [beeneemos en owto]
  I'll drive you home te llevaré a casa en auto [teh yebareh]
driver (man/woman) el/la chofer [chofair]
driving licence la licencia, el carnet de chofer [karneh deh chofair],
  (Arg) el registro [reheestro],
  (Ch) el carné,
  (Col) el pase [paseh],
  (Per) el brevete [brebeteh],
  (Urug) la libreta
drop: just a drop, please (of drink) un poquito nada más [pokeeto]
drug la medicina [medeeseena]
drugs (narcotics) la droga
drunk (adj) borracho
drunken driving manejar en estado de embriaguez [maneHar – deh embr-yag-es]
dry (adj) seco
dry-cleaner la tintorería [teentorairee-a]
duck el pato
due: he was due to arrive yesterday tenía que llegar ayer [keh yegar i-yair]
  when is the train due? ¿a qué hora llega el tren? [ora yega]
dull (pain) sordo
  (weather) gris [grees]
dummy (baby's) el chupete [choopeteh],
  (Col) el chupo,
  (Ven) la chupa

during durante [dooranteh]
dust el polvo [polbo]
dustbin el cubo de la basura,
(Ch) el tarro de la basura,
(Col) la caneca de la basura,
(Csur, Per) el tacho de la basura,
(Mex) el bote de la basura [boteh],
(Ven) el tobo de la basura
dusty polvoriento [polboryento]
duty-free (goods) (los productos) sin impuestos [seen eempwestos]
duty-free shop el duty free
duvet el edredón

E

each cada
how much are they each? ¿a cómo está cada uno?
ear el oído [o-eedo]
earache: I have earache tengo dolor de oídos [deh]
early pronto
early in the morning de madrugada
I called by earlier pasé antes [paseh ant-es]
earring el arete [areteh],
(CSur) el aro,
(Urug) la caravana
earthquake el temblor, el terremoto
east oriente [or-yenteh]
in the east en el oriente

Easter la Semana Santa
easy fácil [faseel]
eat comer [komair]
we've already eaten, thanks ya comimos, gracias [gras-yas]
eau de toilette la colonia
economy class la clase turista [klaseh]
Ecuador Ecuador [ekwador]
Ecuadorian (adj) ecuatoriano [ekwator-yano]
(man) el ecuatoriano
(woman) la ecuatoriana
Edinburgh Edimburgo [edeemboorgo]
egg el huevo [webo]
eggplant la berenjena [berenHena]
either: either ... or ... o ... o ...
either of them cualquiera de los dos [kwalk-yaira deh]
elastic el elástico
elastic band la goma,
(Ch) el elástico,
(Col) el caucho [kowcho],
(Mex) la liga,
(Rpl) la gomita
elbow el codo
electric eléctrico
electrical appliances los electrodomésticos
electric fire la cocina,
(Col, Mex) la estufa eléctrica
electrician el electricista [elektreeseesta]
electricity la electricidad [elektreeseeda]
elevator el ascensor [asensor]

else: something else otra cosa
  somewhere else en otra parte
  [parteh]

dialogue

> would you like anything
> else? ¿algo más?
> no, nothing else, thanks
> nada más, gracias [gras-yas]

embassy la embajada
  [embaHada]
emergency la emergencia
  [emairHens-ya]
  this is an emergency! ¡es una
  emergencia!
emergency exit la salida de
  emergencia [deh]
empty vacío [basee-o]
end el final [feenal]
  (verb) terminar [tairmeenar]
  at the end of the street al
  final de la calle [deh la ka-yeh]
  when does it end? ¿cuándo
  termina? [kwando]
engaged (toilet, telephone)
  ocupado
  (to be married) comprometido
engine (car) el motor
England Inglaterra
  [eenglatairra]
English inglés [eeng-les]
  I'm English (man/woman) soy
  inglés/inglesa
  do you speak English? ¿habla
  inglés? [abla]
enjoy disfrutar
  to enjoy oneself divertirse

[deebairteerseh]

dialogue

> how did you like the film?
> ¿le gustó la película? [leh
> goosto]
> I enjoyed it very much, did
> you enjoy it? me gustó
> mucho, ¿le gustó a usted?
> [meh – moocho – leh – oosteh]

enjoyable divertido
  [deebairteedo]
enlargement (of photo) la
  ampliación [ampl-yas-yon]
enormous enorme [enormeh]
enough bastante [bastanteh]
  there's not enough no hay
  bastante [ī]
  it's not big enough no es
  lo suficientemente grande
  [soofees-yentementeh]
  that's enough basta
entrance la entrada
envelope el sobre [sobreh]
epileptic (adj) epiléptico
equipment el equipo [ekeepo]
error el error
especially sobre todo [sobreh]
essential imprescindible
  [eempreseendeebleh]
  it is essential that ... es
  imprescindible que ... [keh]
Europe Europa [eh-ooropa]
European europeo
  [eh-ooropeh-o]
even incluso [eenklooso]
  even if ... incluso si ...

evening (early evening) la tarde
[tardeh]
(after nightfall) la noche [nocheh]
this evening esta tarde/noche
in the evening por la tarde/
noche
evening meal la cena [sena]
eventually finalmente
[feenalmenteh], por fin [feen]
ever alguna vez [bes]

dialogue

have you ever been to
Monterrey? ¿estuvo
alguna vez en Monterrey?
[estoobo – montairray]
yes, I was there two years
ago sí, estuve allí hace dos
años [estoobeh a-yee aseh
– an-yos]

every cada
every day todos los días [dee-
as]
everyone todos
everything todo
everywhere en todas partes
[part-es]
exactly! ¡exactamente!
[eksaktamenteh]
exam el examen
example el ejemplo [eнemplo]
for example por ejemplo
excellent excelente [ekselenteh]
excellent! ¡estupendo!
except excepto [eksepto]
excess baggage el exceso de
equipaje [ekseso deh ekeepaнeh]

exchange rate el tipo de
cambio [teepo deh kamb-yo]
exciting emocionante [emos-
yonanteh]
excuse me (to get past) con
permiso
(to get attention) ¡por favor!
[fabor]
(to say sorry) disculpe
[deeskoolpeh]
exhaust (pipe) el tubo de
escape [toobo deh eskapeh],
(C.Am) el mofle [mofleh],
(Col) el exhosto,
(Rpl) el caño de escape [kan-yo]
exhausted (tired) agotado
exhibition la exposición
[eksposees-yon]
exit la salida
where's the nearest exit?
¿cuál es la salida más
cercana? [kwal – sairkana]
expect esperar [espairar]
expensive caro
experienced con experiencia
[espair-yens-ya]
explain explicar [espleekar]
can you explain that? ¿puede
explicármelo? [pwedeh]
express (mail) urgente
[oorнenteh]
(train) el exprés
extension (phone) la extensión
[estens-yon],
(Rpl) el interno [eentairno],
(Ch) el anexo
extension 221, please
extensión doscientos
veintiuno, por favor [fabor]

extension lead el alargador, la extensión, el alargue (RpI)

extra: can we have an extra one? ¿nos puede dar otro? [pwedeh]

do you charge extra for that? ¿cobra extra por esto?

extraordinary extraordinario [ekstra-ordeenar-yo]

extremely extremadamente [estremadamenteh]

eye el ojo [oHo]

will you keep an eye on my suitcase for me? ¿me cuida la maleta? [meh kweeda]

eyebrow pencil el lápiz de cejas [lapees deh seHas]

eye drops el colirio [koleer-yo]

eyeglasses las gafas

eyeliner el delineador

eye make-up remover el desmaquillador de ojos [desmakee-yador]

eye shadow la sombra de ojos

F

face la cara

factory la fábrica

Fahrenheit* Fahrenheit

faint (verb) desmayarse [desma-yarseh]

she's fainted se desmayó [seh desma-yo]

I feel faint (said by man/woman) estoy mareado/mareada [mareh-ado]

fair la feria [fair-ya]

(adj: just) justo [Hoosto]

fairly bastante [bastanteh]

fake (thing) la imitación [eemeetas-yon]

(adj) falsificado

fake fur la piel de imitación [p-yel], la piel sintética [seenteteeka]

Falkland Islands las Islas Malvinas [eeslas mal-beenas]

fall (verb) caerse [ka-airseh]

she's had a fall se cayó [seh ka-yo]

fall (US: noun) el otoño [oton-yo]

in the fall en otoño

false falso [fal-so]

family la familia [fameel-ya]

famous famoso

fan (electrical) el ventilador [benteelador]

(handheld) el abanico

(sports) el/la hincha [eencha]

fan belt la correa del ventilador [korreh-a del benteelador]

fantastic fantástico

far lejos [leHos]

dialogue

is it far from here? ¿está lejos de aquí? [deh akee]

no, not very far no, no muy lejos [mwee]

well how far? bueno, ¿qué tan lejos? [bweno keh]

it's about 20 kilometres son unos veinte kilómetros

fare el pasaje [pasaHeh]
farm (large) la hacienda [asyenda]
(small) la finca
fashionable de moda [deh]
fast rápido
fat (person) gordo
(on meat) la grasa
father el padre [padreh]
father-in-law el suegro [swegro]
faucet la llave [yabeh],
(C.Am) la paja [paHa],
(Per) el caño [kan-yo],
(Rpl) la canilla [kanee-ya]
fault el defecto
sorry, it was my fault
disculpe, fue culpa mía
[deeskoolpeh fweh]
it's not my fault no es mi
culpa
faulty defectuoso [defektwoso]
favourite preferido
[prefaireedo]
fax el fax
(verb: person) mandar un fax
(document) mandar por fax
February febrero [febrairo]
feel sentir
I feel hot tengo calor
I feel unwell no me siento
bien [meh s-yento b-yen]
I feel like going for a walk se
me antoja un paseo [seh meh
antoHa]
how are you feeling today?
¿cómo se encuentra hoy?
[enkwentra oy]
I'm feeling better me siento
mejor [meHor]

felt-tip (pen) el rotulador,
(SAm) el marcador
fence la cerca [sairka]
fender la defensa
ferry el ferry
festival el festival [festeebal],
la fiesta
fetch: I'll fetch him lo pasaré a
recoger [pasareh a rekoHair]
will you come and fetch me
later? ¿vendrás a buscarme
más tarde? [bendras a
booskarmeh mas tardeh]
feverish con fiebre
[f-yebreh]
few: a few unos pocos
a few days unos días
fiancé el novio [nob-yo]
fiancée la novia [nob-ya]
field el campo
fight la pelea [peleh-a]
figs los higos [eegos]
fill (verb) llenar [yenar]
fill in rellenar [reh-yenar]
do I have to fill this in?
¿tengo que rellenar esto?
[keh]
fill up llenar [yenar]
fill it up, please lleno, por
favor [yeno por fabor]
filling (in cake, sandwich) el
relleno [reh-yeno]
(in tooth) el empaste
[empasteh],
(Ch, Mex) la tapadura,
(Col) la calza [kalsa],
(Rpl) la emplomadura
film (movie, for camera) la
película

dialogue

do you have this kind of film? ¿tiene películas de este tipo? [t-yeneh – deh esteh teepo]
yes, how many exposures? sí, ¿de cuántas fotos? [kwantas]
36 treinta y seis

film processing el revelado [rebelado]
filter coffee el café de filtro [kafeh deh feeltro]
filter papers los papeles de filtro [papel-es]
filthy muy sucio [mwee soos-yo]
find (verb) encontrar
I can't find it no lo encuentro [enkwentro]
I've found it ya lo encontré [enkontreh]
find out enterarse [enterarseh]
could you find out for me? ¿me lo puede averiguar? [meh lo pwedeh abaireegwar]
fine (noun) la multa [moolta]
it's fine today hoy hace buen tiempo [oy aseh bwen t-yempo]

dialogues

how are you? ¿cómo estás?
I'm fine, thanks bien, gracias [b-yen gras-yas]

is that OK? ¿va bien así? [ba]

that's fine, thanks está bien, gracias

finger el dedo
finish (verb) terminar [tairmeenar], acabar
I haven't finished yet no he terminado todavía [eh tairmeenado todabee-a]
when does it finish? ¿cuándo termina? [kwando tairmeena]
Finland Finlandia [feenland-ya]
Finnish (adj) finlandés [feenland-es]
fire el fuego [fwego]
(blaze) el incendio [eensend-yo]
fire! ¡fuego!
can we light a fire here? ¿se puede prender fuego aquí? [seh pwedeh prendair – akee]
it's on fire está ardiendo [ard-yendo]
fire alarm la alarma de incendios [deh eensend-yos]
fire brigade los bomberos [bombairos]
fire escape la salida de incendios [deh eensend-yos]
fire extinguisher el extintor [esteentor], (SAm) el extinguidor [esteengeedor]
first primero [preemairo]
I was first (said by man/woman) fui el primero/la primera [fwee]
at first al principio [preenseep-yo]

the **first time** la primera vez [bes]

first on the left la primera a la izquierda [eesk-**yair**da]

first aid primeros auxilios [ows**ee**l-yos]

first aid kit el botiquín [botee**kee**n]

first class (travel etc) de primera (clase) [preem**ai**ra (**kla**seh)]

first floor la primera planta, (Andes) el segundo piso [**pee**so]
(US) la planta baja [**ba**Ha], (Andes) el primer piso

first name el nombre de pila [**nom**breh deh]

fish el pez [pes]
(food) el pescado
(verb) pescar

fishing village el pueblo de pescadores [**pwe**blo deh peskad**or**-es]

fishmonger's la pescadería [peskada**ree**-a]

fit (attack) el ataque [a**ta**keh]

fit: it doesn't fit me no me viene bien [b-**ye**neh b-**yen**]

fitting room el probador

fix (repair) arreglar
(arrange) fijar [fee**Har**]

can you fix this? ¿puede arreglar esto? [**pwe**deh]

fizzy con gas

flag la bandera [band**ai**ra]

flannel la manopla, (SAm) la toallita [to-a –**yee**ta]

flash (for camera) el flash

flat (noun: apartment) el

departamento
(adj) llano [**ya**no]

I've got a flat tyre se me pinchó la llanta [seh meh – **yan**ta],
(Mex) se me ponchó la llanta

flavour el sabor

flea la pulga

flight el vuelo [**bwe**lo]

flight number el número de vuelo [**noo**mairo deh]

flippers las aletas

flood la inundación [eenoondas-**yon**]

floor el piso

florist la florería [florai**ree**-a], (Col, Ven) la floristería [floreestai**ree**-a]

flour la harina [a**ree**na]

flower la flor

flu el gripe [**gree**peh], (Col, Mex) la gripa

fluent: he speaks fluent Spanish domina el español [espan-**yol**]

fly la mosca
(verb) volar [bo**lar**]
can we fly there? ¿podemos ir en avión? [eer en ab-**yon**]

fly in llegar en avión [ye**gar**]

fly out irse en avión [**eer**seh]

fog la niebla [n-**yebla**]

foggy: it's foggy hay niebla [ī]

folk dancing el baile tradicional [**bī**leh tradees-yo**nal**]

folk music la música folklórica [**moo**seeka]

follow seguir [se**geer**]
follow me sígame [**see**gameh]

food la comida

food poisoning la intoxicación alimenticia [eentokseekas-yon aleementees-ya]

food shop/store la tienda de alimentos [t-yenda deh], el ultramarinos [ooltramareenos], (Andes, C.Am, Mex) la tienda de abarrotes,
(CSur) el almacén [almasen], (Cu, Per, Ven) la bodega

foot* (of person, measurement) el pie [p-yeh]
on foot a pie

football (game) el fútbol
(ball) el balón, la pelota, (Mex) el futbol

football match el partido de fútbol

for para, por
do you have something for ...? (headache/diarrhoea etc)
¿tiene algo para ...? [t-yeneh]

dialogues

who's the mole poblano for? ¿para quién es el mole poblano? [k-yen]
that's for me es para mí
and this one? ¿y éste? [ee esteh]
that's for her ése es para ella [eseh – eh-ya]

where do I get the bus for Quito? ¿dónde se toma el autobús para Quito? [dondeh seh – keeto]

the bus for Quito leaves from the bus station el autobús para Quito sale de la terminal [saleh deh la termeenal]

how long have you been here for? ¿cuánto tiempo lleva aquí? [kwanto t-yempo yeba akee]
I've been here for two days, how about you? llevo aquí dos días, ¿y usted? [yebo – ee oosteh]
I've been here for a week llevo aquí una semana

forehead la frente [frenteh]
foreign extranjero [estranHairo]
foreigner (man/woman) el extranjero, la extranjera
forest el bosque [boskeh]
forget olvidar [olbeedar]
I forget no me acuerdo [meh akwairdo]
I've forgotten se me olvidó [seh meh olbeedo]
fork el tenedor
(in road) la bifurcación [beefoorkas-yon]
form (document) el formulario [formoolar-yo]
formal (dress) de etiqueta [deh eteeketa]
fortnight quince días [keenseh dee-as], la quincena [keensena]
fortunately por suerte [swairteh]
forward: could you forward my mail? ¿puede enviarme el

correo? [pwedeh emb-yarmeh el korreh-o]

forwarding address la nueva dirección [nweba deereks-yon]

foundation (make-up) la crema base [baseh]

fountain la fuente [fwenteh]

foyer el vestíbulo [besteeboolo]

fracture la fractura [fraktoora]

France Francia [frans-ya]

free libre [leebreh]

(no charge) gratuito [gratweeto]

is it free (of charge)? ¿es gratis?

freeway la autopista [owtopeesta]

freezer el congelador [konHelador]

French francés [frans-es]

French fries las papas fritas

frequent frecuente [frekwenteh]

how frequent is the bus to La Paz? ¿cada cuánto tiempo hay autobús a La Paz [kwanto t-yempo ī – la pas]

fresh fresco

fresh orange el jugo de naranja [Hoogo de naranHa]

Friday viernes [b-yairn-es]

fridge la refrigeradora [refreeHairadora], (Rpl) la heladera [eladaira], (SAm) la nevera [nevaira]

fried frito

fried egg el huevo frito [webo]

friend (male/female) el amigo, la amiga

friendly simpático

from de [deh], desde [desdeh]

when does the next train from Guadalajara arrive? ¿cuándo llega el próximo tren de Guadalajara? [kwando yega – deh gwadalaHara]

from Monday to Friday de lunes a viernes [deh]

from next Thursday a partir del próximo jueves [parteer]

dialogue

where are you from? ¿de dónde es usted? [dondeh es oosteh]

I'm from Los Angeles soy de Los Angeles [anHel-es]

front la parte delantera [parteh delantaira]

in front delante [delanteh]

in front of the hotel delante del hotel

at the front en la parte de delante [deh]

frost la escarcha

frozen congelado [konHelado]

frozen food los congelados

fruit la fruta

fruit juice el jugo de frutas [Hoogo deh]

fry freír [freh-eer]

frying pan la sartén

full lleno [yeno]

it's full of ... está lleno de ... [deh]

I'm full (said by man/woman) estoy lleno/llena

full board pensión completa
[pens-yon]

fun: it was fun fue muy
divertido [fweh mwee
deebairteedo]

funeral el funeral [foonairal]

funny (strange) raro
(amusing) divertido
[deebairteedo]

furniture los muebles [mweb-
les]

further más allá [a-ya]
it's further down the road
está más adelante
[adelanteh]

dialogue

how much further is it to
Iguazú? ¿cuánto falta para
Iguazú? [kwanto – eegwasoo]
about 5 kilometres unos
cinco kilómetros

fuse el fusible [fooseebleh],
(CSur) el tapón
the lights have fused se
fundieron los fusibles [seh
foond-yairon]

fuse box la caja de fusibles
[kaHa deh fooseeb-les]

fuse wire el alambre de fusible
[alambreh]

future el futuro [footooro]
in the future en el futuro

G

gallon* el galón

game (cards etc) el juego
[Hwego]
(match) el partido
(meat) la caza [casa]

garage (for fuel) la gasolinera
[gasoleenaira]
(for repairs) el taller (de
reparaciones) [ta-yair (deh
reparas-yon-es)]
(for parking) el garaje [garaHeh],
la cochera [kochaira]

garden el jardín [Hardeen]

garlic el ajo [aHo]

gas el gas
(US) la gasolina,
(Ch) la bencina [benseena],
(Rpl) la nafta

gas cylinder (camping gas) la
bomba de gas

gasoline la gasolina

gas permeable lenses los
lentes porosos

gas station la gasolinera
[gasoleenaira],
(Andes, Ven) la bomba,
(Ch) la bencinera
[benseenaira],
(Pe) el grifo,
(Rpl) la estación de nafta
[estas-yon deh]

gate la puerta [pwairta]
(at airport) la puerta de
embarque [deh embarkeh]

gay gay

gay bar el bar gay

gearbox la caja de cambios [kaHa deh kamb-yos]

gear lever el cambio

gears la marcha

general general [Heneral]

gents (toilet) el baño de hombres [ban-yo deh omb-res]

genuine (antique etc) auténtico [owtenteeko]

German (adj, language) alemán

German measles la rubeola [roobeh-ola]

Germany Alemania [aleman-ya]

get (fetch) traer [tra-air]

will you get me another one, please? me trae otro, por favor [meh tra-eh – fabor]

how do you get to ...? ¿cómo se va a ...? [seh ba]

do you know where I can get them? ¿sabe dónde las puedo conseguir? [sabeh dondeh las pwedo konsegeer]

dialogue

can I get you a drink? ¿puedo ofrecerle algo de beber? [pwedo ofresairleh – deh bebair]

no, I'll get this one – what would you like? no, yo invito – ¿qué se le antoja? [eenbeeto keh seh leh antoHa]

a glass of red wine una copa de vino tinto [deh]

get back (return) regresar

get in (arrive) llegar [yegar]

get off bajarse [baHarseh]

where do I get off? ¿dónde tengo que bajarme? [dondeh – keh baHarmeh]

get on (to train etc) subirse [soobeerseh]

get out (of car etc) bajarse [baHarseh]

get up (in the morning) levantarse [lebantarseh]

gift el regalo

gift shop la tienda de regalos [t-yenda]

gin la ginebra [Heenebra]

a gin and tonic, please un gintónic, por favor [Heentoneek – fabor]

girl la chica [cheeka], la joven [Hoben], (Arg) la mina, (Col, Ven) la nena, (Mex) la chava [chaba], (Ven) la jeba [Heba]

girlfriend la novia [nob-ya]

give dar

can you give me some change? ¿me da suelto? [meh]

I gave it to him se lo di (a él) [seh]

will you give this to ...? ¿podría entregarle esto a ...? [entregarleh]

dialogue

how much do you want for this? ¿cuánto vale esto? [kwanto baleh]

1,000 pesos mil pesos

I'll give you 800 le doy ochocientos [leh]

give back devolver [debolbair]
glad feliz [felees]
glass (material) el vidrio [beedr-yo]
(tumbler) el vaso [baso]
(wine glass) la copa
a glass of wine una copa de vino [deh]
glasses las gafas
gloves los guantes [gwant-es]
glue el pegamento
go (verb) ir [eer]
we'd like to go to the swimming-pool nos gustaría ir a la piscina
where are you going? ¿adónde va? [adondeh ba]
where does this bus go? ¿adónde va este autobús? [esteh]
let's go! ¡vamos! [bamos]
she's gone (left) se fue [seh fweh]
where has he gone? ¿dónde se ha ido? [dondeh seh a]
I went there last week estuve la semana pasada [estoobeh]
go away irse [eerseh]
go away! ¡lárguese! [largeh-seh]
go back (return) regresar
go down (the stairs etc) bajar [baHar]
go in entrar
go out (in the evening) salir
do you want to go out

tonight? ¿quiere salir esta noche? [k-yaireh – nocheh]
go through pasar por
go up (the stairs etc) subir
goat la cabra
God Dios [d-yos]
goggles las gafas protectoras
gold el oro
golf el golf
golf course el campo de golf [deh]
good bueno [bweno]
good! ¡muy bien! [mwee b-yen]
it's no good es inútil [eenooteel]
goodbye hasta luego [asta lwego]
good evening buenas tardes [bwenas tard-es]
Good Friday el Viernes Santo [b-yairn-es]
good morning buenos días [bwenos]
good night buenas noches [bwenas noch-es]
goose el ganso
got: we've got to ... tenemos que ... [keh]
have you got any apples? ¿tiene manzanas? [t-yeneh]
government el gobierno [gob-yairno]
gradually poco a poco
grammar la gramática
gram(me) el gramo
granddaughter la nieta [n-yeta]
grandfather el abuelo [abwelo]
grandmother la abuela [abwela]

grandson el nieto [n-yeto]

grapefruit la toronja [toronHa], (CSur) el pomelo

grapefruit juice el jugo de toronja [Hoogo deh]

grapes las uvas [oobas]

grass el pasto, el césped [sesped]

grateful agradecido [agradeseedo]

gravy la salsa

great (excellent) muy bueno [mwee bweno]

that's great! ¡estupendo! [estoopendo]

a great success un gran éxito [ekseeto]

Great Britain Gran Bretaña [bretan-ya]

greedy guloso, (Col) garoso, (CSur) angurriento [angoorr-yento]

green verde [bairdeh]

green card (car insurance) la tarjeta verde [tarHeta] (in US) el permiso de residencia y trabajo [trabaHo]

greengrocer's la frutería [frootairee-a]

grey gris [grees]

grill la parrilla [parree-ya]

grilled a la parrilla, a la plancha

grocer's (Andes, C.Am, Mex) (la tienda de) abarrotes [(t-yenda deh) abarrot-es], (esp Csur) el almacén [almasen],

(Cu, Per, Ven) la bodega

ground el piso

on the ground en el piso

ground floor la planta baja [baHa], (Andes) el primer piso [preemair]

group el grupo

guarantee la garantía

is it guaranteed? ¿tiene garantía? [t-yeneh]

Guatemalan (adj) guatemalteco [gwatemalteko]

guest (man/woman) el invitado [eembeetado], la invitada

guesthouse la pensión [pens-yon]

guide el/la guía [gee-a]

guidebook la guía

guided tour la visita con guía [beeseeta]

guitar la guitarra [geetarra]

Gulf of Mexico el Golfo de México

gum (in mouth) la encía [ensee-a]

gun la pistola

Guyana Guyana [gooyana]

Guyanese (adj) guyanés [gooyan-es] (man) el guyanés (woman) la guyanesa

gym el gimnasio [Heemnas-yo]

H

hair el pelo

hairbrush el cepillo para el pelo [sepee-yo]

haircut el corte de pelo [korteh deh]

hairdresser's la peluquería [pelookairee-a]

hairdryer el secador de pelo [deh]

hair gel el fijador (para el pelo) [feeHador]

hairgrip la horquilla [orkee-ya]

hair spray la laca

half* la mitad [meeta]

half an hour media hora [med-ya ora]

half a litre medio litro [med-yo]

about half that aproximadamente la mitad de eso [aprokseemadamenteh – deh]

half board media pensión [med-ya pens-yon]

half fare el medio boleto [med-yo], el boleto con descuento [deskwento]

half price a mitad del precio [meeta del pres-yo]

ham el jamón [Hamon]

hamburger la hamburguesa [amboorgesa]

hammer el martillo [martee-yo]

hammock la hamaca [amaka]

hand la mano

handbag la cartera, (Col) el bolso, (Mex) la bolsa

handbrake el freno de mano [deh]

handkerchief el pañuelo [pan-ywelo]

handle (on door) el mango (on suitcase etc) el asa

hand luggage el equipaje de mano [ekeepaHeh]

hang-gliding el ala delta, (Mex) el deslizador [desleesador]

hangover la resaca, (C.Am, Mex) la cruda, (Col) el guayabo [gwa-yabo], (Ven) el ratón

I've got a hangover tengo resaca

happen suceder [soosedair]

what's happening? ¿qué pasa? [keh]

what has happened? ¿qué pasó?

happy contento

I'm not happy about this esto no me convence [meh konbenseh]

harbour el puerto [pwairto]

hard duro [dooro] (difficult) difícil [deefeeseel]

hard-boiled egg el huevo duro [webo]

hard lenses los lentes duros

hardly apenas

hardly ever casi nunca

hardware shop la ferretería [fairretairee-a], (Ch) la mercería [mairseree-a], (Mex) la tlapalería [tlapalairee-a]

hat el sombrero [sombrairo]

hate (verb) odiar [od-yar]

have* tener [tenair]

can I have a ...? ¿me da ...? [meh]

do you have ...? ¿tiene ...? [t-yeneh]

what'll you have? ¿qué va a tomar? [keh ba]

I have to leave now tengo que irme ahora [eermeh a-ora]

do I have to ...? ¿tengo que ...?

can we have some ...? ¿nos pone ...? [poneh]

hayfever la fiebre del heno [f-yebreh del eno]

hazelnut la avellana [abeh-yana]

he* él

head la cabeza [kabesa]

headache el dolor de cabeza [deh], la jaqueca [Hakeka]

headlights las luces de cruce [loos-es de krooseh]

headphones los auriculares [owreekoolar-es]

health food shop la tienda naturista [t-yenda natooreesta]

healthy sano

hear oír [o-eer]

dialogue

can you hear me? ¿me escuchas? [meh eskoochas]
I can't hear you, could you repeat that? no le escucho, ¿podría repetirlo? [leh]

hearing aid el audífono [owdeefono]

heart el corazón [korason]

heart attack el infarto

heat el calor

heater (in room) la estufa
(in car) la calefacción [kalefaks-yon]

heating la calefacción

heavy pesado

heel (of foot) el talón
(of shoe) el tacón

could you heel these? ¿podría cambiar los tacones? [kamb-yar – takon-es]

heelbar el zapatero [sapatairo]

height la altura

helicopter el helicóptero

hello! ¡hola! [ola]
(answer on phone)
(Mex) ¡bueno! [bweno],
(SAm) aló

helmet el casco

help la ayuda [a-yooda]
(verb) ayudar [a-yoodar]

help! ¡socorro!

can you help me? ¿puede ayudarme? [pwedeh a-yoodarmeh]

thank you very much for your help muchas gracias por su ayuda [moochas gras-yas]

helpful amable [amableh]

hepatitis la hepatitis [epateetees]

her*: I haven't seen her no la he visto [eh beesto]

to her a ella [eh-ya]

with her con ella

for her para ella

that's her ella es

that's her towel ésa es su toalla

herbal tea el té de hierbas [teh

deh y**ai**rbas],
(C.Am, Andes) el agua de
hierbas [**a**gwa],
(Per, Rpl) el té de yuyos [**yoo**-yos]
herbs las hierbas,
(Per, Rpl) los yuyos
here aquí [ak**ee**]
here is/are ... aquí está/
está**n** ...
here you are (offering) aquí
tiene [t-y**e**neh]
hers* (el) suyo [**soo**-yo], (la)
suya
that's hers es de ella [deh **eh**-ya], es suyo/suya
hey! ¡oiga! [**oy**ga]
hi! (hello) ¡hola! [**o**la]
hide (verb) esconder [eskond**ai**r]
high alto
highchair la silla alta para
bebés [**see**-ya – beh-b**e**s]
highway (US) la autopista
[owtop**ee**sta]
hill el cerro [s**ai**rro]
him*: I haven't seen him no lo
he visto [eh b**ee**sto]
to him a él
with him con él
for him para él
that's him él es
hip la cadera [kad**ai**ra]
hire (verb) alquilar [alke**e**lar],
arrendar
for hire de alquiler [deh
alke**e**lair]
where can I hire a bike?
¿dónde puedo alquilar una
bicicleta? [**d**ondeh pw**e**do]

his*: it's his car es su auto
[**ow**to]
that's his eso es de él [deh],
eso es suyo [**soo**-yo]
history la historia [eest**or**-ya]
hit (verb) golpear [golpeh-**ar**]
hitch-hike hacer autostop
[as**ai**r owtost**o**p],
(Col) echar dedo,
(Col, Mex) pedir aventón
[abent**o**n],
(Mex) pedir ráid [r**ī**d],
(Ven) pedir cola
hobby el pasatiempo [pasat-y**e**mpo]
hold (verb) tener en la mano
[ten**ai**r]
hole el agujero [agoo**H**airo], el
hoyo [**oy**-o]
holiday las vacaciones [bakas-y**o**n-es]
on holiday de vacaciones
[deh]
home la casa
at home (in my house) en casa
(in my country) en mi país [pa-**ee**s]
we go home tomorrow
regresamos a casa mañana
Honduran hondureño
[ondoor**e**n-yo]
(man) el hondureño
(woman) la hondureña
Honduras Honduras [ond**oo**ras]
honest honrado [onr**r**ado]
honey la miel [m-yel]
honeymoon la luna de miel
[**loo**na deh]
hood (US: of car) el capó, el

capote [kapoteh],
(Mex) el cofre [kofreh]
hope la esperanza [espairansa]
 I hope so espero que sí
 [espairo keh]
 I hope not espero que no
 hopefully it won't rain no
 lloverá, eso espero [yobaira]
horn (of car) el klaxon
horrible horrible [orreebleh]
horse el caballo [kaba-yo]
horse racing las carreras de
 caballos [karrairas deh kaba-yos]
horse riding la equitación
 [ekeetas-yon]
 I like horse riding me gusta
 montar a caballo [meh – kaba-
 yo]
hospital el hospital [ospeetal]
hospitality la hospitalidad
 [ospeetaleeda]
 thank you for your hospitality
 gracias por su hospitalidad
 [gras-yas]
hot caliente [kal-yenteh]
 (spicy) picante [peekanteh],
 picoso
 I'm hot tengo calor
 it's hot today hoy hace calor
 [oy aseh]
hotel el hotel [otel]
hotel room el cuarto de hotel
 [kwarto deh otel]
hour la hora [ora]
house la casa
house wine el vino de la casa
 [beeno deh]
hovercraft el aerodeslizador
 [a-airodesleesador]

how cómo
 how many? ¿cuántos?
 [kwantos]
 how do you do? ¡mucho
 gusto! [moocho goosto]

dialogues

 how are you? ¿cómo le va?
 [leh ba]
 fine, thanks, and you? bien
 gracias, ¿y a usted? [b-yen
 gras-yas ee a oosteh]

 how much is it? ¿cuánto
 vale? [kwanto baleh]
 1,000 pesos mil pesos
 [pesos]
 I'll take it me lo quedo
 [meh lo kedo]

humid húmedo [oomedo]
humour el humor [oomor]
hungry hambriento [ambr-
 yento]
 I'm hungry tengo hambre
 [ambreh]
 are you hungry? ¿tiene
 hambre? [t-yeneh]
hurry (verb) apurarse
 [apoorarseh]
 I'm in a hurry tengo prisa
 there's no hurry no hay prisa
 [i]
 hurry up! ¡apúrese! [apooreseh]
hurt doler [dolair]
 it really hurts me duele
 mucho [meh dweleh moocho]
husband el marido

hydrofoil la hidroala [eedro-**a**la]
hypermarket el hipermercado [eepairmair**ka**do]

I

I yo
ice el hielo [**ye**lo]
 with ice con hielo
 no ice, thanks sin hielo, por favor [seen – fab**or**]
ice cream el helado [e**la**do]
ice-cream cone el cucurucho [kookoor**oo**cho]
iced coffee el café helado [kaf**eh** e**la**do]
ice lolly la paleta
idea la idea [eed**eh**-a]
idiot el/la idiota [eed-y**o**ta]
if si
ignition el encendido [ensend**ee**do]
ill enfermo [enf**air**mo]
 I feel ill me encuentro mal [meh enk**we**ntro]
illness la enfermedad [enfairme**da**]
imitation (leather etc) de imitación [deh eemeetas-y**on**]
immediately en seguida [seg**ee**da]
important importante [eemport**an**teh]
 it's very important es muy importante [mwee]
 it's not important no tiene importancia [t-y**e**neh eemport**ans**-ya]

impossible imposible [eempos**ee**bleh]
impressive impresionante [eempres-yon**an**teh]
improve mejorar [meHor**ar**]
 I want to improve my Spanish quiero mejorar mi español [k-y**ai**ro – espan-y**ol**]
in: **it's in the centre** está en el centro
 in my car en mi auto
 in Havana en La Habana [ab**a**na]
 in two days from now en dos días más
 in five minutes dentro de cinco minutos [deh]
 in May en mayo
 in English en inglés [eeng-l**es**]
 in Spanish en español [espan-y**ol**]
 is he in? ¿se encuentra? [seh enk**we**ntra]
inch* la pulgada
include incluir [eenkloo-**ee**r]
 does that include meals? ¿están incluidas las comidas? [eenkloo-**ee**das]
 is that included? ¿está incluido en el precio? [eenkloo-**ee**do en el pres-yo]
inconvenient inoportuno [eenoport**oo**no]
incredible increíble [eenkreh-**ee**bleh]
Indian (adj: from India) indio [**een**d-yo]
 (South American: adj) indígena [eend**ee**Hena]

73

(man/woman) el/la indígena

indicator el intermitente [eentairmeetenteh], (Ch) el señalizador [senyaleesador], (Col, Mex) la direccional [deereks-yon-al]

indigestion la indigestión [eendeeHest-yon]

indoor pool la piscina cubierta [peeseena koob-yairta], (Mex) la alberca cubierta [albairka], (Rpl) la pileta cubierta [peeleta]

indoors dentro de la casa [deh]

inexpensive económico

infection la infección [eenfeks-yon]

infectious contagioso [kontaH-yoso]

inflammation la inflamación [eenflamas-yon]

informal (occasion, meeting) informal [eenformal], (dress) de sport [deh]

information la información [eenformas-yon]

  do you have any information about ...? ¿tiene información sobre ... ? [t-yeneh – sobreh]

information desk la información

injection la inyección [eenyeks-yon]

injured herido [ereedo]

  she's been injured está herida

in-laws la familia política [fameel-ya]

inner tube (for tyre) la cámara

de aire [deh **a-ee**reh]

innocent inocente [eenosenteh]

insect el insecto [eensekto]

insect bite la picadura de insecto [deh]

  do you have anything for insect bites? ¿tiene algo para la picadura de insectos? [t-yeneh]

insect repellent el repelente de insectos [repelenteh deh]

inside dentro de [deh]

  inside the hotel dentro del hotel

  let's sit inside vamos a sentarnos adentro [bamos]

insist insistir [eenseesteer]

  I insist insisto

insomnia el insomnio [eensomn-yo]

instant coffee el café instantáneo [kafeh eenstantaneh-o]

instead: give me that one instead deme ese otro [demeh eseh]

  instead of ... en lugar de ... [deh]

intersection el cruce [krooseh]

insulin la insulina [eensooleena]

insurance el seguro [segooro]

intelligent inteligente [eenteleeHenteh]

interested: I'm interested in ... me interesa ... [meh eentairesa]

interesting interesante [eentairesanteh]

  that's very interesting es muy interesante [mwee]

international internacional
[eentairnas-yonal]

interpret actuar de intérprete
[actoo-ar deh eentairpreteh]

interpreter el/la intérprete

interval (at theatre) el
intermedio [eentairmed-yo]

into en

I'm not into ... no me gusta ...
[meh goosta]

introduce presentar

may I introduce ...? le
presento a ... [leh]

invitation la invitación
[eembeetas-yon]

invite invitar [eembeetar]

Ireland Irlanda [eerlanda]

Irish irlandés [eerland-es]

I'm Irish (man/woman) soy
irlandés/irlandesa

iron (for ironing) la plancha
(metal) el hierro [yairro]

can you iron these for me?
¿puede planchármelos?
[pwedeh]

is* es, está

island la isla [eesla]

it ello, lo [eh-yo]

it is ... es ...; está ...

is it ...? ¿es ...?; ¿está ... ?

where is it? ¿dónde está?
[dondeh]

it's him es él

it was ... era ... [aira]; estaba
...

Italian (adj) italiano [eetal-yano]

Italy Italia

itch la comezón [komeson]

it itches me pica [meh]

J

jack (for car) el gato

jacket el saco

jam la mermelada [mairmelada]

jammed: it's jammed se atoró
[seh]

January enero [enairo]

jar el pote [poteh]

jaw la mandíbula

jazz el jazz

jealous celoso [seloso]

jeans los vaqueros [bakairos],
(SAm) los jeans [yeens]

jellyfish la medusa [medoosa],
(Col, Mex) la aguamala
[agwamala],
(Per) la malagua [malagwa], la
aguaviva [agwabeeba]

jersey el jersey [Hairseh]

jetty el muelle [mweh-yeh]

jeweller's shop la joyería [Ho-
yairee-a]

jewellery las joyas [Ho-yas]

Jewish judío [Hoodee-o]

job el trabajo [trabaHo], el
puesto [pwesto]

jogging el footing

to go jogging hacer footing
[asair]

joke el chiste [cheesteh]

journey el viaje [b-yaHeh]

have a good journey! ¡buen
viaje! [bwen]

jug la jarra [Harra]

a jug of water una jarra de
agua [deh]

juice el jugo [Hoogo]

July julio [Hool-yo]
jump (verb) brincar
jumper el jersey [Hairseh]
jump leads las pinzas (para la batería) [peensas (para la batairee-a)]
junction el cruce [krooseh]
June junio [Hoon-yo]
jungle la selva
just (only) solamente [solamenteh]
just two sólo dos
just for me sólo para mí
just here aquí mismo [akee meesmo],
(Mex) aquí mero [mairo]
not just now ahora no [a-ora]
we've just arrived acabamos de llegar [deh yegar]

K

kayak el kayak
keep quedarse [kedarseh]
keep the change quédese con el cambio [kedeseh – kamb-yo]
can I keep it? ¿puedo quedármelo? [pwedo kedarmelo]
please keep it por favor, quédeselo [fabor kedeselo]
ketchup la salsa de tomate [salsa deh tomateh],
(Mex) el catsup [katsoop]
kettle el hervidor [airbeedor]
key la llave [yabeh]
the key for room 201, please la llave del doscientos uno,

por favor [fabor]
keyring el llavero [yabairo]
kidneys los riñones [reen-yon-es]
kill matar
kilo* el kilo
kilometre* el kilómetro
how many kilometres is it to ...? ¿cuántos kilómetros hay a …? [kwantos – ī]
kind (nice) amable [amableh]
that's very kind es muy amable [mwee]

dialogue

which kind do you want? ¿qué tipo quiere? [keh teepo k-yaireh]
I want this/that kind quiero este/aquel tipo [k-yairo esteh/akel]

king el rey [ray]
kiosk el quiosco [k-yosko]
kiss el beso
(verb) besarse [besarseh]
kitchen la cocina [koseena]
kitchenette la cocina pequeña [peken-ya]
Kleenex® el klínex
knee la rodilla [rodee-ya]
knickers los pantis,
(C.Am) las calzonetas,
(Col) los cucos,
(Mex, Ven) las pantaletas,
(Rpl) las bombachas
knife el cuchillo [koochee-yo]

knock (verb: on door) llamar
[yamar]
knock down atropellar
[atropeh-yar]
he's been knocked down lo
atropellaron [atropeh-yaron]
knock over (object) volcar
[bolkar]
(pedestrian) atropellar [atropeh-
yar]
know (somebody, a place)
conocer [konosair]
(something) saber [sabair]
I don't know no sé [seh]
I didn't know that no lo sabía
do you know where I can
find ...? ¿sabe dónde puedo
encontrar …? [sabeh dondeh
pwedo]

dialogue

do you know how this
works? ¿sabe cómo
funciona esto? [foons-yona]
sorry, I don't know lo
siento, no sé [s-yento no seh]

L

label la etiqueta [eteeketa]
ladies' room, ladies' (toilet) el
baño de señoras [ban-yo deh
sen-yoras]
ladies' wear la ropa de señoras
lady la señora [sen-yora]
lager la cerveza clara [sairbesa]
lagoon la laguna

lake el lago
lamb (meat) el cordero
[kordairo]
lamp la lámpara
land la tierra [t-yairra]
(verb) aterrizar [aterreesar]
lane (motorway) el carril
(small road) la callejuela [ka-
yeh-Hwela]
language el idioma [eed-yoma]
language course el curso de
idiomas [koorso deh]
large grande [grandeh]
last último [oolteemo]
last week la semana pasada
last Friday el viernes pasado
last night anoche [anocheh]
what time is the last train to
Buenos Aires? ¿a qué hora es
el último tren para Buenos
Aires? [keh ora – bwenos īres]
late tarde [tardeh]
sorry I'm late disculpe,
me retrasé [deeskoolpeh meh
retraseh]
the train was late el tren se
demoró
we must go – we'll be late
debemos irnos – llegaremos
tarde [eernos – yegaremos]
it's getting late se está
haciendo tarde [seh – as-
yendo]
later más tarde [tardeh]
I'll come back later regresaré
más tarde [regresareh]
see you later hasta luego
[asta lwego]
later on más tarde

latest lo último [**oo**lteemo]
 by Wednesday at the latest
 para el miércoles a más
 tardar
Latin America Latinoamérica
 [lateeno-am**ai**reeka]
Latin American (adj)
 latinoamericano [lateeno-
 amaireek**a**no]
 (man) el latinoamericano
 (woman) la latinoamericana
laugh (verb) reírse [reh-**ee**rseh]
launderette/laundromat la
 lavandería automática
 [labandair**ee**-a owtom**a**teeka]
laundry (clothes) la ropa sucia
 [**soos**-ya]
 (place) la lavandería
 [labandair**ee**-a]
lavatory el baño [**ban**-yo]
law la ley [lay]
lawn el césped [**ses**ped]
lawyer (man/woman) el
 abogado, la abogada
laxative el laxante [lak**san**teh]
lazy flojo [flo**H**o]
lead (electrical) el cable [**kab**leh]
lead (verb) llevar [ye**var**]
 where does this lead to?
 ¿adónde va esto? [ad**on**deh ba]
leaf la hoja [**o**Ha]
leaflet el folleto [fo-**ye**to]
leak (in roof) la gotera [go**tai**ra]
 (gas, water) el escape [es**ka**peh]
 (verb) filtrar [feel**trar**]
 the roof leaks el tejado tiene
 goteras [te**Ha**do t-yeneh go**tai**ras]
learn aprender [apren**dair**]
least: not in the least de

ninguna manera [deh
 – man**ai**ra]
 at least al menos
leather (fine) la piel [p-yel]
 (heavy) el cuero [**kwai**ro]
leave (verb) irse [**eer**seh]
 I am leaving tomorrow me
 voy mañana [meh]
 he left yesterday se fue ayer
 [seh fweh]
 may I leave this here? ¿puedo
 dejar esto aquí? [pwedo deh-**H**ar
 esto ak**ee**]
 I left my coat in the bar dejé
 el abrigo en el bar [deh-**H**e**h**]

dialogue

when does the bus
for Montevideo leave?
¿cuándo sale el autobús
para Montevideo? [kwando
saleh – montebeedeo]
it leaves at 9 o'clock sale a
las nueve

leek el puerro [**pwai**rro]
left izquierda [eesk-**yair**da]
 on the left a la izquierda
 to the left hacia la izquierda
 [as-ya]
 turn left dé vuelta a la
 izquierda [deh bwelta]
 there's none left no queda
 ninguno [**ke**da]
left-handed zurdo [**soor**do]
left luggage (office) la
 consigna [kon**seeg**na], la
 paquetería [paket**ai**ree-a]

leg la pierna [p-yairna]
lemon el limón
lemonade la limonada
lemon tea el té con limón [teh]
lend prestar
  will you lend me your ... ? ¿podría prestarme su ...? [prestarmeh]
lens (of camera) el objetivo [obHeteebo]
lesbian la lesbiana [lesb-yana]
less menos
  less expensive menos caro
  less than 10 menos de diez [deh]
  less than you menos que tú [keh too]
lesson la lección [leks-yon]
let (allow) dejar [deh-Har]
  will you let me know? ¿me tendrás al corriente? [meh – korr-yenteh]
  I'll let you know le avisaré [leh abeesareh]
  let's go for something to eat vamos a comer algo [bamos a komair]
  let off: will you let me off at ...? ¿me deja en...? [meh deh-Ha]
letter la carta
  do you have any letters for me? ¿tiene cartas para mí? [t-yeneh]
letterbox el buzón [booson]
lettuce la lechuga [lechooga]
lever la palanca
library la biblioteca [beebl-yoteka]

licence el permiso
lid la tapa
lie (verb: tell untruth) mentir
lie down acostarse [akostarseh], echarse [echarseh]
life la vida [beeda]
lifebelt el salvavidas [salbabeedas]
lifeguard el/la socorrista
life jacket el chaleco salvavidas [salbabeedas]
lift (in building) el ascensor [asensor]
  could you give me a lift? ¿me podría llevar? [meh – yebar]
  would you like a lift? ¿quiere que lo lleve? [k-yaireh keh lo yebeh]
light la luz [loos]
  (not heavy) ligero [leeHairo]
  do you have a light? (for cigarette) ¿tiene fuego? [t-yeneh fwego]
light green verde claro [bairdeh]
light bulb la bombilla, (Ch) la ampolleta [ampo-yeta], (Col, Ven) el bombillo, (Mex) el foco, (Rpl) la bombita
  I need a new light bulb necesito una bombilla nueva [neseseeto – nweba]
lighter (cigarette) el encendedor [ensendedor]
lightning el relámpago
like (verb) gustar [goostar]
  I like it me gusta [meh]
  I like going for walks me

gusta pasear
I like you me gustas
I don't like it no me gusta
do you like ...? ¿le gusta ...? [leh]
I'd like a beer quisiera una cerveza [kees-yaira]
I'd like to go swimming me gustaría ir a bañarme
would you like a drink? ¿quiere beber algo? [k-yaireh]
would you like to go for a walk? ¿quieres dar un paseo? [k-yair-es]
what's it like? ¿cómo es?
I want one like this quiero uno como éste [k-yairo – esteh]
lime la lima [leema]
lime cordial el jarabe de lima [Harabeh deh]
line la línea [leeneh-a]
could you give me an outside line? ¿puede darme línea? [pwedeh darmeh]
lips los labios [lab-yos]
lip salve la crema de labios [deh]
lipstick el lápiz de labios [lapees]
liqueur el licor
listen escuchar [eskoochar]
litre* el litro
a litre of white wine un litro de vino blanco [deh]
little chico
just a little, thanks un poquito, gracias [pokeeto gras-yas]
a little milk un poco de leche

a little bit more un poquito más
live (verb) vivir [beebeer]
we live together vivimos juntos [beebeemos Hoontos]

dialogue

> where do you live? ¿dónde vive? [dondeh beebeh]
> I live in London vivo en Londres [beebo en lond-res]

lively alegre [alegreh], animado
liver el hígado [eegado]
lizard la lagartija [lagarteeHa]
loaf el pan
lobby (in hotel) el vestíbulo [besteeboolo]
lobster la langosta
local local
can you recommend a local wine/restaurant? ¿puede recomendarme un vino/un restaurante local? [pwedeh rekomendarmeh]
lock la cerradura [sairradoora] (verb) cerrar [sairrar]
it's locked está cerrado con llave [sairrado kon yabeh]
lock in dejar encerrado [deH-Har ensairrado]
lock out: I've locked myself out he cerrado la puerta con las llaves dentro [eh sairrado la pwairta – yab-es]
locker (for luggage etc) la consigna automática [konseegna owtomateeka]

lollipop la paleta

London Londres [lond-res]

long largo

how long will it take to fix it? ¿cuánto tiempo tardará en arreglarlo? [kwanto t-yempo]

how long does it take? ¿cuánto tiempo lleva? [yeba]

a long time mucho tiempo [moocho]

one day/two days longer un día/dos días más

long distance call la llamada de larga distancia [yamada deh – deestans-ya]

look: I'm just looking, thanks sólo estoy mirando, gracias [gras-yas]

you don't look well tienes cara de enfermo [t-yen-es kara deh enfairmo]

look out! ¡cuidado! [kweedado]

can I have a look? ¿me deja ver? [meh deh-Ha bair]

look after cuidar [kweedar]

look at mirar

look for buscar

I'm looking for ... estoy buscando ...

look forward to: I'm looking forward to seeing it tengo muchas ganas de verlo [moochas – deh bairlo]

loose (handle etc) suelto [swelto]

lorry el camión [kam-yon], el tráiler [trilair]

lose perder [pairdair], extraviarse [estrab-yarseh]

I've lost my way me extravié

[estrab-yeh]

I'm lost, I want to get to ... me perdí, quiero ir a ... [k-yairo eer]

I've lost my bag perdí el bolso

lost property (office) (la oficina de) objetos perdidos [(ofeeseena deh) obHetos pairdeedos]

lot: a lot, lots mucho, muchos [moocho]

not a lot no mucho

a lot of people mucha gente

a lot bigger mucho mayor

I like it a lot me gusta mucho [meh goosta]

lotion la loción [los-yon]

loud fuerte [fwairteh]

lounge (in house, hotel) el salón (in airport) la sala de espera [deh espaira]

love el amor (verb) querer [kairair]

I love Guatemala me encanta Guatemala [meh – gwatemala]

lovely encantador

low bajo [baHo]

luck la suerte [swairteh]

good luck! ¡buena suerte! [bwena]

luggage el equipaje [ekeepaH-eh]

luggage trolley el carrito portaequipajes [porta-ekeepaH-es]

lump (on body) la hinchazón [eenchason]

lunch el almuerzo [almwairso]

lungs los pulmones [poolmon-es]

luxurious (hotel, furnishings) de lujo [deh looHo]

luxury el lujo

M

machine la máquina [makeena]

mad (insane) loco

(angry) furioso [foor-yoso]

magazine la revista [rebeesta]

maid (in hotel) la mucama [mookama]

maiden name el apellido de soltera [apeh-yeedo deh soltaira]

mail el correo [korreh-o]

is there any mail for me? ¿hay correspondencia para mí? [ī korrespondens-ya]

mailbox el buzón [booson]

main principal [preenseepal]

main course el plato principal

main post office la oficina central del correo [ofeeseena sentral del korreh-o]

main road (in town) la calle principal [ka-yeh preenseepal] (in country) la carretera principal [karretaira]

mains (for water) la llave de paso [yabeh deh]

mains switch (for electricity) el interruptor de la red eléctrica [eentairrooptor deh la reh]

make (brand name) la marca (verb) hacer [asair]

I make it 500 pesos son quinientos pesos en total

what is it made of? ¿de qué está hecho? [deh keh esta echo]

make-up el maquillaje [makee-yaHeh]

man el hombre [ombreh]

manager el gerente [Hairenteh]

I'd like to speak to the manager quisiera hablar con el gerente [kees-yaira ablar]

manageress la gerente

manual (car with manual gears) el auto de marchas [deh], (Andes) el auto manual [manwal]

many muchos [moochos]

not many pocos

map (city plan) el plano (road map, geographical) el mapa

March marzo [marso]

margarine la margarina

market el mercado [mairkado], (Col) la plaza (de mercado), (Csur, Per) la feria [fair-ya], (Mex) el tianguis [t-yangees]

marmalade la mermelada de naranja [mairmelada deh naranHa]

married: I'm married (said by a man/woman) estoy casado/casada

are you married? (to a man/woman) ¿está casado/casada?

mascara el rímel, (Col) la pestañina [pestan-yeena]

match (football etc) el partido

matches las cerillas [sairee-yas]

material (fabric) el tejido
[teHeedo]
matter: it doesn't matter no
importa
what's the matter? ¿qué pasa?
[keh]
mattress el colchón
May mayo [ma-yo]
may: may I have another one?
¿me da otro? [meh]
may I come in? ¿se puede?
[seh pwedeh]
may I see it? ¿puedo verlo?
[pwedo bairlo]
may I sit here? ¿puedo
sentarme aquí? [sentarmeh
akee]
maybe quizás [keesas]
mayonnaise la mayonesa
[ma-yonesa]
me*: that's for me ése es para
mí [eseh]
send it to me mándemelo
me too yo también [tamb-yen]
meal la comida

dialogue

did you enjoy your meal?
¿te gustó la comida? [teh
goosto]
it was excellent, thank you
estuvo riquísima, gracias
[reekeeseema gras-yas]

mean (verb) querer decir
[kairair deseer]
what do you mean? ¿qué
quiere decir? [keh k-yaireh]

dialogue

what does this word
mean? ¿qué significa esta
palabra?
it means ... in English
significa ... en inglés
[eeng-les]

measles el sarampión [saramp-
yon]
meat la carne [karneh]
mechanic el mecánico
medicine la medicina
[medeeseena]
medium (adj: size) medio
[med-yo]
medium-dry semi-seco
medium-rare poco hecho
[echo]
medium-sized de tamaño
medio [taman-yo med-yo]
meet encontrarse [enkontrarseh]
(for the first time) conocerse
[konosairseh]
nice to meet you (said to
man/woman) encantado de
conocerlo/la [deh]
where shall I meet you?
¿dónde nos vemos? [dondeh
nos bemos]
meeting la reunión [reh-oon-yon]
meeting place el lugar
de encuentro [loogar deh
enkwentro]
melon el melón
men los hombres [omb-res]
mend (clothes) remendar
could you mend this for me?

¿puede arreglarme esto?
[pwedeh arreglarmeh]

men's toilet el baño de
hombres [ban-yo deh omb-res]

menswear la ropa de hombre
[deh ombreh]

mention (verb) mencionar
[mens-yonar]

don't mention it de nada [deh]

menu la carta

may I see the menu, please?
¿me deja ver la carta? [meh
deh-Ha bair]

see menu reader page XYZ

message: are there any
messages for me? ¿hay algún
recado para mí? [i]

I want to leave a message
for ... quisiera dejar un recado
para ... [kees-yaira deh-Har]

metal el metal

metre* el metro

Mexican (adj) mexicano
[meHeekano]

(man) el mexicano

(woman) la mexicana

Mexico México [meHeeko]

Mexico City la ciudad de
México [s-yooda deh], el
Distrito Federal [fedairal], el
D.F. [deh efeh]

microwave (oven) el (horno)
microondas [(orno) meekro-
ondas]

midday el mediodía [med-
yodee-a]

at midday a mediodía

middle: in the middle en el
centro [sentro]

in the middle of the night en
las altas horas de la noche
[oras deh la nocheh]

the middle one el de en
medio

midnight la medianoche [med-
yanocheh]

at midnight a medianoche

might: I might es posible
[poseebleh]

I might not go puede que no
vaya [pwedeh keh no ba-ya]

I might want to stay another
day quizás decida quedarme
otro día [keesas deseeda
kedarmeh]

migraine la jaqueca [Hakeka]

mild (taste) suave [swabeh]

(weather) templado

mile* la milla [mee-ya]

milk la leche [lecheh]

milkshake

(Col) malteada [malteh-ada],

(Mex) el licuado [leekwado],

(Ven) merengada [mairengada]

millimetre* el milímetro

minced meat la carne molida
[karneh]

mind: never mind! ¡no
importa!

I've changed my mind
cambié de idea [kamb-yeh deh
eedeh-a]

dialogue

do you mind if I open the
window? ¿le importa
que abra la ventana? [leh

eempo**r**ta keh – benta**na**]
no, I don't mind no, no me
importa [meh]

mine*: it's mine es mío
mineral water el agua mineral
[**a**gwa meen**ai**ral],
(Mex) el Tehuacán® [teh-
wak**an**]
mint-flavoured con sab**o**r a
menta
mints las pastillas de menta
[past**ee**-yas deh]
minute el minuto [meen**oo**to]
in a minute ahorita [a-or**ee**ta]
just a minute un momento
mirror el espejo [esp**e**Ho]
Miss señorita [sen-yor**ee**ta]
miss: I missed the bus perdí el
autobús [pairde**e**]
missing: one of my ... is missing
falta uno de mis ... [deh]
there's a suitcase missing
falta una maleta
mist la neblina
mistake el error
I think there's a mistake
me parece que hay una
equivocación [meh par**e**seh keh
ī **oo**na ekeebokas-yon]
sorry, I've made a mistake
perdón, me equivoqué [meh
ekeebok**eh**]
misunderstanding el
malentendido
mix-up: sorry, there's been
a mix-up perdón hubo una
confusión [**oo**bo **oo**na konfoos-
yon]

modern moderno [mod**ai**rno]
modern art gallery la galería
de arte moderno [galair**ee**-a
deh **a**rteh]
moisturizer la crema
hidratante [eedrat**a**nteh]
moment: I won't be a moment
no me tardo [meh]
monastery el monasterio
[monast**ai**r-yo]
Monday lunes [**loo**n-es]
money el dinero [deen**ai**ro]
month el mes
monument el monumento
[mono**o**mento]
(statue) la estatua [est**a**twa]
moon la luna
moped el ciclomotor
[seeklomot**o**r]
more* más
can I have some more water,
please? me da más agua, por
favor [meh – fab**o**r]
more expensive/interesting
más caro/interesante
more than 50 más de
cincuenta [deh]
more than that más que eso
[keh]
a lot more mucho más
[m**oo**cho]

dialogue

would you like some
more? ¿quiere más? [k-
y**ai**reh]
no, no more for me, thanks
no, para mí no, gracias

[gras-yas]
how about you? ¿y usted?
[ee oosteh]
**I don't want any more,
thanks** nada más, gracias

morning la mañana [man-yana]
 this morning esta mañana
 in the morning por la mañana
mosquito el mosquito, el
 zancudo [sankoodo]
mosquito coil el espiral
 antimosquitos
mosquito net el mosquitero
 [moskeetairo]
mosquito repellent el
 repelente de mosquitos
 [repelenteh deh]
most: I like this one most of all
 éste es el que más me gusta
 [esteh – keh mas meh goosta]
 most of the time la mayor
 parte del tiempo [ma-yor
 parteh del t-yempo]
 most tourists la mayoría de
 los turistas [ma-yoree-a deh]
 mostly generalmente
 [Henairalmenteh]
mother la madre [madreh]
motorbike la moto
motorboat la (lancha) motora
motorway la autopista
 [owtopeesta]
mountain la montaña [montan-
 ya]
 in the mountains en la sierra
 [s-yaira]
mountaineering el
 montañismo [montan-yeesmo]

mountain range la sierra, la
 cordillera [kordee-yaira]
mouse el ratón
moustache el bigote [beegoteh]
mouth la boca
mouth ulcer la llaga [yaga]
**move: he's moved to another
 room** se trasladó a otro
 cuarto [seh – kwarto]
 could you move your car?
 ¿podría cambiar de lugar el
 auto? [kamb-yar deh]
 could you move up a little?
 ¿puede correrse un poco?
 [pwedeh korrairseh]
 where has it moved to?
 ¿adónde se trasladó? [adondeh
 seh]
movie la película [peleekoola]
movie theater el cine
 [seeneh]
Mr señor [sen-yor]
Mrs señora [sen-yora]
Ms señorita [sen-yoreeta]
much mucho [moocho]
 much better/worse mucho
 mejor/peor [meHor/peh-or]
 much hotter mucho más
 caliente [kal-yenteh]
 not (very) much no mucho
 I don't want very much un
 poco nada más
mud el barro, el lodo
mug (for drinking) la taza [tasa]
 I've been mugged me
 asaltaron
mum la mamá
mumps las paperas [papairas]
museum el museo [mooseh-o]

mushrooms los champiñones [champeen-yon-es]
music la música [mooseeka]
musician el músico [mooseeko], la música
Muslim (adj) musulmán [moosoolman]
mussels los mejillones [meHee-yon-es]
must: I must tengo que [keh]
I mustn't drink alcohol no debo beber alcohol [bebair alko-ol]
mustard la mostaza [mostasa]
my* mi; (pl) mis
myself: I'll do it myself (said by man/woman) lo haré yo mismo/misma [areh]
by myself (said by man/woman) yo solo/sola

N

nail (finger) la uña [oon-ya]
(metal) el clavo [klabo]
nailbrush el cepillo para las uñas [sepee-yo – oon-yas]
nail varnish el esmalte para uñas [esmalteh]
name el nombre [nombreh]
my name's John me llamo John [meh yamo]
what's your name? ¿cómo se llama? [seh yama], ¿cuál es su nombre? [kwal – nombreh]
what is the name of this street? ¿cómo se llama esta calle?

napkin la servilleta [sairbee-yeta]
nappy el pañal [pan-yal]
narrow (street) estrecho [estrecho]
nasty (person) desagradable [desagradableh]
(weather, accident) malo
national nacional [nas-yonal]
nationality la nacionalidad [nas-yonaleeda]
natural natural [natooral]
nausea la náusea [nowseh-a]
navy (blue) azul marino [asool]
near cerca [sairka]
is it near the city centre? ¿está cerca del centro? [sentro]
do you go near the museum? ¿pasa usted cerca del museo? [oosteh – mooseh-o]
where is the nearest ...? ¿dónde está el ... más cercano? [dondeh – sairkano]
nearby por aquí cerca [akee]
nearly casi
necessary necesario [nesesar-yo]
neck el cuello [kweh-yo]
necklace el collar [ko-yar]
necktie la corbata
need: I need ... necesito un ... [neseseeto]
do I need to pay? ¿necesito pagar?
needle la aguja [agooHa]
negative (film) el negativo [negateebo]
neither: neither (one) of them

ninguno (de ellos) [neengoono (deh eh-yos)]
neither ... nor ... ni ... ni ...
nephew el sobrino
net (in sport) la red
Netherlands Los Países Bajos [pa-ees-es baHos]
network map el mapa
never nunca, jamás [Hamas]

dialogue

have you ever been to Tegucigalpa? ¿ha estado alguna vez en Tegucigalpa? [bes – tegooseegalpa]
no, never, I've never been there no, nunca estuve [estoobeh]

new nuevo [nwebo]
news (radio, TV etc) las noticias [notees-yas]
newspaper el periódico [pair-yodeeko]
newspaper kiosk el puesto de periódicos [pwesto deh]
New Year el Año Nuevo [an-yo nwebo]
Happy New Year! ¡Feliz Año Nuevo! [felees]
New Year's Eve Nochevieja [nocheh-b-yeHa]
New Zealand Nueva Zelanda [nweba selanda]
New Zealander: I'm a New Zealander (man/woman) soy neocelandés/neocelandesa

[neh-o-seland-es]
next próximo
the next street on the left la próxima calle a la izquierda [ka-yeh a la eesk-yairda]
at the next stop en la siguiente parada [seeg-yenteh]
next week la semana que viene [keh b-yeneh]
next to al lado de [deh]
Nicaragua Nicaragua [neekaragwa]
Nicaraguan (adj) nicaragüense [neekaragwenseh]
(person) el/la nicaragüense
nice (food) bueno [bweno]
(looks, view etc) lindo
(person) simpático
niece la sobrina
night la noche [nocheh]
at night de noche [deh], por la noche
good night buenas noches [bwenas noch-es]

dialogue

do you have a single room for one night? ¿tiene un cuarto individual para una noche? [t-yeneh oon kwarto eendeebeedwal]
yes, madam sí, señora [sen-yora]
how much is it per night? ¿cuánto es la noche? [kwanto]
it's 3,000 pesos for one night son tres mil pesos la

noche
thank you, I'll take it
gracias, me lo quedo [gras-yas meh la kedo]

nightclub la discoteca [deeskoteka]
nightdress el camisón
night porter el portero [portairo]
no no
 I've no change no tengo cambio [kamb-yo]
 there's no ... left no queda ... [keda]
 no way! ¡ni hablar! [ablar]
 oh no! (upset, annoyed) ¡Dios mío! [d-yos]
nobody nadie [nad-yeh]
 there's nobody there no hay nadie [ī]
noise el ruido [rweedo]
noisy: it's too noisy hay demasiado ruido [ī demas-yado]
non-alcoholic sin alcohol [seen alko-ol]
none ninguno
non-smoking compartment no fumadores [foomador-es]
noon el mediodía [med-yodee-a]
no-one nadie [nad-yeh]
nor: nor do I yo tampoco
normal normal [nor-mal]
north norte [norteh]
 in the north en el norte
 north of El Salvador al norte de El Salvador
North America América del

norte [amaireeka del norteh]
North American (man) el norteamericano, el estadounidense [estado-ooneedenseh], (Arg) el yanqui [yankee] (woman) la norteamericana, la estadounidense, (Arg) la yanqui (adj) norteamericano, estadounidense, (Arg) yanqui
northeast nordeste [nordesteh]
northern del norte [norteh]
Northern Ireland Irlanda del Norte [eerlanda del norteh]
northwest noroeste [noro-esteh]
Norway Noruega [norwega]
Norwegian (adj) noruego
nose la nariz [narees]
nosebleed la hemorragia nasal [emorraH-ya]
not* no
 no, I'm not hungry no, no tengo hambre [ambreh]
 I don't want any, thank you no quiero, gracias [k-yairo gras-yas]
 it's not necessary no es necesario [nesesar-yo]
 I didn't know that no lo sabía
 not that one – this one ése no – éste [eseh – esteh]
note (banknote) el billete [bee-yeteh]
notebook el cuaderno [kwadairno]
notepaper (for letters) el papel de carta [deh]

nothing nada

nothing for me, thanks para
mí nada, gracias [gras-yas]

nothing else nada más

novel la novela [nobela]

November noviembre [nob-
yembreh]

now ahora [a-ora]

number el número [noomairo]

I've got the wrong number
me equivoqué de número
[meh ekeebokeh deh]

what is your phone number?
¿cuál es su número de
teléfono? [kwal]

number plate la placa,
(CSur) la patente [patenteh],
(RpI) la chapa

nurse (man/woman) el
enfermero [enfairmairo], la
enfermera

nursery slope la pista de
principiantes [deh preenseep-
yant-es]

nut (for bolt) la tuerca [twairka]

nuts las nueces [nwes-es]

O

o'clock: at two o'clock a las
dos

occupied (US: toilet etc)
ocupado [okoopado]

October octubre [oktoobreh]

odd (strange) extraño [ekstran-
yo]

of de [deh]

off (lights) apagado

it's just off calle Corredera
está cerca de calle Corredera
[sairka deh ka-yeh]

we're off tomorrow nos
vamos mañana [bamos]

offensive (language, behaviour)
ofensivo [ofenseebo]

office (place of work) la oficina
[ofeeseena]

officer (said to policeman) señor
oficial [sen-yor ofee-syal]

often a menudo

not often pocas veces [bes-es]

how often are the buses?
¿cada cuánto pasa el
autobús? [kwanto]

oil el aceite [asayteh]

ointment la pomada

OK bueno [bweno]

are you OK? ¿está bien?
[b-yen]

is that OK with you? ¿le
parece bien? [leh pareseh]

is it OK to ...? ¿se puede ...?
[seh pwedeh]

that's OK thanks (it doesn't
matter) está bien, gracias [gras-
yas]

I'm OK (nothing for me) para mí
nada

(I feel OK) me siento bien [meh
s-yento]

is this train OK for ...? ¿este
tren va a...? [esteh – ba]

I said I'm sorry, OK? ya pedí
disculpas ¿okey? [deeskoolpas
okay]

old viejo [b-yeHo]

dialogue

how old are you? ¿cuántos años tiene? [kwantos an-yos t-yeneh]
I'm twenty-five tengo veinticinco años
and you? ¿y usted? [ee oosteh]

old-fashioned pasado de moda [deh]
old town (old part of town) el barrio antiguo [barr-yo anteegwo]
　in the old town en el barrio antiguo
olive la aceituna [asaytoona], la oliva [oleeba]
　black/green olives las aceitunas negras/verdes [baird-es]
olive oil el aceite de oliva [asayteh deh oleeba]
omelette la tortilla de huevo [tortee-ya deh webo]
on en
　on the street/beach en la calle/playa
　is it on this road? ¿está en esta calle?
　on the plane en el avión
　on Saturday el sábado
　on television en la tele
　I haven't got it on me no lo traigo [trīgo]
　this one's on me (drink) ésta me toca a mí [meh]
　the light wasn't on la luz no

estaba prendida
　what's on tonight? ¿qué ponen esta noche? [keh]
once (one time) una vez [bes]
　at once (immediately) en seguida [segeeda]
one* uno [oono], una
　the white one el blanco, la blanca
one-way: a one-way ticket to ... un boleto de ida para ... [deh eeda]
onion la cebolla [sebo-ya]
only sólo
　only one sólo uno
　it's only 6 o'clock son sólo las seis
　I've only just got here acabo de llegar [deh yegar]
on/off switch el interruptor [eentairrooptor]
open (adj) abierto [ab-yairto] (verb) abrir [abreer]
　when do you open? ¿a qué hora abre? [keh ora abreh]
　I can't get it open no puedo abrirlo [pwedo]
　in the open air al aire libre [īreh leebreh]
opening times el horario [orar-yo]
open ticket el boleto abierto [ab-yairto]
opera la ópera
operation (medical) la operación [opairas-yon]
operator (telephone: man/ woman) el operador, la operadora

opposite: the opposite direction el sentido contrario

the bar opposite el bar de enfrente [deh enfrenteh]

opposite my hotel enfrente de mi hotel

optician el óptico

or o

orange (fruit) la naranja [naranHa]
(colour) (color) naranja

orange juice (fresh) el jugo de naranja [Hoogo deh]
(fizzy, diluted) el refresco de naranja

orchestra la orquesta [orkesta]

order: can we order now? (in restaurant) ¿podemos pedir ya?

I've already ordered, thanks ya pedí, gracias [gras-yas]

I didn't order this no pedí esto

out of order averiado [abair-yado], fuera de servicio [fwaira deh sairbees-yo]

ordinary corriente [korr-yenteh]

other otro

the other one el otro

the other day el otro día

I'm waiting for the others estoy esperando a los demás

do you have any others? ¿tiene otros? [t-yeneh]

otherwise de otra manera [deh – manaira]

our* nuestro [nwestro], nuestra; (pl) nuestros, nuestras

ours* (el) nuestro, (la) nuestra

out: he's out no está

three kilometres out of town a tres kilómetros de la ciudad

outdoors al aire libre [īreh leebreh]

outside ... fuera de ...

can we sit outside? ¿podemos sentarnos fuera?

oven el horno [orno]

over: over here por aquí [akee]

over there por allá [a-ya]

over 500 más de quinientos [deh]

it's over se acabó [seh]

overcharge: you've overcharged me me cobró de más [meh – deh]

overcoat el abrigo

overlook: I'd like a room overlooking the courtyard quiero un cuarto que da al patio [k-yairo oon kwarto keh da]

overnight (travel) toda la noche [nocheh]

overtake adelantarse a [adelantarseh]

owe: how much do I owe you? ¿cuánto le debo? [kwanto leh]

own: my own ... mi propio ... [prop-yo]

are you on your own? (to a man/woman) ¿está solo/sola?

I'm on my own (said by man/ woman) estoy solo/sola

owner (man/woman) el propietario [prop-yetar-yo], la propietaria

P

Pacific Ocean el Océano Pacífico [oseh-ano]
pack: a pack of ... un paquete de ... [paketeh deh]
(verb) hacer las maletas [asair]
a pack of cigarettes una cajetilla de cigarrillos [kaHetee-ya deh seegarree-yos]
package (parcel) el paquete [paketeh]
package holiday el paquete
packed lunch la bolsa con la comida
packet: a packet of cigarettes una cajetilla de cigarrillos [kaHetee-ya deh seegarree-yos]
padlock el candado
page (of book) la página [paHeena]
could you page Mr ...? ¿podría llamar al señor ... (por altavoz)? [yamar – altabos]
pain el dolor
I have a pain here me duele aquí [meh dweleh akee]
painful doloroso
painkillers los analgésicos [analHeseekos]
paint la pintura
painting el cuadro [kwadro]
pair: a pair of ... un par de ... [deh]
Pakistani (adj) paquistaní [pakeestanee]
palace el palacio [palas-yo]
pale pálido

pale blue azul claro [asool]
pan la olla [o-ya]
Panama Panamá [panama]
Panamanian (adj) panameño [panamen-yo]
(man) el panameño
(woman) la panameña
panties (women's) los pantis, (C.Am) las calzonetas [kalsonetas], (Col) los cucos, (Mex, Ven) las pantaletas, (Rpl) las bombachas
pants (underwear: men's) los calzoncillos [kalsonsee-yos], (Col, Ven) los interiores [eentairee-or-es], (Mex) los calzones [kalson-es] (women's) los pantis (US: trousers) pantalones [pantalon-es]
pantyhose las medias [med-yas], (Col) las medias pantalón [pantalon], (Mex) pantimedias, (Rpl) las medias bombacha, (Ven) las medias panty
paper el papel
(newspaper) el periódico [pair-yodeeko]
a piece of paper un pedazo de papel [pedaso deh]
paper handkerchiefs los klínex®
Paraguay Paraguay [paragwī]
Paraguayan (adj) paraguayo [paragwa-yo]

(man) el paraguayo
(woman) la paraguaya
parcel el paquete [pa**ke**teh]
pardon (me)? (didn't understand/
hear) ¿cómo?,
(Mex) ¿mande? [**man**deh]
parents: my parents mis
padres [pad-res]
parents-in-law los suegros
[**sweg**ros]
park el parque [**par**keh]
(verb) estacionar [estas-yo**nar**]
can I park here? ¿puedo
estacionarme aquí? [**pwe**do
estas-yo**nar**meh a**kee**]
parking lot el estacionamiento
[estas-yonam-**yen**to]
part la parte [**par**teh]
partner (boyfriend, girlfriend etc) el
compañero [kompan-**ya**iro], la
compañera
party (group) el grupo
(political) el partido
(celebration) la fiesta
pass (in mountains) el paso
passenger (man/woman) el
pasajero [pasa**Ha**iro], la
pasajera
passport el pasaporte
[pasa**por**teh]
past*: in the past
antiguamente
[anteeg**wa**menteh]
just past the information
office justo después de la
oficina de información
[**Hoo**sto desp**wes** deh]
path el camino
pattern el dibujo [dee**boo**Ho]

pavement la acera [a**sai**ra]
on the pavement en la acera
pavement café el café terraza
[ka**feh** te**rra**sa]
pay (verb) pagar
can I pay, please? me pasa
la cuenta, por favor [meh
– **kwen**ta por fa**bor**]
it's already paid for ya está
pagado

dialogue

who's paying? ¿quién
paga? [k-yen]
I'll pay pago yo
no, you paid last time,
I'll pay no, usted pagó
la última vez, pago yo
[oos**teh** – **ool**teema bes]

pay phone el teléfono público
[**poo**bleeko], la caseta telefónica
peaceful tranquilo [tran**kee**lo]
peach el durazno [doo**ras**no]
peanuts los cacahuates
[kakawat-es]
pear la pera [**pai**ra]
peas las arvejas [ar**be**Has]
peculiar extraño [eks**tran**-yo]
pedestrian crossing el paso de
peatones [peh-a**ton**-es]
pedestrian precinct la calle
peatonal [ka-yeh peh-ato**nal**]
peg (for washing) la pinza
[**peen**sa]
(for tent) la estaca
pen la pluma [**ploo**ma],
(Col) el estilógrafo

[esteelografo],
(CSur) la lapicera fuente
[lapeesaira fwenteh]
pencil el lápiz [lapees]
penfriend (male/female)
el amigo/la amiga
por correspondencia
[korrespondens-ya]
penicillin la penicilina
[peneeseeleena]
penknife la navaja [nabaHa]
pensioner el jubilado
[Hoobeelado], la jubilada
people la gente [Henteh]
  the other people in the hotel
  los otros huéspedes en el
  hotel [wesped-es]
  too many people demasiada
  gente [demas-yada]
pepper (spice) la pimienta
[peem-yenta]
  (vegetable) el pimiento,
  (SAm not Rpl) el pimentón
  [peementon]
peppermint (sweet) el dulce de
menta [doolseh deh]
per: per night por noche
[nocheh]
  how much per day? ¿cuánto
  es por día? [kwanto]
  per cent por ciento [s-yento]
perfect perfecto [pairfekto]
perfume el perfume
[pairfoomeh]
perhaps quizás [keesas]
  perhaps not quizás no
period (of time) el período
[pairee-odo]
  (menstruation) la regla

perm la permanente
[pairmanenteh]
permit el permiso [pairmeeso]
person la persona [pairsona]
personal stereo el walkman®
[wolkman]
Peru Perú [peroo]
Peruvian (adj) peruano [peroo-
ano]
  (man) el peruano
  (woman) la peruana
petrol la gasolina,
  (Ch) la bencina [benseena],
  (Rpl) la nafta
petrol can la lata de gasolina
[deh]
petrol station la gasolinera
[gasoleenaira],
  (Andes, Ven) la bomba,
  (Ch) la bencinera [benseenaira],
  (Pe) el grifo,
  (Rpl) la estación de nafta
pharmacy la farmacia [far-
mas-ya]
phone el teléfono
  (verb) llamar por teléfono
  [yamar]
phone book la guía telefónica
[gee-a]
phone box la caseta
telefónica
phonecard la tarjeta de
teléfono [tarHeta deh]
phone number el número de
teléfono [noomairo deh]
photo la foto
  excuse me, could you take a
  photo of us? ¿le importaría
  sacarnos una foto? [leh]

phrasebook el libro de frases [deh fras-es]

piano el piano [p-yano]

pickpocket el/la carterista [kartaireesta], (Mex) el/la bolsista [bolseesta]

pick up: will you come and pick me up? ¿pasarás a recogerme? [rekoHairmeh]

picnic el picnic

picture el cuadro [kwadro]

pie (meat) la empanada (fruit) la tarta

piece el pedazo [pedaso]
a piece of ... un pedazo de ... [deh]

pig el chancho, el cerdo [sairdo]

pill la píldora
I'm on the pill estoy tomando la píldora

pillow la almohada [almo-ada]

pillow case la funda (de almohada) [foonda (deh)]

pin el alfiler [alfeelair]

pineapple la piña [peen-ya], (Rpl) el ananá [anana]

pineapple juice el jugo de piña [Hoogo deh]

pink rosa

pipe (for smoking) la pipa [peepa] (for water) el tubo [toobo]

pipe cleaners los limpiapipas [leemp-yapeepas]

pity: it's a pity! ¡qué pena! [keh]

pizza la pizza

place el lugar [loogar]
at your place en tu casa

at his place en su casa

plain el llano [yano] (not patterned) liso

plane el avión [ab-yon]
by plane en avión

plant la planta

plaster cast la escayola [eska-yola], (Col) el yeso

plasters las curitas

plastic plástico (credit cards) las tarjetas de crédito [tarHetas deh kredeeto]

plastic bag la bolsa de plástico

plate el plato

platform el andén [anden]
which platform is it for San Juan, please? ¿de qué andén sale el tren para San Juan, por favor? [deh keh anden saleh – san jwan por fabor]

play (in theatre) la obra (verb) jugar [Hoogar] (instrument) tocar

playground el patio de recreo [pat-yo deh rekreh-o]

pleasant agradable [agradableh]

please por favor [fabor]
yes please sí, por favor
could you please ...? ¿podría hacer el favor de ...? [asair – deh]
please don't no, por favor

pleased: pleased to meet you (said by man/woman) encantado/ encantada de conocerlo/la [deh konosairlo/la]

pleasure: my pleasure es un gusto [goosto]

plenty: plenty of ... mucho ... [**moo**cho]

there's plenty of time tenemos mucho tiempo [t-**yem**po]

that's plenty, thanks es suficiente, gracias [soofees-**yen**teh gras-yas]

pliers los alicates [aleekat-es]

plug (electrical) el enchufe [en**choo**feh]
(for car) la bujía [boo**Hee**-a]
(in sink) el tapón

plumber el plomero [plo**mair**o],
(Ch) el gásfiter [**gas**feetair],
(Per) el gasfitero [gasfee**tair**o]

p.m. de la tarde [deh la **tar**deh]

poached egg el huevo escalfado [**we**bo],
(Rpl) el huevo poché

pocket el bolsillo [bol**see**-yo]

point: two point five dos coma cinco

there's no point no vale la pena [**baleh**]

points (in car) los platinos

poisonous venenoso [bene**no**so]

police la policía [polee**see**-a]
call the police! ¡llame a la policía! [**yameh**]

policeman el (agente de) policía [a**Hen**teh deh]

police station la comisaría de policía

policewoman la (agente de) policía

polish el betún [be**toon**],
(Ch) la pasta,

(Rpl) la pomada

polite educado [edoo**kado**]

polluted contaminado

pony el poney

pool (for swimming) la piscina [pees**ee**na],
(Mex) la alberca [al**bair**ka],
(Rpl) la pileta [pee**le**ta]

poor (not rich) pobre [**pobreh**]
(quality) de baja calidad [deh ba**Ha** kalee**dad**]

pop music la música pop [**moo**seeka]

pop singer el/la cantante de música pop [kan**tan**teh deh]

population la población [poblas-yon]

pork la carne de cerdo [**kar**neh deh **sair**do],
(Ch, Per) la carne de chancho,
(Col) la carne de marrano

port (for boats) el puerto [**pwair**to]
(drink) el Oporto

porter (in hotel) el portero [por**tair**o]

portrait el retrato

posh (restaurant) de lujo [deh **loo**Ho]

possible posible [po**see**bleh]
is it possible to ...? ¿es posible ...?
as ... as possible lo más ... posible

post (mail) el correo [kor**reh**-o]
(verb) echar al correo
could you post this for me? ¿podría echarme esto al correo? [e**char**meh]

postbox el buzón [booson]
postcard la postal [pos-tal]
postcode el código postal
poster el póster [postair], el cartel
poste restante la lista de correos [leesta deh korreh-os], (CSur) el poste restante [posteh restanteh]
post office el correo [korreh-o]
potato la papa
potato chips (US) las papas fritas (de bolsa), (Urug) las papas chips
pots and pans los cacharros de cocina [deh koseena], las ollas [o-yas]
pottery (objects) la cerámica [sairameeka]
pound* (money, weight) la libra
power cut el apagón
power point la toma de corriente [deh korr-yenteh]
practise: I want to practise my Spanish quiero practicar el español [k-yairo – espan-yol]
prawns los camarones, (CSur) los langostinos
prefer: I prefer ... prefiero ... [pref-yairo]
pregnant embarazada [embarasada]
prescription (for chemist) la receta [reseta]
present (gift) el regalo
president (of country) el presidente [preseedenteh], la presidenta
pretty lindo

it's pretty expensive es bastante caro [bastanteh]
price el precio [pres-yo]
priest el sacerdote [sasairdoteh]
prime minister (man/woman) el primer ministro [preemair], la primera ministra
printed matter los impresos
priority (in driving) la preferencia [prefairens-ya]
prison la cárcel [karsel]
private privado [preebado], particular [parteekoolar]
private bathroom el baño privado [ban-yo]
probably probablemente [probableh-menteh]
problem el problema
no problem! ¡con mucho gusto! [moocho goosto]
program(me) el programa
promise: I promise lo prometo
pronounce: how is this pronounced? ¿cómo se pronuncia esto? [seh pronoons-ya]
properly (repaired, locked etc) bien [b-yen]
protection factor (of suntan lotion) el factor de protección [deh proteks-yon]
Protestant (adj) protestante [protestanteh]
public convenience los baños públicos [ban-yos poobleekos]
public holiday el día feriado [dee-a fer-yado]
pudding (dessert) el postre [postreh]

Puerto Rica Puerto Rico
[pwairto]
Puerto Rican (adj)
portorriqueño [portorreeken-yo]
(man) el portorriqueño
(woman) la portorriqueña
pull jalar [Halar]
pullover el suéter [swetair]
puncture el pinchazo,
(Mex) la ponchadura
purple morado
purse (for money) el monedero
[monedairo]
(US: handbag) la cartera
[kartaira],
(Col) el bolso,
(Mex) la bolsa
push empujar [empoo-Har]
pushchair la sillita de ruedas
[see-yeeta deh rwedas],
(Mex) la carreola [karreh-ola],
(SAm) el cochecito [kocheseeto]
put poner [ponair]
where can I put ...? ¿dónde
pongo ...? [dondeh]
could you put us up for the
night? ¿podría alojarnos esta
noche? [aloHarnos – nocheh]
pyjamas el pijama [peeHama]
pyramid la pirámide
[peerameedeh]

Q

quality la calidad [kaleeda]
(personal) la cualidad
[kwaleeda]

quarantine la cuarentena
[kwarentena]
quarter la cuarta parte [kwarta
parteh]
quayside: on the quayside en
el muelle [mweh-yeh]
question la pregunta
[pregoonta]
queue la cola
quick rápido [rapeedo]
that was quick ¡qué rápido!
[keh]
what's the quickest way
there? ¿cuál es el camino más
directo? [kwal – deerekto]
fancy a quick drink? ¿se te
antoja una copa? [seh teh
antoHa]
quickly rápidamente
[rapeedamenteh]
quiet (place, hotel) tranquilo
[trankeelo]
(person) callado [ka-yado]
quiet! ¡cállese! [ka-yeseh]
quite (fairly) bastante
[bastanteh]
(very) muy [mwee]
that's quite right eso es cierto
[s-yairto]
quite a lot bastante

R

rabbit el conejo [koneHo]
race (for runners, cars) la carrera
[karraira]
racket (tennis etc) la raqueta
[raketa]

radiator (of car, in room) el radiador [rad-yador]

radio la radio [rad-yo]

on the radio por radio

raft la balsa

rail: by rail en tren

railway el ferrocarril

rain la lluvia [yoob-ya]

in the rain bajo la lluvia [baHo]

it's raining está lloviendo [yob-yendo]

raincoat el impermeable [eempairmeh-ableh]

rape la violación [b-yolas-yon]

rare (uncommon) poco común (steak) (muy) poco hecho [mwee – echo]

rash (on skin) la erupción cutánea [airoops-yon kootaneh-a]

raspberry la frambuesa [frambwesa]

rat la rata

rate (for changing money) el tipo de cambio [teepo deh kamb-yo]

rather: it's rather good es bastante bueno [bastanteh bweno]

I'd rather ... prefiero ... [pref-yairo]

razor la cuchilla de afeitar [koochee-ya deh afaytar] (electric) la máquina de afeitar eléctrica [makeena]

razor blades las hojas de afeitar [oHas]

read leer [leh-air]

ready preparado

are you ready? (to man/woman)

¿estás listo/lista?

I'm not ready yet (said by man/woman) aún no estoy listo/lista [a-oon]

dialogue

when will it be ready?
¿cuándo estará listo?
[kwando]
it should be ready in a couple of days estará listo en un par de días

real verdadero [bairdadairo], auténtico [owtenteeko].

really realmente [reh-almenteh]

that's really great es estupendo

really? (doubt) ¿no puede ser? [pwedeh sair] (polite interest) ¿de veras? [deh bairas]

rear lights las luces traseras [loos-es], (Mex) las calaveras [kalabairas]

rearview mirror el (espejo) retrovisor [espeHo retrobeesor]

reasonable (prices etc) modesto

receipt el recibo [reseebo]

recently recientemente [res-yentementeh], recién [res-yen]

reception la recepción [reseps-yon]

at reception en la recepción

reception desk la recepción

receptionist el/la recepcionista [reseps-yoneesta]

recognize reconocer
[rekonos**air**]

recommend: could you
recommend ...? ¿puede
recomendar ...? [p**we**deh]

record (music) el disco [d**ee**sko]

red rojo [r**o**Ho]

red wine el vino tinto [b**ee**no
t**ee**nto]

refund la devolución [deboloos-
yon]

can I have a refund? ¿puede
devolverme el dinero?
[p**we**deh debolb**air**meh el d**ee**nairo]

region la zona [s**o**na], la
región [reH-yon]

registered: by registered
mail por correo certificado
[korr**eh**-o sairteefeek**a**do]

registration number el número
de placa [n**oo**mairo deh],
(CSur) el número de patente
[pat**e**nteh],
(Rpl) el número de chapa

relatives los parientes [par-
y**e**nt-es]

religion la religión [releeH-yon]

remember: I don't remember
no recuerdo [rekw**air**do]

I remember recuerdo

do you remember? ¿recuerda?

rent (for apartment etc) la
renta, el arriendo [arr-y**e**ndo]
(verb) rentar, arrendar,
alquilar [alk**ee**lar]

to/for rent se alquila [seh
alk**ee**la]

rented car el auto rentado
[**ow**to]

repair (verb) arreglar

can you repair it? ¿puede
arreglarlo? [p**we**deh]

repeat repetir

could you repeat that?
¿puede repetir? [p**we**deh]

reservation la reservación
[resairbas-yon]

I'd like to make a reservation
quisiera hacer reservación
[kees-y**ai**ra as**air**]

dialogue

I have a reservation tengo
cuarto reservado [kw**ar**to
resairb**a**do]
yes sir, what name please?
sí, señor, ¿a nombre de
quién, por favor? [sen-y**or** a
n**o**mbreh deh k-y**en** por fab**or**]

reserve reservar [resairb**ar**]

dialogue

can I reserve a table for
tonight? ¿puedo reservar
una mesa para esta noche?
[pw**e**do – n**o**cheh]
yes madam, for how
many people? sí, señora,
¿para cuántos? [sen-y**ora**
– kw**a**ntos]
for two para dos
and for what time? ¿y para
qué hora? [ee para keh **o**ra]
for eight o'clock para las
ocho

and could I have your name please? ¿me deja su nombre, por favor? [meh deh-Ha soo nombreh por fabor] see **alphabet** for spelling

rest: I need a rest necesito un descanso [neseseeto]
the rest of the group el resto del grupo [groopo]
restaurant el restaurante [restowranteh]
restaurant car el coche-comedor [kocheh komedor]
rest room el baño [ban-yo]
retired: I'm retired estoy jubilado/jubilada [Hoobeelado]
return (ticket) el boleto de ida y vuelta [deh eeda ee bwelta] see **ticket**
reverse charge call la llamada por cobrar [yamada]
reverse gear la marcha atrás
revolting asqueroso [askairoso]
rib la costilla [kostee-ya]
rice el arroz [arros]
rich rico [reeko]
ridiculous ridículo [reedeekoolo]
right (correct) correcto
(not left) derecho
you were right tenía razón [rason]
that's right es cierto [s-yairto]
this can't be right esto no puede ser [pwedeh sair]
right! ¡bueno! [bweno]
is this the right road for ...? ¿es éste el camino para ...? [esteh]

on the right a la derecha
turn right dé vuelta a la derecha [deh bwelta]
right-hand drive con el volante a la derecha [bolanteh]
ring (on finger) el anillo [anee-yo]
I'll ring you te llamaré [teh yamareh]
ring back volver a llamar [bolbair a yamar]
ripe (fruit) maduro
rip-off: it's a rip-off es una estafa
rip-off prices los precios exagerados [pres-yos eksaHairados]
risky arriesgado [arr-yesgado]
river el río
road la carretera [karretaira]
is this the road for ...? ¿es ésta la carretera para ...?
down the road calle abajo [ka-yeh abaHo]
road accident el accidente de tránsito [akseedenteh deh]
road map el mapa de carreteras
roadsign la señal de tráfico [sen-yal deh]
rob: I've been robbed! ¡me robaron! [meh]
rock la roca
(music) el rock
on the rocks (with ice) con hielo [yelo]
rodeo el rodeo [rodeh-o], (Mex) la charreada [charreh-ada]
roll (bread) el pancito [panseeto],

(Mex) el bolillo [bolee-yo]
roof el tejado [teHado]
roof rack el portaequipajes
 [porta-ekeepaHes]
room el cuarto [kwarto]
 in my room en mi cuarto
room service el servicio de
 cuarto [sairbees-yo deh]
rope la cuerda [kwairda]
rosé (wine) el vino rosado
 [beeno]
roughly (approximately)
 aproximadamente [–menteh]
round: it's my round me toca
 [meh]
roundabout (for traffic) la
 glorieta [glor-yeta],
 (Per) el óvalo [obalo]
round trip ticket el boleto
 de ida y vuelta [deh eeda ee
 bwelta]
 see ticket
route la ruta [roota]
 what's the best route? ¿cuál
 es la mejor ruta? [kwal es la
 meHor]
rubber (material) caucho
 [kowcho],
 (Mex) el hule [ooleh]
 (eraser) la goma de borrar
rubber band la goma,
 (Ch) el elástico,
 (Col) el caucho,
 (Mex) la liga,
 (Rpl) la gomita
rubbish (waste) la basura
 (poor quality goods) las
 porquerías [porkairee-as]
rubbish! (nonsense) ¡babosadas!

rucksack la mochila,
 (Col, Ven) el morral
rude grosero [grosairo]
rug (mat) la alfombra, el tapete
 [tapeteh]
 (blanket) la cobija [kobeeHa], la
 manta, la frazada [frasada]
ruins las ruinas [rweenas]
rum el ron
 rum and Coke® el cubalibre
 [koobaleebreh],
 (Mex) la cubata (de ron)
run (verb: person) correr [korrair]
 how often do the buses
 run? ¿cada cuánto pasan los
 autobuses? [kwanto]
 I've run out of money se me
 acabó el dinero [seh meh
 – deenairo]
rush hour la hora pico [ora]

S

sad triste [treesteh]
saddle (for horse) la silla de
 montar [see-ya deh]
 (on bike) el sillín [see-yeen]
safe seguro [segooro]
safety pin el seguro
sail la vela [bela]
sailboard el windsurf
sailboarding el windsurf
salad la ensalada
salad dressing el aliño para la
 ensalada [aleen-yo]
sale: for sale se vende [seh
 bendeh]
salmon el salmón [sal-mon]

Sa

103

salt la sal
Salvadorean (adj) salvadoreño [salbadoren-yo]
same: the same el mismo, la misma
the same as this igual a éste [eegwal a esteh]
the same again, please otro igual, por favor [fabor]
it's all the same to me me da igual [meh]
sand la arena [areh-na]
sandals las sandalias [sandal-yas],
(Mex) los guaraches [warach-es]
sandwich el sándwich [sandweech], la torta
(Ch) el sánguche [sangoocheh]
sanitary napkin/towel la compresa,
(SAm) la toalla sanitaria [to-a-ya saneetar-ya]
sardines las sardinas
Saturday sábado
sauce la salsa
saucepan la cacerola [kaserola]
saucer el platillo [platee-yo]
sauna la sauna [sowna]
sausage la salchicha
say: how do you say ... in Spanish? ¿cómo se dice ... en español? [seh deeseh en espan-yol]
what did he say? ¿qué dijo? [keh deeHo]
I said ... dije ... [deeHeh]
he said ... dijo ...
could you say that again?

¿podría repetirlo?
scarf (for neck) la bufanda
(for head) el pañuelo [pan-ywelo]
scenery el paisaje [pīsaHeh]
schedule (US) el horario [orar-yo]
scheduled flight el vuelo regular [bwelo regoolar]
school la escuela [eskwela]
scissors: a pair of scissors las tijeras [teeHairas]
scotch el whisky
Scotch tape® el scotch, el Durex®
Scotland Escocia [eskos-ya]
Scottish escocés [eskos-es]
I'm Scottish (man/woman) soy escocés/escocesa
scrambled eggs los huevos revueltos [webos rebweltos]
scratch el rasguño [rasgoon-yo]
scream gritar
screw el tornillo [tornee-yo]
screwdriver el destornillador [destornee-yador]
sea el mar
by the sea junto al mar [Hoonto]
seafood los mariscos
seafood restaurant la marisquería [mareeskairee-a]
seafront el paseo marítimo [paseh-o mareeteemo]
on the seafront en la playa [pla-ya]
seagull la gaviota [gab-yota]
search for (verb) buscar
seashell la concha marina

seasick: I feel seasick (said by man/woman) est**oy** mareado/ mareada [mareh-**ado**]
I get seasick me mareo [meh mar**eh**-o]
seaside: by the seaside en la playa [pl**a**-ya]
seat el asiento [as-y**e**nto]
is this seat taken? ¿está ocupado este asiento? [**e**steh]
seat belt el cinturón de seguridad [seentoor**o**n deh seg**oo**reeda]
sea urchin el erizo de mar [air**ee**so]
seaweed el alga
secluded apartado
second (adj) seg**u**ndo
(of time) el segundo
just a second! ¡un moment**i**to!
second class (travel) de segunda clase [seg**oo**nda kl**a**seh]
secondhand usado [oos**a**do]
see ver [b**ai**r]
can I see? ¿me deja ver? [meh d**e**Ha]
have you seen ...? ¿ha visto ...? [a b**ee**sto]
I saw him this morning lo vi esta mañana [b**ee**]
see you! ¡hasta luego! [**a**sta lw**e**go]
I see (I understand) entiendo [ent-y**e**ndo]
self-service autoservicio [owtosairb**ee**s-yo]

sell vender [bend**air**]
do you sell ...? ¿vende ...? [b**e**ndeh]
Sellotape® el scotch®, el D**u**rex®
send enviar [emb-y**ar**], mand**a**r
I want to send this to England quiero enviar esto a Inglat**e**rra [k-y**ai**ro]
senior citizen el jubilado, [Hoobeel**a**do], la jubilada
separate separ**a**do
a separate room un cu**a**rto ap**a**rte [ap**a**rteh]
separated: I'm separated (said by man/woman) est**oy** separado/ separada
separately (pay, travel) por separado
September septiembre [sept-y**e**mbreh]
septic s**é**ptico
serious serio [s**ai**r-yo]
(illness) grave [gr**a**beh]
service charge el servicio [sairb**ee**s-yo]
service station la estación de servicio [estas-y**o**n deh]
serviette la servilleta [sairbee-y**e**ta]
set menu el men**ú** [men**oo**], (Mex) la comida corrida
several varios [b**a**r-yos]
sew coser [kos**air**]
could you sew this back on? ¿podría coserme esto? [kos**ai**rmeh]
sex el sexo

sexy sexy

shade: in the shade a la sombra

shallow (water) poco profundo

shame: what a shame! ¡qué pena! [keh]

shampoo el champú

a shampoo and set un lavado y marcado [labado ee]

shanty town la barriada, (Arg) la villa miseria [bee-ya meeseree-a], (Ch) la población callampa [poblas-yon ka-yampa], (Urug) el cantegril [kantegreel], (Ven) los ranchos

share (verb) compartir

sharp (knife) afilado (taste) ácido [aseedo] (pain) agudo

shattered (very tired) agotado

shaver la máquina de afeitar [makeena deh afaytar]

shaving foam la espuma de afeitar

shaving point el enchufe (para la máquina de afeitar) [enchoofeh – makeena]

shawl el rebozo [reboso]

she* ella [eh-ya]

is she here? ¿está (ella) aquí? [akee]

sheet (for bed) la sábana

shelf la estantería [estantairee-a]

shellfish los mariscos

sherry el jerez [Her-es]

ship el barco

by ship en barco

shirt la camisa

shit! ¡mierda! [m-yairda]

shock el susto

I got an electric shock me dio una descarga eléctrico [meh]

shock-absorber el amortiguador [amorteegwador]

shocking chocante [chokanteh]

shoes los zapatos [sapatos]

a pair of shoes un par de zapatos [deh]

shoelaces los cordones [kordon-es], (Mex) las agujetas [a-ooHetas], (Per) los pasadores

shoe polish el betún [betoon], (Ch) la pasta, (Rpl) la pomada [pomada]

shoe repairer's la zapatería [sapatairee-a]

shop la tienda [t-yenda]

shopping: I'm going shopping voy de compras [boy deh]

shopping centre el centro comercial [sentro komairs-yal]

shop window el escaparate [eskaparateh], (Ch, Col, Ven) la vitrina [beetreena], (Mex) el aparador, (Rpl) la vidriera [beedr-yaira]

shore la orilla [oree-ya]

short (time, journey) corto (person) bajo [baHo]

it's only a short distance queda bastante cerca [keda bastanteh sairka]

shortcut el atajo [ataHo]

shorts los pantalones cortos

[pantal**o**n-es]

should: what should I do?
¿qué hago? [keh **a**go]

he shouldn't be long no debe
tardar [d**e**beh]

you should have told me me
lo hubieras dicho [meh oob-
y**ai**ras]

shoulder el hombro [**o**mbro]

shout (verb) gritar

show (in theatre) el espectáculo
[espekt**a**koolo]

could you show me? ¿me lo
enseña? [meh lo ensen-ya]

shower (in bathroom) la regadera
[regad**ai**ra]
(of rain) el chubasco
[choob**a**sko]

with shower con baño [ban-
yo]

shower gel el gel de baño
[нel deh]

shut (verb) cerrar [s**ai**rrar]

when do you shut? ¿a qué
hora cierran? [keh **o**ra
s-y**ai**rran]

when do they shut? ¿a qué
hora cierran?

they're shut está cerrado
[s**ai**rrado]

I've shut myself out cerré y
dejé la llave dentro [s**ai**rr**eh** ee
deh-н**eh** la yab**e**h]

shut up! ¡cállese! [ka-y**e**seh]

shutter (on camera) el obturador
(on window) la contraventana
[kontrabent**a**na]

shy tímido [t**ee**meedo]

sick (ill) enfermo [enf**ai**rmo]

I'm going to be sick (vomit)
voy a devolver [boy a
debolb**ai**r]

side el lado

the other side of town al
otro lado de la ciudad [deh la
s-y**oo**da]

sidelights los pilotos,
(Col, Ven) los cocuyos [kok**oo**-
yos],
(Mex) las calaveras [kalab**ai**ras]

side salad la ensalada aparte
[ap**a**rteh]

side street la callejuela [ka-
yeh-н**we**la]

sidewalk la acera [as**ai**ra],
(C.Am) el andén [and**e**n],
(Csur, Per) la vereda [b**ai**reda],
(Mex) la banqueta [bank**e**ta]

sight: the sights of ... los
lugares de interés de ...
[loog**a**r-es deh eent**ai**r-es]

**sightseeing: we're going
sightseeing** vamos a hacer
un recorrido turístico [b**a**mos
a as**ai**r oon]

sightseeing tour el recorrido
turístico

sign (notice) el letrero [letr**ai**ro]
(roadsign) la señal de tráfico
[sen-y**a**l deh]

signal: he didn't give a signal
no hizo ninguna señal [**ee**so]

signature la firma [f**ee**rma]

signpost el letrero [letr**ai**ro]

silence el silencio [seel**e**ns-yo]

silk la seda

silly tonto

silver la plata

silver foil el papel de aluminio [aloomeen-yo]

similar parecido [pareseedo]

simple (easy) sencillo [sensee-yo]

since: since yesterday desde ayer [desdeh a-yair]

since we got here desde que llegamos aquí [keh yegamos akee]

sing cantar

singer el/la cantante [kantanteh]

single: a single to ... un boleto de ida para ... [deh eeda]

I'm single (said by man/woman) soy soltero/soltera [soltairo]

single bed la cama individual [eendeebeedwal]

single room el cuarto individual [kwarto]

single ticket el boleto de ida [deh eeda]

sink (in kitchen) el fregadero [fregadairo], (Andes, Mex) el lavaplatos [labaplatos], (Rpl) la pileta [peeleta]

sister la hermana [airmana]

sister-in-law la cuñada [koon-yada]

sit: can I sit here? ¿puedo sentarme aquí? [pwedo sentarmeh akee]

is anyone sitting here? ¿está ocupado este asiento? [esteh as-yento]

sit down sentarse [sentarseh]

sit down! ¡siéntese!

[s-yenteseh]

size el tamaño [taman-yo] (of clothes) la talla [ta-ya]

skin la piel [p-yel]

skin-diving el buceo [booseh-o]

skinny flaco

skirt la falda

sky el cielo [s-yelo]

sleep (verb) dormir

did you sleep well? ¿dormiste bien? [dormeesteh b-yen]

I need a good sleep necesito dormir bien [neseseeto]

sleeper (on train) el coche-cama [kocheh kama]

sleeping bag la bolsa de dormir [deh]

sleeping car el coche-cama [kocheh-kama]

sleeping pill la pastilla para dormir [pastee-ya]

sleepy: I'm feeling sleepy tengo sueño [swen-yo]

sleeve la manga

slide (photographic) la diapositiva [d-yaposeeteeba]

slip (under dress) la enagua [enagwa], (Mex) el fondo, (Rpl) el viso [beeso]

slippery resbaladizo [resbaladeeso]

slow lento

slow down! ¡cálmese! [kalmeseh]

slowly: could you say it slowly? ¿podría decirlo despacio? [deseerlo despas-yo]

very slowly muy lento [mwee]

small chico

smell: it smells! (smells bad)
¡apesta!

smile (verb) sonreír [sonreh-**eer**]

smoke el humo [**oo**mo]
do you mind if I smoke? ¿le
importa que fume? [leh – keh
foo**meh**]

I don't smoke no fumo

do you smoke? ¿fuma?

snack la comida ligera
[leeHaira]

snake la culebra, la víbora
[beebora]

sneeze (verb) estornudar

snorkel el tubo de buceo
[**too**bo deh boos**eh**-o],
(Col) la careta [kareta]

snow la nieve [n-yebeh]
it's snowing está nevando
[nebando]

so: it's so good es tan bueno
[bweno]
not so fast no tan de prisa
[deh **pree**sa]
so am I yo también [tamb-yen]
so do I yo también
so-so más o menos

soaking solution (for contact
lenses) el líquido preservador
[leekeedo presairbador]

soap el jabón [Habon]

soap powder el jabón en
polvo [em polbo]

sober sobrio [sobr-yo]

sock el calcetín [kalseteen]

socket (electrical) el enchufe
[enchoofeh]

soda (water) la soda

sofa el sofá

soft (material etc) suave [swabeh]

soft-boiled egg el huevo
pasado por agua [webo –
agwa]

soft drink el refresco

soft lenses los lentes blandos
[lent-es]

sole (of shoe, of foot) la suela
[swela]
could you put new soles on
these? ¿podría cambiarles las
suelas? [kamb-yarl-es]

some: can I have some water?
¿me da agua? [meh]
can I have some rolls? ¿me
da unos pancitos?
can I have some? ¿me da
unos?

somebody, someone alguien
[algen]

something algo
something to drink algo de
beber [deh bebair]

sometimes a veces [bes-es]

somewhere en alguna parte
[parteh]

son el hijo [eeHo]

song la canción [kans-yon]

son-in-law el yerno [yairno]

soon dentro de poco [deh]
I'll be back soon no me tardo
[meh]
as soon as possible lo antes
posible [ant-es poseebleh]

sore: it's sore me duele [meh
dweleh]

sore throat el dolor de
garganta [deh]

sorry: (I'm) sorry disculpe [deeskoolpeh]
sorry? (didn't understand) ¿cómo?, (Mex) ¿mande? [mandeh]
sort: what sort of ...? ¿qué clase de ...? [keh klaseh deh]
soup la sopa
sour (taste) ácido [aseedo]
south el sur [soor]
  in the south al sur
South Africa Sudáfrica
South African (adj) sudafricano
I'm South African (man/woman) soy sudafricano/sudafricana
South America América del Sur [amaireeka]
South American (adj) sudamericano
  (man/woman) el sudamericano
  (man/woman) la sudamericana
southeast el sudeste [sood-esteh]
southwest el sudoeste [soodo-esteh]
souvenir el recuerdo [rekwairdo]
Spain España [espan-ya]
Spaniard (man/woman) el español [espan-yol], la española
Spanish español
spanner la llave inglesa [yabeh]
spare parts los repuestos [repwestos], las refacciones [refaks-yon-es]
spare tyre la llanta de repuesto [yanta deh]
sparkplug la bujía [booHee-a]
speak hablar [ablar]

do you speak English? ¿habla inglés? [abla eeng-les]
I don't speak ... no hablo ... [ablo]

dialogue

can I speak to Pablo? ¿puedo hablar con Pablo? [pwedo]
who's calling? ¿quién lo llama? [k-yen lo yama]
it's Patricia Patricia
I'm sorry, he's not in, can I take a message? lo siento, no está, ¿quiere dejar recado? [s-yento – k-yaireh deh-Har]
no thanks, I'll call back later no gracias, llamaré más tarde [gras-yas yamareh mas tardeh]
please tell him I called por favor, dígale que llamé [fabor deegaleh keh yameh]

speciality la especialidad [espes-yaleeda]
spectacles las gafas
speed la velocidad [beloseeda]
speed limit el límite de velocidad [leemeeteh deh]
speedometer el velocímetro [beloseemetro]
spell: how do you spell it? ¿cómo se escribe? [seh eskreebeh]
  see alphabet
spend gastar

spider la araña [aran-ya]

spin-dryer la secadora

splinter la astilla [astee-ya]

spoke (in wheel) el radio [rad-yo]

spoon la cuchara

sport el deporte [deporteh]

sprain: I've sprained my ... me torcí el ... [meh torsee]

spring (season) la primavera [preemabaira]
(of car, seat) el resorte [resorteh]

square (in town) la plaza [plasa]

stairs la escalera [eskalaira]

stale (bread) duro
(food) pasado

stall: the engine keeps stalling el motor se para cada rato [seh]

stamp la estampilla [estampee-ya], el timbre [teembreh]

dialogue

a stamp for England, please una estampilla para Inglaterra, por favor [fabor]
what are you sending? ¿qué es lo que envía? [keh – embee-a]
this postcard esta postal

standby el vuelo standby [bwelo]

star la estrella [estreh-ya]
(in film) el/la protagonista

start el principio [preenseep-yo]
(verb) comenzar [komensar]

when does it start? ¿cuándo comienza? [kwando com-yensa]

the car won't start el carro no arranca

starter (of car) el motor de arranque [arrankeh]
(food) la entrada

starving: I'm starving me muero de hambre [meh mwairo deh ambreh]

state (country) el estado
the States (USA) los Estados Unidos [ooneedos]

station la estación de ferrocarril [estas-yon deh fairrokarreel]

statue la estatua [estatwa]

stay: where are you staying? ¿dónde está alojado? [dondeh – aloHado]

I'm staying at ... (said by man/woman) estoy alojado/alojada en ...

I'd like to stay another two nights me gustaría quedarme dos noches más [meh – kedarmeh – noch-es]

steak el filete [feeleteh]

steal robar

my bag has been stolen me robaron el bolso [meh]

steep (hill) empinado, escarpado

steering la dirección [deereks-yon]

step: on the steps en las escaleras [eskalairas]

stereo el estéreo [estaireh-o]

sterling la libra esterlina [estairleena]

steward (on plane) el auxiliar de vuelo [owseel-yar deh bwelo]

stewardess la azafata [asafata]

sticking plaster la curita [kooreeta]

still: I'm still waiting sigo esperando

is he still there? ¿sigue ahí? [seegeh a-ee]

keep still! ¡quédese quieto! [kedeseh k-yeto]

sting: I've been stung algo me ha picado [meh a]

stockings las medias [med-yas]

stomach el estómago

stomach ache el dolor de estómago [deh]

stone (rock) la piedra [p-yedra]

stop (verb) parar

please, stop here (to taxi driver etc) pare aquí, por favor [pareh akee por fabor]

do you stop near ...? ¿para cerca de ...? [sairka deh]

stop doing that! ¡deje de hacer eso! [deh-Heh deh asair]

stopover la escala

storm la tormenta

straight: it's straight ahead todo recto

a straight whisky un whisky solo

straightaway en seguida [segeeda]

strange (odd) extraño [estran-yo]

stranger (man/woman) el forastero [forastairo], la

forastera

I'm a stranger here no soy de aquí [deh akee]

strap la correa [korreh-a]

strawberry la fresa, la frutilla [frootee-ya]

stream el arroyo [arro-yo]

street la calle [ka-yeh]

on the street en la calle

streetmap el plano de la ciudad [deh la s-yooda]

string la cuerda [kwairda]

strong fuerte [fwairteh]

stuck: the key's stuck la llave se atascó [yabeh seh]

student el/la estudiante [estood-yanteh]

subway (US) el metro

suburb el suburbio [sooboorb-yo]

suddenly de repente [deh repenteh]

suede el ante [anteh]

sugar el azúcar [asookar]

suit el traje [traHeh]

it doesn't suit me (jacket etc) no me queda bien [meh keda b-yen]

it suits you te queda muy bien [teh – mwee]

suitcase la maleta, (Mex) la petaca, (Rpl) la valija [baleeHa]

summer el verano [bairano]

in the summer en verano

sun el sol

in the sun al sol

out of the sun a la sombra

sunbathe tomar el sol

sunblock (cream) la crema protectora, el filtro solar

sunburn la quemadura de sol [kemadoora deh]

sunburnt quemado [kemado]

Sunday domingo

sunglasses las gafas de sol [deh]

sun lounger la tumbona, (Col, Per) la perezosa, (Rpl) la reposera, (Urug) el perezoso

sunny: it's sunny hace sol [aseh]

sunroof (in car) el techo corredizo [korredeeso]

sunset la puesta del sol [pwesta]

sunshade la sombrilla [sombree-ya]

sunshine la luz del sol [loos]

sunstroke la insolación [eensolas-yon]

suntan el bronceado [bronseh-ado]

suntan lotion la loción bronceadora [los-yon bronseh-adora]

suntanned bronceado [bronseh-ado]

suntan oil el aceite bronceador [asayteh]

super fabuloso

supermarket el supermercado [soopairmairkado]

supper la cena [sena]

supplement (extra charge) el suplemento [sooplemento]

sure: are you sure? ¿está seguro?

sure! ¡por supuesto! [soopwesto]

surfboard la tabla de surf [deh soorf]

surfing el surfing

surname el apellido [apeh-yeedo]

swearword la grosería [grosairee-a]

sweater el suéter [swetair]

sweatshirt la sudadera [soodadaira]

Sweden Suecia [swes-ya]

Swedish (adj) sueco [sweko]

sweet (dessert) el postre [postreh]
(adj: taste) dulce [doolseh]

sweetcorn el maíz, (Mex) el elote [eloteh], (SAm) el choclo, (Ven) el jojoto [Hohoto]

sweets los dulces [dools-es]

swelling la hinchazón [eenchason]

swim (verb) bañarse [ban-yarseh]
I'm going for a swim voy a bañarme [boy a ban-yarmeh]
let's go for a swim vamos a bañarnos [bamos a ban-yarnos]

swimming costume el traje de baño [traHeh deh ban-yo]

swimming pool la piscina [peeseena], (Mex) la alberca [albairka], (Rpl) la pileta [peeleta]

swimming trunks el traje de baño [traHeh deh ban-yo]

switch el interruptor
[eentairooptor]
switch off apagar
switch on prender [prendair]
swollen hinchado
[eenchado]

T

table la mesa
 a table for two una mesa para
 dos
tablecloth el mantel
table tennis el ping-pong
table wine el vino de mesa
 [beeno deh]
tailback (of traffic) la caravana
 de carros [karabana deh]
tailor el sastre [sastreh]
take (lead) tomar
 (accept) aceptar [aseptar]
 **can you take me to the
 airport?** ¿me lleva al
 aeropuerto? [meh yeba al a-
 airopwairto]
 do you take credit cards?
 ¿acepta tarjetas de crédito?
 [asepta tarHetas deh kredeeto]
 fine, I'll take it me llevo éste
 [meh yebo esteh]
 can I take this? (leaflet etc)
 ¿puedo llevarme esto? [pwedo
 yebarmeh]
 how long does it take?
 ¿cuánto tarda? [kwanto]
 it takes three hours tarda tres
 horas [oras]
 is this seat taken? ¿está

ocupado este asiento? [esteh
as-yento]
 a hamburger to take away
 una hamburguesa para llevar
 [yebar]
 **can you take a little off
 here?** (to hairdresser) ¿puede
 quitarme un poco de aquí?
 [pwedeh keetarmeh – deh akee]
talcum powder el talco
talk (verb) hablar,
 (C.Am, Mex) platicar
tall alto
tampons los tampones
 [tampon-es]
tan el bronceado [bronseh-ado]
 to get a tan broncearse
 [bronseh-arseh]
tank (in car) el depósito
 [deposeeto]
tap la llave [la yabeh],
 (C.Am) la paja [paHa],
 (Per) el caño [kan-yo],
 (Rpl) la canilla [kanee-ya]
tape (for cassette) la cinta
 [seenta]
 (sticky) la cinta adhesiva
 [adeseeba]
tape measure la cinta métrica
tape recorder la grabadora
taste el sabor
 can I taste it? ¿puedo
 probarlo? [pwedo]
taxi el taxi, el colectivo
 [kolekteebo]
 will you get me a taxi? ¿me
 consigue un taxi? [meh
 konseegeh]
 where can I find a taxi?

¿dónde encuentro un taxi?
[dondeh enkwentro]

dialogue

to the airport/to the
Sol Hotel please al
aeropuerto/al hotel Sol,
por favor [a-airopwairto/al
otel – fabor]
how much will it be?
¿cuánto va a ser? [kwanto
ba a sair]
1,000 pesos mil pesos
that's fine, right here,
thanks está bien aquí
mismo, gracias [b-yen akee
meesmo gras-yas]

taxi-driver el/la taxista
taxi rank la parada de taxis
[deh]
tea (drink) el té [teh]
  tea for one/two please un
  té/dos tés, por favor [fabor]
teabags las bolsas de té [deh]
teach: could you teach me?
  ¿podría enseñarme? [ensen-
  yarmeh]
teacher (primary: man/woman) el
  maestro [ma-estro], la maestra
  (secondary) el profesor, la
  profesora
team el equipo [ekeepo]
teaspoon la cucharita
tea towel el trapo de cocina
  [deh koseena],
  (Col) el limpión [leemp-yon],
  (Rpl) el repasador

teenager el/la adolescente
  [adolesenteh]
telephone el teléfono
  see phone
television la televisión
  [telebees-yon]
tell: could you tell him ...?
  ¿podría decirle ...? [deseerleh]
temperature (weather) la
  temperatura [tempairatoora]
  (fever) la fiebre [f-yebreh]
temple el templo
tennis el tenis
tennis ball la pelota de tenis
  [deh]
tennis court la cancha de tenis
tennis racket la raqueta de
  tenis [raketa]
tent la tienda de campaña [t-
  yenda deh kampan-ya], la carpa
term (at university, school) el
  trimestre [treemestreh]
terminus (rail) la terminal
  [tairmeenal]
terrible malísimo
terrific fabuloso [fabooloso]
text (message) el mensaje (de
  texto) [mensaHeh]
than* que [keh]
  smaller than más pequeño
  que [peken-yo]
thanks, thank you gracias
  [gras-yas]
  thank you very much muchas
  gracias [moochas]
  thanks for the lift gracias por
  traerme [tra-airmeh]
  no thanks no gracias

dialogue

thanks gracias
that's OK, don't mention it
no hay de qué [ī deh keh]

that: that man ese hombre
[eseh **o**mbreh]
that woman esa mujer
[moo**H**air]
that one ése [**e**seh]
I hope that ... espero que ...
[esp**ai**ro keh]
that's nice (clothes, souvenir etc)
qué lindo
is that ...? ¿es ése ...?
that's it (that's right) eso es
the* el, la; (pl) los, las
theatre el teatro [teh-**a**tro]
their* su; (pl) sus [soos]
theirs* su, sus; (pl) suyos
[soo-yos], suyas; de ellos [deh
eh-yos], de ellas
them* (things) los, las
(people) les
for them para ellos/ellas [**eh**-
yos/**eh**-yas]
with them con ellos/ellas
I gave it to them se lo di a
ellos/ellas [seh]
who? – them ¿quiénes? –
ellos/ellas [k-**yen**-es]
then luego [lwego]
there allí [a-yee]
over there allá [a-ya]
up there allá arriba
is/are there ...? ¿hay ...? [ī]
there is/are ... hay ...
there you are (giving something)

aquí tiene [ak**ee** t-yeneh]
thermometer el termómetro
[tairm**o**metro]
Thermos® flask el termo
[**tair**mo]
these: these men estos
h**o**mbres
these women estas mujeres
can I have these? ¿me puedo
llevar éstos? [meh pwedo yebar]
they* (male) ellos [**eh**-yos]
(female) ellas [**eh**-yas]
thick grueso [grw**e**so]
(stupid) bruto
thief (man/woman) el ladrón, la
ladrona
thigh el muslo
thin flaco
thing la cosa
my things mis cosas [mees]
think pensar
(believe) creer [kreh-**air**]
I think so creo que sí [kr**e**h-o
keh]
I don't think so no creo
I'll think about it lo pensaré
[pensar**eh**]
third party insurance el seguro
contra terceros [tairs**ai**ros]
thirsty: I'm thirsty tengo sed
[seh]
this: this man este hombre
[**e**steh]
this woman esta mujer
this one éste/ésta [**e**steh]
this is my wife le presento a
mi mujer [leh]
is this ...? ¿es éste/ésta ...?
those: those men aquellos

hombres [ak**eh**-yos]
those women aquellas
mujeres [ak**eh**-yas]
which ones? – those ¿cuáles?
– aquéllos/aquéllas [kwal-es]
thread el hilo [**ee**lo]
throat la garganta
throat pastilles las pastillas
para la garganta [past**ee**-yas]
through a través de [trav-**es** deh]
does it go through ...? (train,
bus) ¿pasa por ...?
throw (verb) echar, aventar
[abentar]
throw away (verb) tirar, botar
thumb el pulgar
thunderstorm la tormenta
Thursday jueves [Hw**eb**-es]
ticket el boleto

dialogue

a return to Cartagena un
boleto de ida y vuelta
a Cartagena [deh **ee**da ee
bwelta a kartaHena]
coming back when?
¿cuándo piensa regresar?
[kwando p-yensa]
today/next Tuesday hoy/el
martes que viene [oy/el
mart-es keh b-yeneh]
that will be 2,000 pesos
son dos mil pesos

ticket office (bus, rail) la taquilla
[tak**ee**-ya], la boletería
[boletair**ee**-a]
tide la marea [mar**eh**-a]

tie (necktie) la corbata
tight (clothes etc) ajustado
[aHoostado]
it's too tight me queda
estrecho [meh k**e**da]
tights las medias [m**e**d-yas],
(Col) las medias pantalón
[pantal**on**],
(Mex) pantimedias,
(Rpl) las medias bombacha,
(Ven) las medias panty [p**a**ntee]
till la caja [k**a**Ha]
time* el tiempo [t-y**e**mpo]
what's the time? ¿qué hora
es? [keh **o**ra]
this time esta vez [bes]
last time la última vez
[**oo**lteema]
next time la próxima vez
four times cuatro veces [b**es**-
es]
timetable el horario [or**ar**-yo]
tin (can) la lata, el bote [b**o**teh]
tinfoil el papel de aluminio
[aloom**ee**n-yo]
tin-opener el abrelatas
tiny minúsculo [meen**oo**skoolo]
tip (to waiter etc) la propina
tired cansado
I'm tired (said by a man/woman)
est**oy** cansado/cansada
tissues los klinex®
to: to Santo Domingo/London
a Santo Domingo/L**o**ndres
to Asuncion/England a
Asunci**ó**n/Inglat**e**rra
to the post office al correo
toast (bread) la tostada
today hoy [oy]

toe el dedo del pie [p-yeh]

together juntos [Hoontos]

we're together (in shop etc) estamos juntos

can we pay together? ¿podemos pagar todo junto, por favor? [fabor]

toilet el baño [ban-yo]

where is the toilet? ¿dónde está el baño? [dondeh]

I have to go to the toilet tengo que ir al baño [keh]

toilet paper el papel higiénico [eeH-yeneeko]

tomato el tomate [tomateh], (Mex) el jitomate [Heetomateh]

tomato juice el jugo de tomate [Hoogo deh]

tomato ketchup la salsa de tomate, (Mex) el catsup [katsoop]

tomorrow mañana [man-yana]

tomorrow morning mañana por la mañana

the day after tomorrow pasado mañana

toner (for skin) el tonificador facial [fas-yal]

tongue la lengua [lengwa]

tonic (water) la tónica

tonight esta noche [nocheh]

tonsillitis las anginas [anHeenas]

too (excessively) demasiado [demas-yado]

(also) también [tamb-yen]

too hot demasiado caliente [kal-yenteh]

too much demasiado

me too yo también

tooth el diente [d-yenteh], la muela [mwela]

toothache el dolor de muelas [deh]

toothbrush el cepillo de dientes [sepee-yo deh d-yent-es]

toothpaste la pasta de dientes

top: on top of ... encima de ... [enseema deh], arriba de ...

at the top en la parte de arriba [parteh]

at the top of ... en la parte más alta de ...

top floor el último piso [oolteemo]

topless topless

torch la linterna [leentairna]

total el total [tot-al]

tour la excursión [eskoors-yon]

is there a tour of ...? ¿hay recorrido de ...? [ī – deh]

tour guide el guía turístico [gee-a], la guía turística

tourist el/la turista

tourist information office la oficina de información turística [ofeeseena deh eenformas-yon]

tour operator el operador turístico

towards hacia [as-ya]

towel la toalla [to-a-ya]

town la ciudad [s-yooda]

in town en el centro [sentro]

just out of town a la salida de

la ciudad

town centre el centro de la ciudad [**s**entro deh la s-yood**a**]

town hall el ayuntamiento [a-yoontam-**y**ento], la municipalidad

toy el juguete [Hoog**e**teh]

track (US) la vía [b**ee**-a]

tracksuit el chandal, (Ch, Per) el buzo [b**oo**so], (Col) la sudadera [soodad**ai**ra], (Mex) los pants, (Rpl) el jogging [**y**ogeen]

traditional tradicional [tradees-yon**al**]

traffic el tránsito, la circulación [seerkoolas-y**on**]

traffic jam el embotellamiento [emboteh-yam-y**e**nto]

traffic lights el semáforo

trailer (for carrying tent etc) el remolque [rem**o**lkeh] (US: caravan) la caravana [karab**a**na]

trailer park el camping

train el tren

by train en tren

dialogue

is this the train for ...? ¿es éste el tren para ...? [**e**steh]

sure sí

no, you want that platform there no, tiene que ir a aquel andén [t-y**e**neh keh eer a ak**e**l and**e**n]

trainers (shoes) los tenis [t**e**nees], (Mex) los tráiner [tr**ī**nair]

train station la estación de ferrocarril [estas-y**on** deh fairrokar**ee**l]

tram el tranvía [tramb**ee**-a]

translate traducir [tradoos**eer**]

could you translate that? ¿podría traducir eso?

translation la traducción [tradooks-y**on**]

translator (man/woman) el traductor, la traductora

trashcan el cubo de la basura, (Ch) el tarro de la basura, (Col) la caneca de la basura [kan**e**ka], (Csur, Per) el tacho de la basura, (Mex) el bote de la basura [b**o**teh], (Ven) el tobo de la basura

travel (verb) viajar [b-ya**H**ar]

we're travelling around andamos de paseo [deh pas**eh**-o]

travel agent's la agencia de viajes [a**H**ens-ya deh b-ya**H**-es]

traveller's cheque el cheque de viajero [ch**e**keh deh b-ya**H**airo]

tray la bandeja [band**e**Ha]

tree el árbol

tremendous tremendo

trendy de moda [deh]

trim: just a trim please (to hairdresser) córtemelo sólo un poco, por favor [fab**or**]

trip (excursion) la excursión
[eskoors-yon]
I'd like to go on a trip to ...
me gustaría hacer una
excursión a ... [meh –
asair]
trolley el carrito
trouble problemas
[problemas]
I'm having trouble with ...
tengo problemas con ...
sorry to trouble you
disculpe la molestia
[deeskoolpeh]
trousers los pantalones
[pantalon-es]
true cierto [s-yairto]
that's not true no es cierto
trunk (US) el maletero
[maletairo],
(Ch, Pe) la maleta,
(Col, Rpl) el baúl [ba-ool],
(Mex) la cajuela [kaHwela]
trunks (swimming) el traje de
baño [traHeh deh ban-yo]
try (verb) intentar
can I try it? ¿puedo
intentarlo yo? [pwedo]
try on: can I try it on? ¿puedo
probármelo?
T-shirt la camiseta,
(Mex) la playera [pla-yaira],
(Rpl) la remera [remaira]
Tuesday martes [mart-es]
tuna el atún
tunnel el túnel [toonel]
turn: turn left/right tuerce a la
izquierda/derecha
[twairseh]

turn off: where do I turn off?
¿dónde doy vuelta? [dondeh
doy bwelta]
can you turn the heating off?
¿puede apagar la
calefacción? [pwedeh – kalefaks-
yon]
turn on: can you turn the
heating on? ¿puede
poner la calefacción?
[ponair]
turning (in road) el desvío
[desbee-o]
TV la tele [teleh]
tweezers las pinzas
[peensas]
twice dos veces [bes-es]
twice as much el doble
[dobleh]
twin beds las camas gemelas
[Hemelas]
twin room el cuarto con dos
camas [kwarto]
twist: I've twisted my ankle
me torcí el tobillo [meh torsee
el tobee-yo]
type el tipo [teepo]
a different type of ... otro tipo
de ... [deh]
typical típico [teepeeko]
tyre la llanta [yanta]

U

ugly feo [feh-o]
UK el Reino Unido [rayno
ooneedo]
ulcer la úlcera [oolsaira]

umbrella el paraguas
[paragwas]

uncle el tío

unconscious inconsciente
[eenkons-yenteh]

under (in position) debajo de
[debaHo deh]
(less than) menos de

underdone (meat) poco hecho
[echo]

underground (railway) el
metro

underpants los calzoncillos
[kalsonsee-yos],
(Col, Ven) interiores [eentairee-
or-es],
(Mex) los calzones
[kalson-es]

understand: I understand lo
entiendo [ent-yendo]
I don't understand no
entiendo
do you understand?
¿entiende? [ent-yendeh]

unemployed desempleado
[desempleh-ado]

unfashionable fuera de moda
[fwaira deh]

United States los Estados
Unidos [ooneedos]

university la universidad
[ooneebairseeda]

unleaded petrol la gasolina sin
plomo [seen]

unlimited mileage sin límite
de kilometraje [leemeeteh deh
keelometraHeh]

unlock abrir [abreer]

unpack deshacer las maletas

[desasair]

until hasta que [asta keh]

unusual poco común
[komoon]

up arriba
up there allá arriba [a-ya]
he's not up yet (not out of bed)
todavía no se ha levantado
[todabee-a no seh a lebantado]
what's up? (what's wrong?) ¿qué
pasa? [keh]

upmarket (restaurant, hotel etc) de
lujo [deh looHo]

upset stomach el mal del
estómago

upside down al revés [rebes],
boca abajo [abaHo]

upstairs arriba

urgent urgente [oorHenteh]

Uruguay Uruguay [ooroogwī]

Uruguayan (adj) uruguayo
[ooroogwa-yo]
(man) el uruguayo
(woman) la uruguaya

us*: with us con nosotros/
nosotras
for us para nosotros/
nosotras

USA EE.UU., Estados
Unidos [ooneedos]

use (verb) emplear
[empleh-ar]
may I use ...? ¿me
permite ...? [meh permeeteh]

useful útil [ooteel]

usual de costumbre [deh
kostoombreh]
the usual (drink etc) lo de
siempre [s-yempreh]

vacancy: do you have any vacancies? (hotel) ¿tiene cuartos libres? [t-yeneh kwartos leeb-res]

vacation las vacaciones [bakas-yon-es]

vaccination la vacuna [bakoona]

vacuum cleaner la aspiradora

valid (ticket etc) válido [baleedo]

  how long is it valid for? ¿hasta cuándo tiene validez? [asta kwando t-yeneh baleed-es]

valley el valle [ba-yeh]

valuable (adj) valioso [bal-yoso]

  can I leave my valuables here? ¿puedo dejar aquí mis objetos de valor? [pwedo deh-Har akee mees obHetos deh balor]

value el valor

van la camioneta [kam-yoneta]

vanilla vainilla [bīnee-ya]

  a vanilla ice cream un helado de vainilla [elado deh]

vary: it varies depende [dependeh]

vase el florero [florairo]

veal la ternera [tairnaira]

vegetables las verduras [bairdooras]

vegetarian (man/woman) el vegetariano [beHetar-yano], la vegetariana

vending machine la máquina expendedora [makeena espendedora]

Venezuela Venezuela [beneswayla]

Venezuelan (adj) venezolano [benesolano]
  (man) el venezolano
  (woman) la venezolana

very muy [mwee]
  very little for me muy poquito para mí [pokeeto]
  I like it very much me gusta mucho [meh goosta moocho]

vest (under shirt) la camiseta

via por

video el video [beedeh-o]

view la vista [beesta]

villa el chalet [chaleh]

village el pueblo [pweblo]

vinegar el vinagre [beenagreh]

vineyard el viñedo [been-yedo]

visa la visa

visit (verb) visitar [beeseetar]
  I'd like to visit Honduras me gustaría conocer Honduras [konosair]

vital: it's vital that ... es imprescindible que ... [eempreseendeebleh keh]

vodka el vodka [bodka]

voice la voz [bos]

volcano el volcán [bolkan]

voltage el voltaje [boltaHeh]

vomit vomitar [bomeetar]

vulture el buitre [bweetreh], (Mex) el zopilote [sopeeloteh] (Ven) el zamuro

122

W

waist la cintura [seent**oo**ra]

waistcoat el chaleco

wait esperar [espair**ar**]

wait for me espéreme [esp**ai**remeh]

don't wait for me no me espere [meh esp**ai**reh]

can I wait until my wife/ partner gets here? ¿puedo esperar hasta que llegue mi mujer/compañero? [pw**e**do – **a**sta keh y**e**geh]

can you do it while I wait? ¿puede hacerlo ahora mismo? [pw**e**deh as**ai**rlo a-**o**ra]

could you wait here for me? ¿puede esperarme aquí? [espair**ar**meh ak**ee**]

waiter el mesero [mes**ai**ro]

waiter! ¡señor! [sen-y**or**]

waitress la mesera [mes**ai**ra]

waitress! ¡señorita! [sen-yor**ee**ta]

wake: can you wake me up at 5.30? ¿podría despertarme a las cinco y media? [despair**tar**meh]

wake-up call la llamada para despertar [yam**a**da]

Wales Gales [g**a**l-es]

walk: is it a long walk? ¿se tarda mucho caminando? [seh – m**oo**cho]

it's only a short walk está cerca [s**ai**rka]

I'll walk iré caminando [eer**eh**]

I'm going for a walk voy a dar una vuelta [boy – bw**e**lta]

Walkman® el walkman® [w**o**lkman]

wall (inside) la pared [par**eh**] (outside) el muro

wallet la cartera [kart**ai**ra]

wander: I like just wandering around me gusta caminar sin rumbo fijo [meh g**oo**sta – seen r**oo**mbo fee**Ho**]

want: I want a ... quiero un/ una ... [k-y**ai**ro]

I don't want ... no quiero ninguno/ninguna ...

I want to go home quiero irme a casa [**eer**meh]

I don't want to no quiero

he wants to ... quiere ... [k-y**ai**reh]

what do you want? ¿qué quiere? [keh]

ward (in hospital) el pabellón [pabeh-y**on**]

warm caliente [kal-y**en**teh]

I'm very warm tengo mucho calor [m**oo**cho]

was*: it was ... era ... [**ai**ra]; estaba ...

wash (verb) lavar [lab**ar**]

can you wash these? ¿puede lavar estos? [pw**e**deh]

washer (for bolt etc) la arandela, (CSur) el cuerito [kwair**ee**to], (Col, Ven) el empaque [emp**a**keh]

washhand basin el lavabo
[lababo]
(CSur) el lavatorio [labatoree-o]
(Rpl) la pileta

washing (clothes) la ropa sucia
[soos-ya]

washing machine la lavadora
[labadora]

washing powder el detergente
[detairHenteh]

washing-up liquid el
(detergente) lavavajillas
[lababaHee-yas]

wasp la avispa [abeespa]

watch (wristwatch) el reloj
[reloH]

**will you watch my things for
me?** ¿puede cuidarme mis
cosas? [pwedeh kweedarmeh
mees]

watch out! ¡cuidado!
[kweedado]

watch strap la correa
[korreh-a]

water el agua [agwa]

may I have some water? ¿me
da un poco de agua? [meh
– deh]

waterproof (adj) impermeable
[eempairmeh-ableh]

waterskiing el esquí acuático
[eskee akwateeko]

wave (in sea) la ola

way: it's this way es por aquí
[akee]

it's that way es por allí
[a-yee]

is it a long way to ...? ¿queda
lejos ...? [keda leH-Hos]

no way! ¡de ninguna manera!
[deh – manaira]

dialogue

> **could you tell me the way
> to ...?** podría indicarme el
> camino a ...? [eendeekarmeh]
> **go straight on until you
> reach the traffic lights**
> siga recto hasta llegar al
> semáforo [asta yegar]
> **turn left** tuerza a la
> izquierda [twairsa]
> **take the first on the right**
> tome la primera a la
> derecha [tomeh]
> **see where**

we* nosotros, nosotras

weak débil

weather el tiempo [t-yempo]

dialogue

> **what's the weather going
> to be like?** ¿qué tiempo va
> a hacer? [keh – ba a asair]
> **it's going to be fine** va a
> hacer bueno [bweno]
> **it's going to rain** va a llover
> [yobair]
> **it'll brighten up later**
> despejará más tarde
> [despeH-Hara mas tardeh]

wedding la boda

wedding ring el anillo de
casado [anee-yo]

Wednesday miércoles [m-**yair**kol-es]
week la semana
  a week (from) today dentro de una semana [deh]
  a week (from) tomorrow dentro de una semana a partir de mañana [man-**yana**]
weekend el fin de semana [feen deh]
  at the weekend el fin de semana
weight el peso
weird extraño [ekstran-yo]
weirdo: he's a weirdo es un tipo raro [**tee**po]
welcome: welcome to ... bienvenido a ... [b-yenben**eedo**]
  you're welcome (don't mention it) no hay de qué [ī deh keh]
well: I don't feel well no me siento bien [meh s-**yento** b-yen]
  she's not well no se siente bien [seh s-**yenteh**]
  you speak English very well habla inglés muy bien [**abla** eeng-les mwee]
  well done! ¡bravo! [**brabo**]
  this one as well éste también [**esteh** tamb-**yen**]
  well well! (surprise) ¡vaya, vaya! [**ba**-ya], (Mex) ¡ándale, pues! [**andaleh** pwes]

dialogue

> how are you? ¿cómo le va? [leh ba]
> very well, thanks muy bien, gracias [mwee b-yen gras-yas]
> – and you? – ¿y usted? [ee oosteh]

well-done (meat) bien hecho [b-yen **echo**]
Welsh galés [gal-es]
  I'm Welsh (man/woman) soy galés/galesa
were*: we were estábamos; éramos [**airamos**]
  you were estaban; eran [**airan**]
  they were estaban; eran
west el oeste [o-**esteh**], el occidente [okseed**enteh**]
  in the west en el oeste
West Indian (adj) antillano [antee-**yano**]
wet mojado [mo**Hado**]
what? ¿qué? [keh]
  what's that? ¿qué es eso?
  what should I do? ¿qué hago? [**a**-go]
  what a view! ¡qué vista!
  what number bus is it? ¿qué número de autobús es ese? [**noo**mairo deh – **eseh**]
wheel la rueda [**rweda**]
wheelchair la silla de ruedas [**see**-ya deh **rwedas**]
when? ¿cuándo? [**kwando**]
  when we get back cuando regresamos

when's the train/ferry?
¿cuándo es el tren/ferry?
where? ¿dónde? [dondeh]
I don't know where it is no sé
dónde está [seh]

dialogue

where is the cathedral?
¿dónde está la catedral?
it's over there está por ahí
[a-ee]
could you show me where
it is on the map? ¿puede
enseñarme en el mapa
dónde está? [pwedeh ensen-
yarmeh]
it's just here está aquí
nomás [akee nomas],
(Mex) está aquí mero [akee
mairo]
see way

which: which bus? ¿qué
camión? [keh]

dialogue

which one? ¿cuál?
[kwal]
that one ese [eseh]
this one? ¿éste? [esteh]
no, that one no, aquél
[akel]

while: while I'm here ya
que estoy aquí [keh estoy
akee]
whisky el whisky

white blanco
white wine el vino blanco
[beeno]
who? ¿quién? [k-yen]
who is it? ¿quién es?
the man who ... el hombre
que... [keh]
whole: the whole week toda la
semana
the whole lot todo
whose: whose is this? ¿de
quién es esto? [deh k-yen]
why? ¿por qué? [keh]
why not? ¿por qué no?
wide ancho
wife la mujer [mooHair], la
esposa
will*: will you do it for me?
¿puede hacer esto por mí?
[pwedeh asair]
wind el viento [b-yento]
window (of house) la ventana
[bentana]
(of ticket office, vehicle) la
ventanilla [bentanee-ya]
near the window cerca de la
ventana [sairka deh]
in the window (of shop) en el
escaparate [eskaparateh],
(Ch, Col, Ven) en la vitrina
[beetreena],
(Mex) en el aparador,
(Rpl) en la vidriera [beedr-yaira]
window seat el asiento junto
a la ventana [as-yento Hoonto a
la bentana]
windscreen el parabrisas
windscreen wiper el
limpiaparabrisas [leemp-ya-

parabr**ee**sas]
windsurfing el windsurf
windy: it's very windy hace
mucho viento [aseh m**oo**cho
b-y**e**nto]
wine el vino [b**ee**no]
 can we have some more
 wine? ¿podría traernos más
 vino? [tra-**ai**rnos]
wine list la lista de vinos
 [l**ee**sta deh b**ee**nos]
winter el invierno [eemb-y**ai**rno]
 in the winter en invierno
winter holiday las vacaciones
 de invierno [bakas-y**o**n-es deh]
wire el alambre [al**a**mbreh]
 (electric) el cable eléctrico
 [k**a**bleh]
wish: best wishes saludos
with con
 I'm staying with ... est**o**y en
 casa de ... [deh]
without sin [seen]
witness el/la testigo [test**ee**go]
 will you be a witness for me?
 ¿acepta ser mi testigo? [as**e**pta
 sair]
woman la mujer [moo**H**air]
wonderful estupendo
 [estoop**e**ndo]
won't*: it won't start no
 arranca
wood (material) la madera
 [mad**ai**ra]
woods (forest) el bosque
 [b**o**skeh]
wool la lana
word la palabra
work el trabajo [trab**a**Ho]

it's not working no funciona
 [foons-y**o**na]
 I work in ... trabajo en ...
world el mundo [m**oo**ndo]
worry: I'm worried (said by man/
 woman) est**o**y preocupado/
 preocupada [preh-okoop**a**do]
worse: it's worse es peor
 [peh-**o**r]
worst el peor
worth: is it worth a visit?
 ¿vale la pena visitarlo? [b**a**leh
 – beeseet**a**rlo]
would: would you give this
 to ...? ¿le puede dar esto a ...?
 [leh pw**e**deh]
wrap: could you wrap it up?
 ¿me lo envuelve? [meh lo
 embw**e**lbeh]
wrapping paper el papel de
 envolver [deh embolb**ai**r]
wrist la muñeca [moon-y**e**ka]
write escribir [eskreeb**ee**r]
 could you write it down?
 ¿puede escribírmelo?
 [pw**e**deh]
 how do you write it? ¿cómo
 se escribe? [seh eskr**ee**beh]
writing paper el papel de
 escribir
wrong: it's the wrong key no
 es ésa la llave [y**a**beh]
 this is the wrong train éste no
 es el tren [**e**steh]
 the bill's wrong la cuenta
 está equivocada [kw**e**nta
 – ekeebok**a**da]
 sorry, wrong number
 perdone, me equivoqué

de número [pairdoneh meh
ekeebokeh deh noomairo]
**there's something wrong
with ...** le pasa algo a ...
[leh]
what's wrong? ¿qué pasa?
[keh]

X

X-ray la radiografía [rad-
yografee-a]

Y

yacht el yate [yateh]
yard* (courtyard) el patio
year el año [an-yo]
yellow amarillo [amaree-yo]
yes sí
yesterday ayer [a-yair]
 yesterday morning ayer por
 la mañana [man-yana]
 the day before yesterday
 anteayer [anteh-a-yair]
yet

dialogue

is it here yet? ¿está aquí
ya? [akee]
no, not yet no, todavía no
[todabee-a]
**you'll have to wait a little
longer yet** tendrá que
esperar un poquito más
[keh espairar oon pokeeto]

yobbo el hampón [ampon]
yoghurt el yogur [yogoor]
you* (fam, sing) tú/vos [too, bos]
 (pol, sing) usted [oosteh]
 (pol, pl) ustedes [oosted-es]
 this is for you esto es para
 tí/vos/usted
 with you contigo/con usted
young joven [Hoben]
your* (fam, sing) tu; (pl) tus
 [toos]
 (pol, sing) su; (pl) sus [soos]
yours* (fam, sing) tuyo [too-yo],
 tuya
 (pol, sing) suyo [soo-yo], suya;
 de usted [deh oosteh]
youth hostel el albergue
juvenil [albairgeh Hoobeneel]

Z

zero cero [sairo]
zip el cierre [s-yairreh]
 could you put a new zip in?
 ¿podría cambiar el cierre?
 [kamb-yar]
zip code el código postal
[pos-tal]
zoo el zoo(lógico) [zo(loHeeko)]

Xr

Spanish

→

English

Colloquial Spanish

The following are words you might well hear. Some of them you wouldn't ever want to use and you shouldn't be tempted to use any of the stronger ones unless you are sure of your audience.

¿a quién carajos le importa? [karaHos] who bloody cares?
¡bien! [b-yen] great!
boludo m dickhead
cabrón m bastard
¡cómo no! of course
¡carajo! [karaHo] Christ!, shit!
chingar to fuck
¡chinga tu madre! fuck off!
coger [koHair] to fuck
¡Dios mío! [d-yos mee-o] my God!
¿dónde carajos? [dondeh] where the hell?
¡hijo de la chingada! [eeHo] son of a bitch!
¡hijo de puta! [eeHo deh poota] son of a bitch!
¡hijueputa! [eeHwepoota] son of a bitch!
huevón [webon] jerk!
joder [Hodair] to screw up
¡la puta! [poota] bloody hell!
¡lárguese! [largeseh] go away!
¡lo jodiste! [Hodeesteh] you screwed up!
maldita sea damn!
marica m, maricón m queer
me pega la gana I feel like it
¡me importa un carajo! [eemporta oon karaHo] I don´t give a shit!
¡mierda! [m-yairda] shit!
¡ni modo! well, what can you do?
no me da la gana I couldn't be bothered
¡oiga! [oyga] listen here!; excuse me!
¡qué cagada! [keh kagada] what a fuck-up!
¿qué hubo? [keh oobo] how's it going?
¡qué va! [ba] no way!
tirar [teerar] to fuck

A

a to; at; per; from

abajeño m [abaнen-yo] lowlander

abajo [abaнo] downstairs; down below

abaleo m [abaleh-o] shootout

abarrotes: tienda de abarrotes f [t-yenda deh abarrot-es] grocer's, dry goods store

abierto [ab-yairto] open

abierto de ... a ... open from ... to ...

abierto las 24 horas del día open 24 hours

abogada f, abogado m lawyer

abono m (CAm, Col) instalment

abonos mpl season tickets

aborrezco [aborresko] I hate

ábrase aquí (Mex) open here

ábrase en caso de emergencia open in case of emergency

abrazo m [abraso] embrace

abrebotellas m [abreboteh-yas] bottle-opener

abrelatas m can-opener

abrigo m coat

abrigo de pieles [deh p-yel-es] fur coat

abril m April

abrir to open

abrochador m (Rpl) stapler

abrochar (Rpl) to staple

abróchense los cinturones fasten your seatbelts

abuela f [abwela] grandmother

abuelo m grandfather

abuelos mpl grandparents

abul [abool] (RD) good-bye

abundoso [aboondoso] (CAm, Mex) abundant

aburrido boring; bored

aburrirse [aboorreerseh] to be bored; to get bored

abusador bully

acabar to finish

acabo de ... [deh] I have just ...

acantilado m cliff

acavangado [akabangado] (Nic) sad

acceso a ... access to ...

acceso al andén to the trains

acceso playa to the beach

accidente m [akseedenteh] accident

tener un accidente [tenair] to have an accident

accidente de auto [deh] car accident

accidente de montaña [montanya] mountaineering accident

accidente de tránsito road accident

accidente en cadena [kadena] pile-up

acelerador m [aselairador] accelerator, gas pedal

acelerar [aselairar] to accelerate

acento m [asento] accent

aceptar [aseptar] to accept

acera f [asaira] pavement, sidewalk

acerca de [asairka deh] about, concerning

acere m [asaireh] (Cu) friend, pal

acero m [asairo] steel

acetona f [asetona] nail polish remover

achantado (CAm, Col) down

aciguambado (Guat) [aseeg-wambado] stupid

achicar (Pe) to have a wee

achicarse (Arg) to get frightened

achurar (Rpl) to kill

ácido (m) [aseedo] sour; acid

acolchado m (Rpl) bedspread

acompañar [akompan-yar] to accompany

lo acompaño en el sentimiento my condolences, my thoughts are with you

acondicionador de pelo m [akondees-yonador deh] hair conditioner

aconsejar [akonseh-Har] to advise

acoplado m (Ch) gatecrasher; (Rpl) trailer

acordarse [akordarseh] to remember

acostar to put to bed; to lay down

acostarse [akostarseh] to lie down; to go to bed

al acostarse when you go to bed

acotamiento m [akotamyento] (Mex) hard shoulder

ACPM m [asepeh-emeh] (Col) diesel

actriz f [aktrees] actress

acuerdo m [akwairdo] agreement

estoy de acuerdo [deh] I agree

de acuerdo OK

adaptador m adaptor

adelantado: por adelantado [adelantado] in advance

adelantarse a [–arseh] to overtake

además de [deh] besides, as well as

adentro inside

adeudo m [ade-oodo] (Mex) debt

adición f [adees-yon] (Rpl) check, bill

adolescente m/f [adolesenteh] teenager

aduana f [adwana] Customs

aduanero m [adwanairo] Customs office

aerodeslizador m [a-airo-desleesador] hovercraft

aerolínea f [a-airoleeneh-a] airline

aeropuerto m [a-airopwairto] airport

aerosilla f [a-airoseeya] (Arg, Ch) chairlift

afanador m, **afanadora** f (Mex) cleaner

afano m (Rpl) rip-off

afeitarse [afaytarseh] to shave

afiche m [afeecheh] poster

aficionada f [afees-yonada], **aficionado** m fan, enthusiast

aflatado (Guat) scared

afortunadamente [–menteh] fortunately

afueras fpl [afwairas] suburbs

agarradera f handle

agarrar to hold, to grasp; to catch; to take

agarre m [agarreh] (Ec) lover

agencia f [aHens-ya] agency

agencia de viajes [deh b-yaH-es] travel agency

agenda f [aHenda] diary

agítese antes de usar(se) shake before use

agosto m August

agradable [agradableh] pleasant

agradar to please

agradecer [agradesair] to thank

agradecido [agradeseedo] grateful

agradezco [agradesko] I thank

agresivo [agreseebo] aggressive

agricultor m farmer

agriparse (Mex) to catch the flu

agua f [agwa] water

agua de colonia [deh kolon-ya] (Mex) eau de toilette

agua de cuba f [agwa deh kooba] (Ch) bleach

agua de hierbas f [agwa deh yairbas] (CAm, Andes) herbal tea

agua Jane f [agwa Haneh] (Urug) bleach

agua potable [potableh] drinking water

aguacate m [agwakateh] avocado

aguamala f [agwamala] (Col, Mex) jellyfish

aguantar: no aguanto ... [agwanto] I can't stand ...

aguaviva f [agwabeeba] (Rpl) jellyfish

águila ratonera f [ageela] buzzard

aciguambado [aseegwambado] (Guat) stupid

agüitar [agweetar] (Guat) to frighten

agüite m [agweeteh] (Salv) sadness

agujero m [agooHairo] hole

agujetas fpl [a-ooHetas] (Mex) shoelaces

ahora [a-ora] now

ahorita [a-oreeta] right away; soon; just a moment ago

aire m [īreh] air

aire acondicionado [akondees-yonado] air-conditioning

ajedrez m [aHed-res] chess

ajustado [aHoostado] tight

ajustador m (Cu) bra

ala f wing

ala delta m hang-gliding

alambre m [alambreh] wire

alambre de púas [deh poo-as] barbed wire

alargador m extension lead

alargue m [alargeh] (Rpl) extension lead

alarma f alarm

dar la señal de alarma [sen-yal deh] to raise the alarm

albaricoque m apricot

alberca f [albairka] (Mex) swimming pool

alberca cubierta f (Mex) indoor swimming pool

alberca infantil f [eenfanteel] (Mex) children's pool

albergue juvenil [albairgeh Hoobeneel] youth hostel

alborotador m troublemaker

alcahuete mf [alka-weteh] (Rpl) telltale

alcoba f bedroom; sleeping compartment

alcohómetro m Breathalyzer®

alegre [alegreh] happy

alegro: me alegro I'm pleased; I'm pleased to hear it

alemán (m) German

Alemania f [aleman-ya] Germany

alérgico a [alairHeeko] allergic to

alero m (Hond) pal

aletas fpl flippers

alfiler m [alfeelair] pin

alfombra f rug, carpet

algo something

algo más something else

algodón m cotton; cotton wool, absorbent cotton

alguien [algen] somebody; anybody

algún some; any

alguno someone; anyone; one; any one

alianza f [al-yansa] (Mex) wedding ring

alimentos mpl groceries, foodstuffs

aliscafo m (Rpl) hydrofoil

allá: más allá [a-ya] further (on)

allí [a-yee] there

almacén m [almasen] department store;

warehouse; (CSur) grocer's, dry goods store

almohada f [almo-ada] pillow

almuerzo m [almwairso] lunch

aló (SAm) hello

alojamiento m [aloHam-yento] accommodation

alojamiento y desayuno [desa-yoono] bed and breakfast

alpinismo m mountaineering

alquilar [alkeelar] to rent; to hire

alquiler m [alkeelair] rental

alquiler de autos car rental

alquiler de barcos boat hire

alquiler de bicicletas [beeseekletas] cycle hire

alquiler de esquís [eskees] water-ski hire

alquiler de tablas surfboard hire

alquileres rentals

alrededor (de) [deh] around

alta costura f haute couture, high fashion

alto (m) stop sign; high; tall

¡alto! stop!

en lo alto at the top

altura f altitude; height

altura máxima maximum headroom

aluminio m aluminium

amable [amableh] kind;

si fuera tan amable [fwaira] if you wouldn't mind

amamantar to breastfeed

amanecer m [amanesair] sunrise, daybreak

¿cómo amaneciste? how did you sleep?

amargo bitter

amarillo [amaree-yo] yellow

amarrado (Mex, Col) stingy

amarrete stingy

ambia m [amb-ya] (Cu) pal

ambos both

ambulancia f [amboolans-ya] ambulance

América f [amaireeka] America; Latin America

América del Norte [norteh] North America

América del Sur South America

americana (f), americano (m) American; Latin American

amiga f friend, amigo m friend

amor m love

hacer el amor [asair] to make love

amortiguador m [amorteegwador] shock-absorber

amperio m [ampair-yo] amp

ampliación f [amplee-as-yon] enlargement

amplio broad; loose-fitting

ampolla f [ampo-ya] blister

ampolleta f [ampo-yeta] (Ch) lightbulb

analgésico m [analHeseeko] painkiller

análisis clínicos mpl clinical tests

anaranjado [anaranHado] orange (colour)

ancho (m) width, breadth; wide; loose

anchura f width, breadth

¡ándale pues! [andaleh pwes] (Mex) go on then!, OK!

andaluz [andaloos] Andalusian

andar to walk; to move; to work

andarivel m (Rpl) lane

andén m (CAm) sidewalk

andinismo m mountaineering

anémico anaemic

anestesia f [anestes-ya] anaesthetic

anexo m (Ch) extension

anfiteatro m [anfeeteh-atro] amphitheatre

Angeles Verdes mpl [angel-es baird-es] (Mex) breakdown service

angina (de pecho) f [anHeena] angina

anginas fpl tonsillitis

angurriento [angoorr-yento] (CSur) greedy

anillo m [anee-yo] ring

anoche [anocheh] last night

anochecer m [anochesair] nightfall, dusk

anochece [anocheseh] it's getting dark

ante m [anteh] suede

anteayer [anteh-a-yair] the day before yesterday

anteojos mpl [anteh-oHos] glasses

antepasado m ancestor

antes de [ant-es deh] before

antes de entrar dejen salir let passengers off first

antes de que [keh] before

anticipo m [anteeseepo] advance

anticonceptivo m [anteekonsepteebo] contraceptive

anticongelante m [anteekonHelanteh] antifreeze

anticuado [anteekwado] out of date

anticuario m [anteekwar-yo] antiques dealer

antigüedades: una tienda de antigüedades [t-yenda deh anteegwedad-es] an antique shop

antiguo [anteegwo] old; ancient

antihistamínico m [anteeeestameeneeko] antihistamine

Antillas fpl [antee-yas] the West Indies

antipático unpleasant, nasty

anulado cancelled

anular to cancel

añadir [an-yadeer] to add

año m [an-yo] year

Año Nuevo m [nwebo] New Year

día de Año Nuevo m [dee-a deh] New Year's Day

¡feliz Año Nuevo! [felees] Happy New Year!

apagador m (Mex) switch

apagar to switch off

apagón m power cut

apague el motor switch off your engine

apague las luces switch off your lights

aparador m (Mex) shop window

aparato m device

aparatos electrodomésticos electrical appliances

aparecer [aparesair] to appear

aparezco [aparesko] I appear

apasionante [apas-yonanteh] thrilling

apellido m [apeh-yeedo] surname

apenado sorry; embarrassed, shy

apenarse [–arseh] to be ashamed, to be embarrassed

apenas scarcely

apenas ... (cuando) [kwando] hardly ... when

son las seis apenas it's only just six o'clock

apetecer: me apetece [meh apeteseh] I feel like

apetito m appetite

apodo m nickname

apolar (Urug) to sleep

apoplejía f [apopleHee-a] stroke; fit

aprender [aprendair] to learn

aprensivo [aprenseebo] fearful, apprehensive

apretado (Parag) stingy

apriete el botón para cruzar press button to cross

aprovechar [aprobechar] to take advantage of

¡que aproveche! [keh aprobecheh] enjoy your meal!

aproximadamente [–menteh] about

136

apto para mayores de 14 años y menores acompañados authorized for those over 14 and young people accompanied by an adult

apto para mayores de 18 años for adults only

apto para todos los públicos suitable for all

apunamiento m (CSur) altitude sickness

apurado in a hurry

apurarse [–arseh] to rush, to hurry

¡apúrate! [apoorateh] hurry up!

aquel [akel] that

aquél that (one)

aquella [akeh-ya] that

aquélla that (one)

aquellas [akeh-yas] those

aquéllas those (ones)

aquellos [akeh-yos] those

aquéllos those (ones)

aquí [akee] here

aquí tiene [t-yeneh] here you are

araña f [aran-ya] spider

arañazo m [aran-yaso] scratch

arandela f [arandela] (Andes) washer

árbol m tree

ardor de estómago m [deh] heartburn

área de servicio m [areh-a deh serbees-yo] service area, motorway services

arena f [areh-na] sand

aretes mpl [aret-es] earrings

argel [arHel] (Parag) disgusting

argentino (m) [arHenteeno] Argentine; Argentinian

armario m cupboard

armazón f (Rpl) frame

armería f [armairee-a] gunsmith's

aro m ring; (CSur) earring

arqueología f [arkeh-oloHee-a] archaeology

arrancar to pull out, to tear out; to start up

arrancarse (Pan) to get drunk

arranque m [arrankeh] ignition

arrecho horny; furious; (Col, Ven) gutsy; (CAm) tough

arreglar to mend; to sort out, to arrange

arrendar [arrendar] to rent; to hire

se arrienda to rent, for hire

arriba up; upstairs; on top

arrocero m (Ven) gatecrasher

arroyo m stream

arruga f wrinkle; (Pe) debt

arte m [arteh] art

artesanía f crafts

artículos de artesanía mpl [deh] arts and crafts

artículos de boda wedding presents

artículos de deporte [deporteh] sports goods

artículos de limpieza [leemp-yesa] household cleaning products

artículos de piel [p-yel] leather goods

artículos de playa [pla-ya] beachwear

artículos de viaje [b-yaнeh] travel goods

artículos escolares [eskolar-es] schoolwear

artículos para el bebé [beh-beh] babywear

artista m/f artist

artritis f arthritis

ascensor m [asensor] lift, elevator

asegurar to insure

así like this; like that

así que so (that)

asiento m [as-yento] seat

asma m asthma

asolearse [asoleh-arseh] to sunbathe

aspiradora f vacuum cleaner

asqueroso [askairoso] disgusting

astigmático long-sighted

astilla f (Cu) money

asuntos exteriores foreign affairs

asustado afraid

asustar to frighten

atacar to attack

atado m (Arg) packet

atajo m [ataнo] shortcut

ataque m [atakeh] attack

ataque al corazón [korason] heart attack

atención [atens-yon] please note

¡atención! take care!, caution!

atención al tren beware of trains

ateo [ateh-o] atheist

aterrizaje m landing

aterrizaje forzoso emergency landing

aterrizar [atairreesar] to land

atletismo m athletics

atollar [ato-yar] (CR) to hit

atorado stuck

atorrante [atorranteh] (CSur) good-for-nothing

atorarse [atorarseh] to get stuck

atracar to mug; to hold up

atracciones turísticas fpl [atraks-yon-es] tourist attractions

atraco a mano armada m armed robbery, hold-up

atractivo [atrakteebo] attractive

atrás at the back; behind

¡atrás! get back!

la parte de atrás [parteh deh] the back

está más atrás it's further back

años atrás [an-yos] years ago

atrasado late

atraso m delay

atravesar [atrabesar] to cross

atravieso [atrab-yeso] I cross

atreverse [atrebairseh] to dare

atropellar [atropeh-yar] to knock down

atroz [atros] dreadful

audición f [owdees-yon] (Rpl) radio program(me)

audífono m [owdeefono] hearing aid

aun [a-oon] even

aún [a-oon] still; yet

aunque [ownkeh] although

auto m [owto] car

auto automático automatic

auto manual manual (car)

autobús m [owtoboos] bus, coach, long-distance bus

auto-estopista m/f [owto-estopeesta] (Mex) hitch-hiker

automóvil m [owtomobeel] car

autopista de cuota [deh kwota] (Mex) toll motorway/highway

autopista f [owtopeesta] motorway, freeway, highway

auto-servicio m [owto-sairbeesyo] self-service

autostop: hacer autostop [asair owtostop] to hitchhike

autovía f [owtobee-a] (Mex) slow, local train; dual carriageway, (US) divided highway

auxiliar f [owseel-yar] (Rpl) spare wheel

avalúo m [abaloo-o] valuation

avenida f [abeneeda] avenue

aventar [abentar] (Mex) to throw

aventón: pedir aventón [abenton] (Col, Mex) to hitch a lift

avergonzado [abairgonsado] ashamed

avería f [abairee-a] breakdown

averiarse [abair-yarseh] to break down

avión m [ab-yon] aeroplane, airplane

por avión by air

avisar [abeesar] to inform

aviso m [abeeso] advertisement; notice

aviso a los señores pasajeros passenger information

avispa f [abeespa] wasp

avivarse [abeebarseh] to wise up

ayer [a-yair] yesterday

ayer por la mañana [man-yana] yesterday morning

ayer por la tarde [tardeh] yesterday afternoon

ayuda f [a-yooda] help

ayudar [a-yoodar] to help

ayuntamiento m [a-yoontam-yento] town hall

azotea f [asoteh-a] roof

azteca [asteka] Aztec

azul (m) [asool] blue

azul claro light blue

azul marino navy blue

B

baca f roof rack

bacán (Rpl) cushy; (Andes) fantastic

bache m [bacheh] hole in the road

bagayero m [baga-yairo] (Rpl) smuggler

bahía f [ba-ee-a] bay

bailar [bīlar] to dance

ir a bailar to go dancing

baile m [bīleh] dance; dancing

¡bajan! [baHan] (Mex) next stop please!, people getting off!

bajar [baHar] to go down

bajar de [deh] to get off

bajar la velocidad [beloseeda] to slow down

bajarse (de) [baHarseh (deh)] to get off

bajeño [baHen-yo] from/of Baja California

Bajío m [baHee-yo] Baja California

bajo [baHo] low; short; under; underneath

balaca f (Col) hair band

balacear [balaseh-ar] to shoot at

balacera f [balasaira] exchange of fire

balance de pagos m [balanseh] balance of payments

balanceo m [balanseh-yo] wheel-balancing

balastre [balastreh] (Salv) mean

balcón m balcony

balde m [baldeh] bucket

balón m ball

balonmano m handball

balsa f raft

balurdo (CAm, Ven) uncool, naff

bamba (Pe) fake

banana f (Pe, Rpl) banana

banano m (CAm) banana

bancar (Rpl) to put up with

bancario mf [bankar-yo] (CSur) bank employee

banco m bank; bench

bandeja f [bandeHa] tray

bandera f [bandaira] flag

banderazo m [bandairaso] (Col, Ven) minimum charge

bandido m bandit

banqueta f [banketa] (Mex) pavement, sidewalk

banquina f [bankeena] (Rpl) hard shoulder

bañadera f [ban-yadaira] (Arg) bath

bañarse [ban-yarseh] to go swimming; to have a bath/shower

bañazo [ban-yaso] (CR) ridiculous

bañera f [ban-yaira] bathtub; (Arg) lifeguard

bañero (Arg) lifeguard

baño m [ban-yo] bathroom; toilet, rest room; bath

baños mpl toilets, rest room

baraja f [baraHa] pack of cards

barata f (Ch) cockroach

barato cheap, inexpensive

barba f chin; beard

barbacoa f barbecue; barbecued meat

bárbaro [barbaro] (Rpl) great, fantastic

barbería f [barbairee-a] barber's shop

barbero m [barbairo] barber

barco (m) boat; (Hond) undemanding

barco de remo [deh] rowing boat

barco de vela [bela] sailing boat

barcos para alquilar boats to rent

barda f (Andes, Mex) wall

barra de labios f [deh lab-yos] (Mex) lipstick

barriada f shanty town

barrilete m [barreeleteh] (Arg) kite

barrio m [barr-yo] district, area; neighbourhood; ghetto

barullento [barooyento] (Rpl) noisy

básquet m [basket] basketball

bastante [bastanteh] enough; quite; very

bastante más quite a lot more

basura f rubbish, garbage

bata f dressing gown

bate m [bateh] bat; (CR) man

batería f [batairee-a] battery; drum kit

batería de cocina [deh koseena] pots and pans

baúl m [ba-ool] (Col, Rpl) boot, (US) trunk

bautismo m [bowteesmo] christening

bayuncada (f) [ba-yoonkada] (Salv) silly thing, silly remark; (Nic) rude

bebé m [beh-beh] baby

beber [bebair] to drink

béisbol m [baysbol] baseball

bejuco m [beHooko] (Cu) telephone

Belice [beleeseh] Belize

bello [beh-yo] beautiful

bemba f thick lips

bencina f [benseena] (Ch) petrol, (US) gasoline

bencinera f (Ch) petrol/gas station, filling station

berma f (Andes) hard shoulder

besar to kiss

beso m kiss

betún m [betoon] shoe polish

biberón m baby´s bottle

biblioteca f [beebl-yoteka] library; bookcase

bicha f [beecha] (Cu) prostitute

bicicleta f [beeseekleta] bicycle

bicicleta de carreras f [karrairas] racing bike

bicicleta de montaña f [montan-ya] mountain bike

bicicletear [beeseekleteh-ar] (Arg) to avoid

biel f [bee-el] (Ec) beer

bien [b-yen] well

¡bien! good!

bien ... bien ... either ... or ...

o bien ... o bien ... either ... or ...

bienes mpl [b-yen-es] possessions

¡bienvenido! [b-yenbeneedo] welcome!

bifurcación f [beefoorkas-yon] fork

bigote m [beegoteh] moustache

bilet m [beelet] (Mex) lipstick

billete m [bee-yeteh] banknote, (US) bill

billuzo m [bee-yooso] (Ec) money

binóculos mpl [beenokoolos] binoculars

birome m [beeromeh] (Rpl) biro®

birra f (SAm) beer
birrioso m [beerr-**yoso**] (Pan) sportsman
bizcocho [beesk**ocho**] (Col) attractive
blanco (m) white
blanqueador m [blankeh-ad**or**] (Col, Mex) bleach
bloomer m (Cu) knickers, panties
blusa f blouse
boa boa; (Hond) crawler
boca f mouth
bochinche m [boch**ee**ncheh] brawl
boda f wedding
bodega f wine cellar; (Cu, Pe, Ven) grocer's, dry goods store
boleador m [boleh-ad**or**] shoeshine boy
boletería f ticket office
boleto m ticket
boleto de ida [deh **ee**da] single ticket, one-way ticket
boleto de ida y vuelta [ee b**we**lta] return ticket, round-trip ticket
boliche m [bol**ee**cheh] (Bol, Rpl) bar
bolígrafo m ballpoint pen
bolita f (CSur) marble
bolo m (CAm) drunkard; (Ven) bolivar
bolsa f (Mex) bag; stock exchange
bolsa de dormir [deh] sleeping bag
bolsa de plástico plastic bag

bolsa de viaje [b-ya**Heh**] travel bag
bolsillo m [bols**ee**-yo] pocket
bolsista m [bols**ee**sta] (Mex) pickpocket
bolso m handbag, (US) purse
boludo (Col, Rpl, Ven) idiot
bomba f bomb; (Andes, Ven) petrol/gas station, filling station
bomba de gas [deh] camping gas cylinder
bombachas fpl (Rpl) knickers, panties
bomberos mpl [bomb**ai**ros] fire brigade
bombeta (CR) arrogant
bombilla f [bomb**ee**-ya] light-bulb
bombillo m [bomb**ee**-yo] (Col, Ven) lightbulb
bombita f (Rpl) lightbulb
bordado embroidered
borracho drunk
bosque m [b**o**skeh] forest
bostezo (m) [b**o**steso] yawn; (CR) boring
bota f boot
botanas fpl (Mex) snacks
botar to throw away
bote m [b**o**teh] (Mex, Nic, Ven) jail
botella f [bot**eh**-ya] bottle
botiquín m [boteek**een**] first-aid kit
botón m button
botón desatascador coin return button
boxeo m [boks**eh**-o] boxing
boya f buoy

bracero m [brasairo] (Mex) migrant labourer from Mexico to the US

bragas fpl pants, panties

brasier m [bras-yair] (Mex) bra

brasilera (f) [braseelaira], **brasilero** (m) Brasilian

brazo m [braso] arm

bretear [breteh-ar] (CR) to work

bretel m (CSur) strap

brevete m [brebeteh] (Pe) driving licence

bricolaje m [breekolaHeh] DIY, do-it-yourself

brillar [bree-yar] to shine

brincar to jump

brisa f breeze

británico British

brocha de afeitar f [deh afaytar] (Mex) shaving brush

broche m [brocheh] brooch

bronca f row; anger

bronce m [bronseh] bronze

bronceado (m) [bronseh-ado] suntan; suntanned

bronceador m [bronseh-ador] suntan oil/lotion

bronquitis f [bronkeetees] bronchitis

brújula f [brooHoola] compass

bruta f [broota] (Hond) beer

bruto stupid

buay m [bwa-ee] (Pan) kid

bucear [booseh-ar] to skin-dive

buceo m [booseh-o] skin-diving

buchaca f (Guat) mouth

buco (Pan) a lot of

buenas noches [bwenas noch-es] good night

buenas tardes [tard-es] good afternoon; good evening

bueno [bweno] good; good-natured; hello

buenos días [dee-as] good morning

bufanda f scarf

bufear [boofeh-ar] (RD) to goof around

bufete m [boofeteh] lawyer's office

buitre m [bweetreh] buzzard, vulture; (Ec) traffic police

buitrear [bweetreh-ar] (Parag) to throw up

bujía f [booHee-a] spark plug

bulto m package; lump, swelling

buroca f (Guat) protest

burro m donkey; (Mex) ironing board

burundanga f (Pan) junk food

buscapleitos m [booskaplaytos] troublemaker

buscar to look for

buseta f (Col, Ecu) bus

busqué [booskeh] I looked for

butacas fpl stalls

buzo m (Ch, Pe) tracksuit, (US) sweats

buzón m [booson] letter box, postbox, mailbox

c/ street
caballeros mpl [kaba-yairos] gents, men's rest room
caballo m [kaba-yo] horse
caballos mpl (CR) trousers, pants
cabaña f [kaban-ya] beach hut; (Mex) goal
cabello m [kabeh-yo] hair
cabeza f [kabesa] head
cabida ... personas capacity ... people
cabina telefónica f telephone booth, phone box
cable m [kableh] wire
cable de extensión m [deh ekstens-yon] extension lead
cabra f goat
cabritas (Ch) popcorn
cabrón m bastard
cachetada f slap in the face
cachifo m (Ec, Ven) servant
cachilo m (Rpl) old banger
cachimbón [kacheembon] (Salv) cool
cachina f (Ec) clothes
cachucha f (Andes, CAm, Mex) cap
cacto m cactus
cada every
  cada vez (que) [bes (keh)] every time (that)
cadena f chain
cadera f [kadaira] hip
cadete m [kadeteh] (Rpl) errand boy

caduca ... expires ...
caer [ka-air] to fall
caerse [ka-airseh] to fall over, to fall down
café [kafeh] coffee; café
cafetera f [kafetaira] coffee pot
cafetería f [kafetairee-a] bar-type restaurant; coffee shop
cafúa f [kafoo-a] (Rpl) slammer
cagarla to screw up
caída f [ka-eeda] fall
caimán m [kiman] alligator
caites mpl [kites] (CR) old shoes
caja f [kaHa] cash desk, till; cashier
caja de ahorros [deh a-orros] savings bank
caja de cambios [kamb-yos] gearbox
caja de dientes f (Col) dentures
cajera f [kaHaira], cajero m cashier
cajero automático [owtomateeko] cashpoint, automatic teller, ATM
cajeta f [kaHeta] (Mex) fudge
cajetilla f [kaHetee-ya] packet, (US) pack
cajilla f [kaHee-ya] (Rpl) packet
cajuela f [kaHwela] (Mex) boot (of car), (US) trunk
cajuelita f [kaHweleeta] (CAm, Mex) glove compartment
calambre m [kalambreh] cramp
calancho (Bol) naked
calandria f [kalandr-ya] (Mex) carriage

calaveras fpl [kalabairas] (Mex) rear lights, sidelights

calcetines mpl [kalseteen-es] socks

calculadora f calculator

caldero m (Pe) hangover

calefacción f [kalefaks-yon] heating

calefacción central [sentral] central heating

calefón m [kalefon] (Rpl) (water) heater

calendario m [–dar-yo] calendar

calesita f (Rpl) merry-go-round

caleta f (Ec) house

calidad f [kaleeda] quality

caliente [kal-yenteh] hot

callampas fpl [ka-yampas] (Ch) shanty town

calle f [ka-yeh] street

calle comercial [komairs-yal] shopping street

calle de sentido único one-way street

calle peatonal [peh-atonal] pedestrianized street

calle principal [preenseepal] main street

callejón m [ka-yeh-Hon] lane, alley

callejón sin salida cul-de-sac, dead end

callo m [ka-yo] corn (on foot)

calmante m [kalmanteh] tranquillizer

calor m heat

  hace calor [aseh] it's warm/hot

calvo [kalbo] bald

calza f [kalsa] (Col) filling (in tooth)

calza: ¿qué número calza? [keh noomairo kalsa] what is your shoe size?

calzada deteriorada poor road surface

calzada f [kalsada] street

calzada irregular uneven surface

calzados shoe shop

calzoncillos mpl [kalsonsee-yos] underpants

calzones mpl [kalson-es] (Mex) underpants

calzonetas fpl (CAm) knickers, panties

cama f bed

cama de campaña [deh kampan-ya] campbed

cama individual [eendeebeedwal] single bed

cama matrimonial [matreemon-yal] double bed

cámara f camera; inner tube

cámara fotográfica camera

camarín m (Mex) sleeping berth

camarote m [kamaroteh] cabin

cambalache m [kambalacheh] swap; (Hond) favour

cambiar [kamb-yar] to change

cambiarse (de ropa) [kamb-yarseh (deh)] to get changed

cambio m [kamb-yo] change; exchange; exchange rate

cambio de divisas [deh deebeesas] currency exchange

cambio de moneda currency exchange

cambio de sentido take filter lane to exit and cross flow of traffic

cambur m (Ven) banana

camellar [kameh-yar] (Col) trabajar

camellón m [kameh-yon] (Mex) central reservation

caminar to walk; to work

camino m path

camino cerrado (al tráfico) road closed (to traffic)

camino privado private road

camión m [kam-yon] (C. Am, Mex) bus

camioneta f [kam-yoneta] van

camisa f shirt

camiseta f T-shirt; vest

camisón m nightdress

campana f bell

campaña f [kampan-ya] (Guat) favour

campesino m peasant farmer

camping m camping; campsite; caravan site, trailer park

campo m countryside; pitch; court; field

campo de deportes [deh deportes] sports field

campo de futból football ground

campo de golf golf course

cana f (Col, Cu, Ven) jail

canadiense (m/f) [kanad-yenseh] Canadian

cancelado [kanselado]

cancelled; stamped

cancelar [kanselar] to cancel; to stamp

cancha f court; pitch

canción f [kans-yon] song

candela: en candela (Cu) in danger

caneca de la basura f [kaneka] (Col) bin, dustbin

canguro m/f (Mex) baby-sitter

canilla f (Rpl) tap, (US) faucet

canillita mf [kaneeyeeta] (CSur) newspaper vendor

canoa f canoe; skiff

canoso greying; grey

canotaje m [kanotaheh] (SAm) canoeing

cansado tired

cansón m [kanson] (Col, Ven) annoying

cansona f [kansona] (Col, Ven) annoying

cantaleta: la misma cantaleta the same old story

cantar to sing

cantegril m (Urug) shanty town

cantimplora f [kanteemplora] water bottle; (Nic) poof

cantina f (exc Rpl) bar

canto m song; singing

caña f [kan-ya] sugar cane; sugar cane liquor; (Pe) car

caña de pescar [deh] fishing rod

cañandonga [kan-yandonga] (Ven) booze

cañaveral m sugar cane plantation

cañería f [kan-yairee-a] pipes

cañero mf [kan-yairo] plantation worker

caño m [kan-yo] (Rpl) exhaust;
(Pe) faucet

caño de escape [eskapeh] (Rpl)
exhaust

cañón m [kan-yon] canyon

capaz: ser capaz (de) [sair
kapas (deh)] to be able (to); to
be capable (of)

capazo m [kapaso] carry-cot

capilla f [kapee-ya] chapel

capitalina f, capitalino m
person who lives in the
capital city

capitán m captain

capó(t) m bonnet (of car), (US)
hood

caquero [kakairo] (Guat) arrogant

cara f face

carcacha f (Col, Mex) banger

carácter m [karaktair]
character; nature
tiene mal carácter [t-yeneh]
he's got a bad temper

¡carajo! [karaHo] Christ!, shit!
¿dónde carajos? [dondeh]
where in the hell?

caravana f caravan, (US)
trailer; (Urug) earring

carburador m carburettor

cárcel f [karsel] prison

careta f [kareta] (Col) snorkel

carey m [karay] tortoiseshell

Caribe: el Caribe [kareebeh] the
Caribbean

caricaturas fpl cartoons

cariño m [kareen-yo] love;

affection

carnal m (Mex) mate

carne de chancho f [karneh deh
chancho] (Ch, Pe) pork

carne de marrano f [karneh deh
marrano] (Col) pork

carné m (Ch) driving licence

carnet de chofer m [chofair]
(Mex) driving licence

carnet de identidad m [deh
eedenteeda] (Mex) identity card

carnicería f [karneesairee-a]
butcher's

caro expensive

carpa f large tent, marquee

carpeta f (Cu) reception

carpintería f [karpeentairee-a]
joiner's, carpenter's

carrera f [karraira] race; career;
(Mex, Col, Ven) parting, (US) part

carreras de caballos mpl [deh
kaba-yos] horse racing

carrete m [karreteh] film (for
camera)

carretera f [karretaira] main
road

carretera cortada road
blocked, road closed

carretera de circunvalación
by-pass

carretera de doble carril two-
lane road

carril m lane

carrito m trolley; cart;
pushchair

carrito de niño [deh neen-yo]
pushchair

carrito portaequipajes [porta-
ekeepaH-es] baggage trolley

carro m car

carro rentado m rented car

carrocería f [karrosairee-a] bodywork

carro-comedor m buffet car, restaurant car

carrusel m (Col, Ven) merry-go-round

carta f letter; menu

cartel m poster

cartelera de espectáculos f [kartelaira deh] entertainments guide

cartera f [kartaira] briefcase; handbag; wallet

carterista m pickpocket

cartero m postman, mailman

cartón m cardboard; carton

casa f house

en casa at home

en casa de Juan [deh] at Juan's

está en su casa make yourself at home

casa de cambio [kamb-yo] bureau de change

casa de huéspedes [deh wesped-es] guesthouse

casa de socorro emergency first-aid centre

casa rodante (Col, Rpl, Ven) caravan, (US) trailer

casaca f (Guat) lie

casado married

casarse [kasarseh] to get married

cascada f waterfall

cáscara f shell; peel; rind; skin

caseta telefónica phone box, phone booth

casete f [kaset] cassette

casi almost

caso m case

en caso de que [deh keh] in case

caso urgente [oorHenteh] emergency

caspa f dandruff

castaño (m) [kastan-yo] sweet chestnut; brown

castigar to punish

castigo m punishment

castillo m [kastee-yo] castle

casualidad: de casualidad [deh kaswaleeda] by chance

catarro: tengo catarro I've got a cold

catire [kateereh] (Ven) blond

católico (m) Catholic

catorce [katorseh] fourteen

catracho (m) (Hond) Honduran

caucho m [kowcho] (Col) elastic band; rubber

causa f [kowsa] cause

cauteloso [kowteloso] cautious; careful

cayó [ka-yo] he/she fell

caza f [kasa] hunting

cazadora f [kasadora] bomber jacket, blouson jacket; (CR) bus

cazar [kasar] to hunt

cazuela f [kaswela] casserole; saucepan

c/c current account

cebador m [sebador] (Rpl) choke

ceda el paso give way

ceja f [seHa] eyebrow

celos: tener celos [tenair selos] to be jealous

celoso [seloso] jealous

cementerio m [sementair-yo] cemetery

cena f [sena] dinner

cenar to have dinner

cenicero m [seneesairo] ashtray

cenote m [senoteh] deep pool used for ceremonial purposes by the Mayas

central camionera f [sentral kam-yonaira] (Mex) main bus station

central de autobuses [deh owtoboos-es] main bus station

central telefónica telephone exchange

centro m [sentro] centre

centro ciudad [s-yooda] city/town centre

centro comercial [komairs-yal] shopping centre

centro de salud [deh saloo] health centre

centro deportivo sports centre

centro urbano city/town centre

ceñido [sen-yeedo] tight-fitting

cepillo m [sepee-yo] brush

cepillo de dientes [deh d-yent-es] toothbrush

cepillo de pelo hairbrush

cera f [saira] wax

cerámica f [sairameeka] pottery; ceramics

cerca de [sairka deh] near

cerilla f [sairee-ya] match

cerillo m [sairee-yo] (CAm, Mex) match

cero [sairo] zero

cerquillo m [sairkee-yo] fringe, (US) bangs

cerrada f [sairrada] cul-de-sac

cerrado [sairrado] closed

cerrado por defunción closed due to bereavement

cerrado por descanso del personal closed for staff holidays

cerrado por obras/reforma/vacaciones closed for alterations/renovation/holidays

cerradura f [sairradoora] lock

cerramos los ... we close on ...

cerrar [sairrar] to close

cerrar con llave [yabeh] to lock

cerrojo m [sairroHo] bolt

certificado m [sairteefeekado] certificate; registered letter

cervecería f [sairbesairee-a] bar specializing in beer

césped m [sesped] lawn

cesta f [sesta] basket

cesto de la compra m [sesto deh] (Mex) shopping basket

chabacano m (Mex) apricot

chafa m (Guat) soldier; (Hond) police officer

chaleca f [chaleka] (Ch) cardigan

chaleco m [chaleko] waistcoat, (US) vest

chaleco salvavidas
[salbab**ee**das] life-jacket

chalet m [chal**eh**] villa

chalupa f (Mex, CAm, Col)
dugout

chama mf (Cu) kid

chamaco m (CAm, Cu, Mex) kid

chamarra f (Mex) woollen
jacket; waistcoat, (US) vest

chamba f (Mex, Pe, Ven) work

chamo m (Ven) kid

champión m [champee-**on**]
(Urug) trainer

champú m shampoo

chance m [chanseh] opportunity, chance

chancha f (Pe) whip-round

chancla f (Col) slipper

chancuaco m [chankwako]
(Guat) cigarette

chángana f (Cu) fight

changarro m (Mex) small store

chante m [chanteh] (CR) laziness; (Guat) home

chantin f [chanteen] (Pan) house

chao bye-bye

chapa f (Rpl) number plate, (US)
license plate; (Col, Mex) lock

chapapote m [chapapoteh] (Mex)
tar; pitch

chaparro (Mex) very small

chaparrón m shower;
downpour

chapín (CAm, Mex) Guatemalan

chapulín m (CAm, Mex) grass-
hopper

chaqueta f [chaketa] cardigan;
jacket

charcutería f [charkootair**ee**-a]

(Mex) delicatessen

charlar to chat

charola f (Andes, CAm, Mex) tray

charralear (Hond) to burn

charreada f [charreh-ada] (Mex)
horse-riding display,
rodeo

charro m (Mex) horseman

chasquilla f [chaskee-ya] (Ch)
fringe, (US) bangs

chato (Mex) snub-nosed

chauchas fpl [ch**ow**chas] (Rpl)
runner beans

chava f [chaba] (Mex) girl

chavo m (Mex) boy

chaya (Hond) mean

checar (Mex) to check

chela f beer

chele [cheleh] (CAm) blond

chepa f (Hond) police

cheque de viajero m [chekeh
deh b-yaHairo] traveller's
cheque

chequera f [chekaira] cheque
book

cheto (Rpl) posh

cheve f [chebeh] (Guat) beer

chévere [chebaireh] (Andes)
great, fun

chibolo m (Pe) kid

chica f girl

chichi f (Mex) breast, tit

chicle m [cheekleh] chewing
gum

chico m boy

chiflar to whistle

chilango from/of Mexico
City

chileno (m) Chilean

chillar [chee-yar] to shout, to scream

chimbilín m (Pan) money

chimbo (Col) fake; (Ven) lousy

china f [cheena] (RD) orange

chinampa f (Mex) man-made island

chinche m [cheencheh] drawing pin, (US) thumbtack; bug

chingadera: ¡qué chingadera! [keh cheengadaira] (Mex) what a fuck-up!

chingar (Mex) to fuck

chingo: un chingo de [deh] (Mex) loads of

chino (m) Chinese; (Mex) curly

chiquear [cheekeh-ar] (Parag) to check

chiringue [cheereengeh] (CR) funny

chirote [cheeroteh] (Salv) naked

chiste m [cheesteh] joke

chiva (f) [cheeba] (CR) great; (Ec) bicycle

chivato m (RD) informer

chivo m (Mex) wages; (Cu) bicycle; (Pe) poof

chocar con to run into

choclo m (SAm) sweetcorn

chocolate con leche m [chokolateh kon lecheh] milk chocolate

chofer m [chofair] driver

chompa f (Col, Ec) jacket; (Bol, Pe) sweater; (Arg) polo shirt

chop m (Ch) beer

choque m [chokeh] crash; clash

chorros: a chorros loads

choya f (Hond, Guat) laziness

choyado (Salv) mad

chubasco m sudden short shower

chubasquero m [choobaskairo] cagoule

chuleta m (Hond) poof

chulo m (Col) buzzard, vulture

chulón (Salv) naked

chupa f (Ven) dummy, (US) pacifier

chupar to drink (alcohol)

chupete m [choopeteh] dummy (baby's); (Ch, Pe) lollipop

chupo m (Col) dummy (baby's)

churrasco m roast meat

churro (SAm) gorgeous

Cía. company

cicatriz f [seekatrees] scar

ciclismo m [seekleesmo] cycling

ciclista m/f [seekleesta] cyclist

ciclovía f cycle lane

ciego [s-yego] blind

cielo m [s-yelo] sky

cien [s-yen] hundred

ciencia f [s-yens-ya] science

ciento ... [s-yento] a hundred and ...

cierre m [s-yairreh] zip, zipper

cierren las puertas close the doors

cierro [s-yairro] I close

cigarro m [seegarro] cigarette

cinco [seenko] five

cincuenta [seen-kwenta] fifty

cine m [seeneh] cinema, movie theater

cinta f [seenta] tape; ribbon

cintura f [seentoora] waist; waist measurement

cinturón m [seentooron] belt

cinturón de seguridad [deh segooreeda] seat belt

cipote m [seepoteh] (Hond) kid

circo m [seerko] circus

circulación f [seerkoolas-yon] traffic; circulation

circule despacio drive slowly

circule por la derecha keep to your right

círculo m [seerkoolo] circle

circunvalación f [seerkoonbalas-yon] ring road

cita f [seeta] appointment

citadino m city dweller

ciudad f [s-yooda] town, city

ciudad perdida (Mex) shanty town

claro clear; light

¡claro! of course!

clase f [klaseh] class

clasificado m classified ad

clausurar [klowsoorar] to close down

clavado de acantilado m [klabado] cliff-diving

clavo m [klabo] nail; clove

claxon m [klakson] horn

clima m climate

climatizado [kleemateesado] air-conditioned

clínica f hospital; clinic

cobija f [kobeeHa] rug, blanket

cobrar to charge; to earn

cobre m [kobreh] copper

cocaleca f (RD) pop corn

cocer [kosair] to boil

coche-cama m sleeper, sleeping car

cocheche [kochecheh] (Nic) poof

cochecito m [kocheseeto] pram

coche-comedor m [kocheh komedor] dining car

cochera f (Mex) garage

cocina f [koseena] kitchen

cocinar [koseenar] to cook

cocinera f [koseenaira], cocinero m cook

cocuyos mpl [kokoo-yos] (Col, Ven) sidelights

código de la circulación m highway code

código postal m [pos-tal] postcode, zip code

codo m elbow

cofre m [kofreh] (Mex) bonnet, hood

coger [koHair] (Mex, Rpl, Ven) to fuck

coger botella [boteh-ya] (Cu) to hitch-hike

coima f [koyma] (CSur, Pe) bribe

cojo m [koHo] person with a limp

cojudo [koHoodo] (Ec) stupid

cola f tail; queue

hacer cola to queue

pedir cola (Ven) to hitch-hike

colado m gatecrasher

colcha f bedspread

colchón m mattress

colchoneta inflable f [eenflableh] air mattress

colección f [koleks-yon] collection

colecta f whip-round

colectivo m [kolekteebo] collective taxi; (Arg, Ven) bus

colegio m [koleH-yo] school

collar m [ko-yar] necklace

colocar to place, to put

colonia f [kolon-ya] (Mex) urban district

color m colour

colorete m [koloreteh] blusher

columna vertebral f spine

comadre f [komadreh] godmother; mother of one's godchild

combi m (Mex, Pe, Rpl) collective taxi, minibus

combustible m [komboosteebleh] fuel

comedor m dining room

comenzar [komensar] to begin

comer [komair] to eat

comercial m [komairs-yal] advert

comerciante m [komairs-yanteh] shopkeeper; dealer

comicios mpl [komees-yos] elections

comida f lunch; food; meal

comidas para llevar [yevar] take-away meals, meals to go

comienzo (m) [kom-yenso] I begin; beginning

comisaría f police station

como as; like
¿cómo está? how are you?
¿cómo le va? [leh ba] how are things?
como quieras [k-yairas] it's up to you

compact m compact disc

compadre m [kompadreh] godfather; father of one's godchild

compañera f [kompan-yaira] girlfriend

compañero m mate; boyfriend

compañía f [kompan-yee-a] company

compañía aérea [a-aireh-a] airline

comparar to compare

compartir to share

compinche m [kompeencheh] friend, pal

completamente [–menteh] completely

completo full; no vacancies

complicado complicated

compra: hacer la compra [asair] to do the shopping

compramos a ... buying rate ...

comprar to buy

compras: ir de compras [eer deh] to go shopping

compresa m sanitary towel, sanitary napkin

comprimido efervescente m soluble tablet

comprimidos mpl tablets

computadora f computer

comunicando (Mex) engaged, busy, occupied

con with

concha f shell

concientizar [kons-yenteesar] make aware

concierto m [kons-yairto] concert

condenar to sentence

condición: a condición de que [kondees-yon deh keh] on condition that

condominio m apartment block

condón m condom

confección f [konfeks-yon] clothing industry

confecciones fpl [konfeks-yones] ready-to-wear clothes

conferencia internacional f [konfairens-ya eentairnas-yonal] (Mex) international call

conferencia interurbana (Mex) long-distance call

confesar to admit; to confess

confiable [konf-yableh] reliable

confirmar to confirm

confitería f [konfeetairee-a] sweetshop, candy store

conforme [konformeh] as

estar conforme to agree

congelado [konHelado] frozen

congelador m [konHelador] freezer

congelados mpl [konHelados] frozen foods

conjunto m [konHoonto] group; band

conmigo with me

conmoción cerebral f [konmos-yon sairebral] concussion

conmover [konmobair] to move

conmutadora f switchboard

conocer [konosair] to know

conozco [konosko] I know

conque [konkeh] so, so then

consentido spoiled

consérvese en lugar fresco store in a cool place

consigna f [konseegna] left luggage, baggage check

consigna automática [owtomateeka] left luggage lockers, baggage lockers

consigo with himself; with herself; with yourself; with themselves; with yourselves

constar: me consta I can confirm

consulado m consulate

consulta médica surgery, doctor's office

consúmase antes de ... best before ...

contacto: ponerse en contacto con to contact

contado: pagar al contado to pay cash

contador m, **contadora** f accountant

contagioso [kontaH-yoso] contagious

contaminado polluted

contar to count; to tell

contener [kontenair] to contain

contenido m contents

contento happy

contestar to reply, to answer

contigo with you

continuación: a continuación [konteenwas-yon] then, next; below

continuar [konteenwar] to continue

contra against

contradecir [kontradeseer] to contradict

contraindicaciones fpl contraindications

contraventanas fpl [kontrabentanas] shutters

control de pasaportes m passport control

convalecencia f [konbalesens-ya] convalescence

convencer [konbensair] to persuade

conversa f [konbairsa] chat

coñudo [kon-yoodo] (Ec) stingy

copa f wine glass

coquetear [koketeh-ar] to flirt

corazón m [korason] heart

corbata f tie, necktie

corchete m [korcheteh] (Ch) staple

corchetera f (Ch) stapler

cordillera f [kordee-yaira] mountain range

cordón m (Cu, Rpl) kerb

cordones mpl [kordon-es] shoelaces

corona [korona] crown

corpiño m [korpeen-yo] (Rpl) bra

correa del ventilador f [korreh-a del benteelador] fan belt

correo m [korreh-o] post, mail; post office

correo aéreo [a-aireh-o] airmail

correo central [sen-tral] main post office

correo terrestre [tairrestreh] surface mail

correo urgente [oorHenteh]

express (mail)

correr [korrair] to run

correspondencia f [–dens-ya] transfer, change

hacer correspondencia en ... to change (trains/buses) at ...

corrida de toros f [deh] bullfight

corriente peligrosa dangerous current

corrimiento de tierras danger: landslides

cortadura f cut

cortar to cut

cortarse [kortarseh] to cut oneself

cortauñas m [korta-oon-yas] nail clippers

corte de pelo m [korteh deh] haircut

corte y confección [ee konfeks-yon] dressmaking

cortina f curtain

corto short; short of money

cosa f thing

coser [kosair] to sew

costa f coast

costar to cost

costilla f [kostee-ya] rib

costumbre f [kostoombreh] custom

costurera f [kostooraira] seamstress

cráneo m [kraneh-o] skull

crédito m credit; unit(s)

creer [kreh-air] to believe

crema f cream

crema base [baseh] foundation cream

crema de belleza [deh beh-yesa] cold cream

crema hidratante [eedratanteh] moisturizer

crema limpiadora [leemp-yadora] cleansing cream

crespo (Col, CSur, Ven) curly

creyó [kreh-yo] he/she believed

criticar to criticize

crocante [krokanteh] (Rpl) crunchy

cruce m [krooseh] crossroads; junction, intersection; crossing

cruce de ciclistas danger: cyclists crossing

cruce de ganado danger: cattle crossing

crucero m [kroosairo] cruise

cruda f (CAm, Mex) hangover

Cruz Roja f [kroos roHa] Red Cross

cruzar [kroosar] to cross

cuaderno m [kwadairno] notebook

cuadra f [kwadra] block
está a dos cuadras it's two blocks away

cuadrado [kwadrado] square

cuadro m [kwadro] painting
de cuadros [deh] checked

cual [kwal] which; who;
¿cuál? which?

¿cuándo? [kwando] when?

cuanto: en cuanto ... as soon as ...

¿cuánto? [kwanto] how much?
¡cuánto lo lamento! I'm so sorry!

¿cuántos? how many?

cuarenta [kwarenta] forty

cuartel m [kwartel] barracks

cuartilla f [kwartee-ya] writing paper

cuarto (m) [kwarto] quarter; fourth; room

cuarto con dos camas twin room

cuarto de baño [ban-yo] bathroom

cuarto de estar sitting room

cuarto de hora [deh ora] quarter of an hour

cuarto doble [dobleh] double room

cuarto individual [eendeebeedwal] single room

cuarto piso fourth floor, (US) fifth floor

cuate m [kwateh] (Mex) friend, pal; twin

cuatro [kwatro] four

cuatrocientos [kwatros-yentos] four hundred

cubeta f [koobeta] (Mex) bucket

cubierta f [koob-yairta] deck

cubierto (m) covered; overcast; menu

cubiertos mpl cutlery

cubo m [koobo] (Mex) bucket; cube; bin

cubo de la basura [deh] (Mex) dustbin, trashcan

cucaracha f cockroach

cuchara f spoon

cucharilla f [koocharee-ya] teaspoon

cuchillería f [koochee-yairee-a] cutlery

cuchillo m [koochee-yo] knife

cucho m (Ch, Ec) cat
 hacerse el cucho to act dumb

cucos mpl (Col) knickers, panties

cucufate m [kookoofateh] (Guat) bottom, bum

cueco [kweko] (Pan) poof

cuelgue, espere y retire la tarjeta hang up, wait and remove card

cuello m [kweh-yo] neck; collar

cuenta f [kwenta] bill, (US) check; account

cuenta corriente [korr-yenteh] current account

cuentas fpl beads

cuento m [kwento] tale

cuerda f [kwairda] rope; string; (RD) anger

cuerito m [kwaireeto] (CSur) washer

cuero m [kwairo] leather

cuerpo m [kwairpo] body

cuesta (f) [kwesta] it costs; slope
 cuesta abajo/arriba [abaHo] downhill/uphill

cueva f [kweba] cave

cuidado (m) [kweedado] take care; look out; care

cuidado con ... caution ...

cuidado con el escalón mind the step

cuidado con el perro beware of the dog

cuidar [kweedar] to look after; to nurse

cuilia f [kweel-ya] (Salv) police

culear [kooleh-ar] (SAm) to fuck

culebra f snake

culo m [koolo] bottom; back; rear

culpa f fault, blame; guilt
 es culpa mía it's my fault

culturismo m body building

cumbancha f (Cu) party

cúmbila m/f (Cu) pal

cumplas: ¡que cumplas muchos más! many happy returns!

cumpleaños m [koompleh-an-yos] birthday

cuna f cot, (US) crib

cuneta f gutter

cuñada f [koon-yada] sister-in-law

cuñado m [koon-yado] brother-in-law

cuota m [kwota] contribution; membership fee; motorway toll
 pagar en cuotas to pay by instalments

cura m priest

curado cured; drunk; smoked

curar to cure; to heal

curarse [koorarseh] to heal up

curda: ¡tenía una curda! [koorda] (Parag) he was so drunk!

curepa (mf) (Parag) Argentine

curralar (Cu) to work

curva f [koorba] bend; curve

curva peligrosa dangerous bend

cutear [kooteh-**ar**] (Hond) to throw up

cuyo [**koo**-yo] whose; of which

D

D. (Don) Mr.

D.F. m [deh **e**feh] Mexico City

damas fpl draughts, (US) checkers; ladies' toilet, ladies' room

damasco m (CSur) apricot

danés [dan-**es**] Danish

danza f [**dan**sa] dancing; dance

danzón m [dan**son**] (Mex) popular Mexican dance

dañar [dan-**yar**] to damage

dañarse la espalda [dan-**yarseh**] to hurt one's back

daños mpl [dan-yos] damage(s)

dar to give

dcha. (derecha) right

de [deh] of; from

de dos metros de alto two metres high

debajo de [debaнo deh] under

deber (m) [deb**air**] to have to; to owe; duty

deberes mpl [deb**air**-es] homework

débil weak

decepción f [deseps-**yon**] disappointment

decepcionado [deseps-yon**ado**] disappointed

decidir [deseed**eer**] to decide

décimo [**des**eemo] tenth

decir [des**eer**] to say; to tell

declaración f [deklaras-**yon**] declaration; statement

declarar to declare, to state

dedo m finger

dedo del pie [p-yeh] toe

defectuoso [defektw**oso**] faulty

defensa f (Mex) bumper, (US) fender

dejar [deh-**нar**] to leave; to let

dejar de beber [deh beb**air**] to stop drinking

delante de [del**anteh**] in front of

delantera f [delant**aira**] front (part)

delantero front; forward

la parte delantera [part**eh**] the front (part)

demás: los demás the others, the rest

demasiado [demas-y**ado**] too much

demasiados too many

democracia f [demokr**as**-ya] democracy

demora f delay

demorar: ¿cuánto demora? [**kwanto**] how long does it take?

demorón (Andes, Rpl): **es demorón** he is always late

dentadura postiza f [post**eesa**] dentures

dentista m/f dentist

dentro (de) [deh] inside

dentro de dos semanas in two weeks' time

dentro de poco soon

departamento m apartment

departamento amueblado [amweblado] furnished apartment

departamento sin amueblar [amweblar] unfurnished apartment

depende [dependeh] it depends

dependienta f [–yenta], **dependiente m** [–yenteh] shop assistant

deporte m [deporteh] sport

deportista m/f sportsman/ sportswoman

deportivo [deporteebo] sports

deportivos mpl trainers, (US) sneakers

depósito m tank; deposit

deprimido depressed

derecha f right

a la derecha (de) on the right (of)

derecho: todo derecho straight ahead

derribar to pull down, to demolish

derrota f defeat

desacuerdo m [desakwairdo] disagreement

desagradable [–dableh] unpleasant

desaparecer [–resair] to disappear

desaparecido m victim of illegal arrest

desarmador m screwdriver

desastre m [desastreh] disaster

desayunar [desa-yoonar] to

have breakfast

desayuno m [desa-yoono] breakfast

descansar to rest

descanso m interval; landing

descarado cheeky

descarrilarse to be derailed

deschongue m [deschongeh] (Salv) racket

descolgar el aparato lift receiver

descomponerse [deskomponairseh] to break down

descompostura breakdown, mechanical problem

descompuesto [deskompwesto] broken; broken down

descorchador m (Andes, Rpl) corkscrew

descubierto [deskoob-yairto] discovered; uncovered

descubrir to discover; to uncover

descuelgue el auricular lift the receiver

descuento [deskwento] discount

descuidado [deskweedado] careless

¡descuide! [deskweedeh] don't worry about it!

desde [desdeh] since

desde luego [lwego] of course

desde que [keh] since

desear [deseh-ar] to want; to wish

¿qué desea? [keh deseh-a] what can I do for you?

desembarcadero m
[desembarkadairo] quay

desempleado (m) [desempleh-
ado] unemployed person;
unemployed

desempleo m [desempleh-o]
unemployment

desfile m [desfeeleh] procession

desfile de modas fashion
show

desgracia: por desgracia
[desgras-ya] unfortunately

desgraciadamente [–damenteh]
unfortunately

deshacer las maletas [des-
asair] to unpack

desierto m [des-yairto] desert

desinfectante m [–tanteh]
disinfectant

deslizador m (Mex) hang-gliding

desmadre m [desmadreh] (Mex)
chaos; mess

¡qué desmadre! [keh] what a
bloody mess!

desmaquillarse [desmakee-
yarseh] to remove one's
make-up

desmayarse [desma-yarseh] to
faint

desnudo naked

desnutrición f [desnootrees-yon]
malnutrition

desobediente [desobed-yenteh]
disobedient

desodorante m [–ranteh]
deodorant

desordenado untidy

desorientarse [desor-yentarseh]

to lose one's way

despachador automático m
[owtomateeko] ticket machine

despachar to check in

despacho de petróleo m [deh
petroleh-o] (Mex) store selling
paraffin and oil for heating

despacio [despas-yo] slowly

despedida f farewell

despedirse [despedeerseh] to
say goodbye

despegar to take off

despegue m [despeh-geh]
take-off

despejado [despeHado] clear

despelote m [despeloteh] mess

despertador m [despairtador]
alarm clock

despertar to wake

despertarse [–tarseh] to wake
up

despiche m [despeecheh] (CR)
disorder

despierto [desp-yairto] awake

desprendimiento de terreno
danger: landslides

despreocupado [despreh-
okoopado] thoughtless

después [despwes] afterwards

después de [deh] after

destinatario m addressee

destino m destination

el avión con destino a ... the
plane for ...

destornillador m [destornee-
yador] screwdriver

destruir [destrweer] to destroy

desvestirse [desbesteerseh] to
undress

desviación f [desb-yas-yon]
diversion

desvío m [desbee-o] detour,
diversion

desvío provisional temporary
diversion

detener [detenair] to arrest;
to stop

detergente en polvo m
[detairHenteh] washing powder

detergente lavavajillas
[lababaHee-yas] washing-up
liquid

detrás (de) [deh] behind

deuda f [deh-ooda] debt

devolver [debolbair] to give
back; to vomit

di I gave; tell me

día m [dee-a] day

día de Año Nuevo [deh an-yo
nwebo] New Year's Day

Día de los Muertos [deh los
mwairtos] Day of the Dead,
All Souls' Day

día feriado [fair-yado] public
holiday

diamante m [d-yamanteh]
diamond

diapositiva f [d-yaposeeteeba]
slide

diario (m) [d-yar-yo] diary;
daily newspaper; daily

diarrea f [d-yarreh-a] diarrhoea

días feriados public holidays

días laborables [laborab-les]
weekdays; working days

dibujar [deebooHar] to draw

dibujos animados mpl
[deebooHos] cartoons

diccionario m [deeks-yonar-yo]
dictionary

dice [deeseh] he/she says;
you say

dicho [deecho] said

diciembre m [dees-yembreh]
December

diecinueve [d-yeseenwebeh]
nineteen

dieciocho [d-yesee-ocho]
eighteen

dieciséis [d-yeseesays] sixteen

diecisiete [d-yesees-yeteh]
seventeen

diente m [d-yenteh] tooth

dieron [d-yairon] they gave;
you gave

diesel m [deesel] diesel

dieta f [d-yeta] diet
 a dieta on a diet

diez [d-yes] ten

difícil [deefeeseel] difficult

dificultad f [deefeekoolta]
difficulty

diga tell me

digitar [deeHeetar] to key

digo I say

dije [deeHeh] I said

dijeron [deeHairon] they said;
you said

dijiste [deeHeesteh] you said

dijo [deeHo] he/she said; you
said
 ¿qué dijo? what did you
 say?; what did he/she say?

dilatar to delay; to be late

diminuto tiny

Dinamarca f Denmark

dinero m [deenairo] money

Dios m [d-yos] God
¡Dios mío! [mee-o] my God!
dirección f [deereks-yon]
  direction; address; steering;
  management
direccional f [deereks-yon-**al**]
  (Col, Mex) indicator
director m, **directora** f
  manager; director;
  headteacher
directorio m telephone
  directory
dirigir [deereeнeer] to direct;
  to lead
disco m record
disconformidad f
  [deeskonformeeda]
  disagreement
discoteca f music shop; disco
disculparse [deeskoolparseh] to
  apologize
disculpe [deeskoolpeh] excuse
  me
disculpen las molestias
  we apologize for any
  inconvenience
discurso m speech

discusión f [deeskoos-yon]
  discussion; argument
discutir to argue
diseñador de modas m [deesen-
  yador deh] fashion designer
disimular [deeseemoolar] to
  pretend
disqueta f [deesketa] (Mex)
  diskette
distancia f [deestans-ya]
  distance
distinto different

distraído [deestra-**ee**do] absent-
  minded; distracted
distribuidor m [deestreebweedor]
  distributor
Distrito Federal m [fedairal]
  Federal District, Mexico
  City
distrito postal postcode, zip
  code
disuélvase en agua dissolve
  in water
divertido [deebairteedo]
  entertaining; funny
divertirse [deebairteerseh] to
  have a good time
divisas fpl [deebeesas] foreign
  currency
divorciado [deebors-yado]
  divorced
divorciarse [deebors-yarseh] to
  divorce
divorcio m [deebors-yo] divorce
divulgar [deeboolgar] to
  publicize
dizque [deeskeh] (Andes, Mex)
  apparently, supposedly
doble [dobleh] double
doble sentido two-way
doce [doseh] twelve
docena (de) f [dosena] dozen
dólar m dollar
doler [dolair] to hurt
dolor m pain
dolor de cabeza [kabesa]
  headache
dolor de garganta [deh] sore
  throat
dolor de muelas [mwelas]
  toothache

dolor de oídos [o-**ee**dos] earache

doloroso painful

domicilio m [domee**see**l-yo] place of residence

domingo m Sunday

domingos y feriados Sundays and public holidays

donativa f donations

donde [**don**deh] where

¿dónde? where?

donjuán m [don**H**wan] woman-izer

dorado (m) gold, golden; type of fish

dormido asleep

dormir to sleep

dormitorio m [dormee**tor**-yo] bedroom; dormitory

dos two

doscientos [dos-**yen**tos] two hundred

doy I give

droga f drug

drogadicto m [droga**deek**to] drug addict

drogado drugged; (Mex) in debt

drogarse [dro**gar**seh] to take drugs; (Mex) to get into debt

droguería f [drogai**ree**-a] drugstore

ducha f shower

ducharse [doo**char**seh] to have a shower

dudar to doubt; to hesitate

duele [**dwe**leh] it hurts

dulce [**dool**seh] sweet; gentle

dulces mpl [**dool**s-es] sweets, candies

dunas fpl sand dunes

dundo (Nic) stupid

durante [doo**ran**teh] during

Durex® m Sellotape®, Scotch tape®

duro hard; (Pan) stingy, mean

E

e [eh] and

E parking

echar to throw; to throw away

echar al buzón [boo**son**] to post, to mail

echar al correo [kor**reh**-o] to post, to mail

echar dedo (Col) to hitch-hike

echar el cerrojo [sairro**Ho**] to bolt

echar sangre [**san**greh] to bleed

echarse la siesta [e**char**seh] to have a nap

echarse un polvo to have a shag

ecobio m [ek**ob**-yo] (Cu) pal

ecológico [ekolo**Hee**ko] ecological

ecologista m/f environmentalist, Green

economía f economy

económico cheap, inexpensive; economic; economical

ecuatoriano (m) [ekwator-yano]
Ecuadorean

edad f [eda] age
¿qué edad tienes? [keh – t-
yen-es] how old are you?

edificio m [edeefees-yo]
building

edredón m quilt, eiderdown;
duvet

educado polite

EE.UU. (Estados Unidos) USA

efectivo: en efectivo [efekteebo]
in cash

egresado m graduate

eje m [eHeh] axle

eje del cigüeñal [seegwen-yal]
crankshaft

ejemplo m [eHemplo] example
por ejemplo for example

ejidatario m [eHeedatar-yo] (Mex)
member of an agricultural
community

ejido m [eHeedo] (Mex)
communal land

el the

él he; him

elástico elastic; (Ch) elastic
band

elecciones fpl [eleks-yon-es]
elections

electricidad f [elektreeseeda]
electricity

electricista m [elektreeseesta]
electrician

eléctrico electric

electrodomésticos mpl
electrical appliances

elegir [eleh-Heer] to choose

ella [eh-ya] she; her

ellas [eh-yas] they; them

ellos [eh-yos] they; them

embajada f [embaHada]
embassy

embalse m [embalseh] reservoir

embarazada [embarasada]
pregnant

embarrarla (Col) to make a
mistake

embole m [emboleh] (Rpl) bore

embotellamiento m [emboteh-
yam-yento] traffic jam

embrague m [embrageh]
clutch

emergencia f [emairHens-ya]
emergency

emisión f [emees-yon]
programme; emission;
distribution date; issue

emocionante [emos-yonanteh]
exciting

empacar to pack

empalme m [empalmeh]
junction

empaque m [empakeh] (Col, Ven)
washer

empaquetado m [empaketado]
packing

empaste m [empasteh] (Mex)
filling

empeorar [empeh-orar] to get
worse

empezar [empesar] to begin
empieza a las ocho [emp-yesa]
it starts at eight

empinado steep

empleada f [empleh-ada],
empleado m white collar
worker, employee

emplomadura f [emplomad**oo**ra]
(Rpl) filling (in tooth)

empresa f firm, enterprise

empresario m businessman

empujar [empoo**Har**] to push

en in; at; on; by

**enamorados: día de los
enamorados** m [dee-a deh] St
Valentine's Day

encamotarse [enkamot**ar**seh]
(Pe) to fall for, to fall in love
with

encantado delighted
¡encantado! pleased to meet
you!

encantador lovely

encantar to please

encendedor m [ensended**or**]
lighter

encerrar [ensai**rrar**] to lock in;
to lock up

enchibolarse [encheebol**ar**seh]
(Hond) to get confused

enchufe m [ench**oo**feh] plug;
socket

encima [ens**ee**ma] above
encima de [deh] on top of

encomienda f parcel

encontrar to find

encontrarse (con/a) [–**trar**seh]
to meet

encuentra: se encuentra [seh
enk**wen**tra] is located

encuentro (m) [enk**wen**tro]
meeting, encounter; I find

endrogarse [–**gar**seh] (Mex) to
get into debt

enemigo m enemy

enero m [en**ai**ro] January

enfermarse [–**mar**seh] to
become ill, to get sick

enfermedad f [enfairm**eda**]
disease

enfermedad venérea [ben**ai**reh-
a] VD, venereal disease

enfermera f [enfairm**ai**ra],
enfermero m nurse

enfermo [enf**ai**rmo] ill, sick

enfrente de [enfr**en**teh deh]
opposite

enganche [eng**an**cheh] deposit

engañar [engan-**yar**] to cheat;
to trick

enmicado m [enmeek**a**do]
plastic covering (for documents)

enojado [eno**Ha**do] angry

enojarse [–**Har**seh] to get
angry

enorme [en**or**meh] enormous

enseñar [ensen-**yar**] to teach

entender [entend**air**] to
understand
no entiendo I don't
understand

entero [ent**ai**ro] whole; in one
piece

entiendo [ent-**yen**do] I
understand

entierro m [ent-**yai**rro] funeral

entonces [ent**on**s-es] then;
therefore

entrada f entrance, way in;
ticket

entrada gratis admission free

entrada libre [**lee**breh]
admission free

entrar to go in, to enter

entre [**en**treh] among; between

entretanto meanwhile

entretiempo m [entret-**ye**mpo] (CSur) half-time

entrevista f [entrebe**e**sta] interview

enviar [emb-**yar**] to send

envolver [embol**bair**] to wrap up; to involve

enyesar (SAm) to put in plaster

equipaje m [ekeepa**He**h] luggage, baggage

equipaje de mano [deh] hand luggage

equipajes mpl [ekeepa**H**-es] left-luggage office, (US) baggage check

equipo m [e**kee**po] team; equipment, tools

equivocado [ekeebo**ka**do] wrong

equivocarse [ekeebo**kar**seh] to make a mistake

equivocarse de número [deh **noo**mairo] to dial the wrong number

era [**ai**ra] I/he/she/it was; you were

éramos [**ai**ramos] we were

eran [**ai**ran] they were; you were

eras [**ai**ras] you were

eres [**air**-es] you are

erupción f [airoops-**yon**] rash; eruption

es he is; you are

esa that

ésa that (one)

esas those

ésas those (ones)

escala f intermediate stop; scale; ladder

escalera automática f escalator

escaleras fpl stairs

escaparate m [eskapa**ra**teh] shop window

escarcha f frost

escayola f [eska-**yo**la] plaster cast

escocés [eskos-**es**] (m) Scottish; Scot, Scotsman

Escocia f [es**ko**s-ya] Scotland

escoger [esko**Hair**] to choose

esconder [eskon**dair**] to hide

escorpión m [eskorp-**yon**] scorpion

escribir to write

escrito written

por escrito in writing

escritorio m [eskreetor-yo] office

escritura f deed; document

escuchar to hear

escuela f [es**kwe**la] school

escuela de párvulos [deh par**boo**los] (Mex) kindergarten

escuincle m/f [es**kween**kleh] (Mex) kid, nipper; runt

escurrir a mano to wring by hand

ese [**e**seh] that

ése that (one)

esencial [esens-**yal**] essential

esfero m (Col) biro®, ball point

esfuerzo m [es**fwair**so] effort

esmalte de uñas m [es**mal**teh deh **oo**n-yas] nail polish

esmeralda f emerald
eso that
 eso es that's it, that's right
esos those
ésos those (ones)
espalda f back
España f [espan-ya] Spain
español (m) [espan-yol],
 española (f) Spanish;
 Spaniard
espantoso dreadful;
 frightening
especialista m/f [espes-yaleesta]
 specialist
especialmente [espes-
 yalmenteh] especially
espectáculo m show,
 spectacle
espejo m [espeHo] mirror
esperar [espairar] to wait; to
 hope
 espere [espaireh] please wait
 ¡espéreme! [espairemeh] wait
 for me!
 espero que sí I hope so
espeso thick
esponja f [esponHa] sponge
esposa f wife
esposo m husband
espuma de afeitar f [deh
 afaytar] shaving foam
esquí acuático [eskee
 akwateeko] waterski;
 waterskiing
esquina f [eskeena] corner
esta this
ésta this one
estación f [estas-yon] station;
 season; radio station

estación de autobuses [deh
 owtoboos-es] bus station
estación de ferrocarril train
 station
estación de nafta (Rpl) petrol/
 gas station, filling station
estación de servicio [sairbees-
 yo] service station
estacionamiento m [estas-
 yonam-yento] car park, (US)
 parking lot
estacionamiento limitado
 restricted parking
estacionamiento privado
 private parking
estacionamiento reservado
 this parking place reserved
estacionamiento subterráneo
 underground parking
estacionamiento vigilado
 supervised parking
estacionarse [estas-yonarseh]
 to park
estadía f [estadee-a] stay
estadio de fútbol m [estad-yo
 deh] football stadium
Estados Unidos mpl [ooneedos]
 United States
estadounidense [estado-oonee-
 denseh] American, North
 American
estallar [esta-yar] to explode
estampilla f [estampee-ya]
 stamp
estaño m [estan-yo] tin; pewter
estar to be
estas these
éstas these ones
estatua f [estatwa] statue

este m [esteh] east
este this
éste this (one)
esterilizado [estaireeleesado]
  sterilized
estilógrafo m (Col) fountain
  pen
esto this
estómago m stomach
estornudar to sneeze
estos these
éstos these (ones)
estoy I am
estrecho narrow; tight
estrella f [estreh-ya] star
estrellarse contra [estreh-
  yarseh] to run into; to crash
  into
estreñido [estren-yeedo]
  constipated
estreñimiento m [estren-yeem-
  yento] constipation
estreno m new film/movie
  release
estropear [estropeh-ar] to
  damage
estudiante m/f [estood-yanteh]
  student

estudiar [estood-yar] to study
estufa eléctrica f (Col, Mex)
  electric fire
estupefaciente m [–fas-yenteh]
  hallucinogenic drug
estupendo wonderful, great
estúpido stupid
etiqueta f [eteeketa] label
... de etiqueta [deh] formal ...
europeo [eh-ooropeh-o]
  European

evidente [ebeedenteh] obvious
exactamente [–menteh] exactly
¡exacto! exactly!
excelente [ekselenteh] excellent
excepto [esepto] except
excepto domingos y feriados
  except Sundays and holidays
excepto sábados except
  Saturdays
exceso de equipaje m [ekseso
  deh ekeepaHeh] excess baggage
exceso de velocidad
  [beloseeda] speeding
excursión f [eskoors-yon] trip
excusados mpl [eskoosados]
  toilets, rest rooms
exhosto m [eksosto] (Col)
  exhaust
expedir [espedeer] to despatch
expendio m [ekspend-yo] stall;
  kiosk; shop, store
explicación f [espleekas-yon]
  explanation
explicar to explain
exportación f [esportas-yon]
  export
exposición f [esposees-yon]
  exhibition
exprés m [espres] fast train;
  special delivery
extensión f [extension; extension lead
exterior (m) [estair-yor]
  exterior, outer; foreign;
  overseas
extinguidor m [esteengeedor]
  (SAm) fire extinguisher
extra four-star petrol, (US)
  premium gas

extranjera (f) [estranHaira], **extranjero (m)** [estranHairo] foreign; foreigner

en el extranjero abroad, overseas

extrañar [estran-yar] to miss

extraño [estran-yo] strange

F

fábrica f factory

fabricado por ... made by ...

fachento (CR) eccentric

facho m fascist

fácil [faseel] easy

facilidad: con facilidades payment by instalments

factura f bill, (US) check; invoice

facturación f [faktooras-yon] check-in

facturar el equipaje [ekeepaHeh] to check in luggage/baggage

faena f [fa-ena] (Rpl) slaughtering

faenar (Rpl) to slaughter

fajasón m [faHason] (Guat) fight

falda f skirt; hillside

fallar [fa-yar] to fail; to break down

falso false

falta f lack; mistake; defect; fault

no hace falta ... [aseh] it's not necessary to ...

falta de visibilidad poor visibility

faltaba más don't mention it

faltar to be missing; to be absent

faltan tres there are three missing

faltan seis kilómetros para llegar there are six kilometres to go before we get there

¿cuánto falta (para) ...? how much further is it (to) ...?

echar a faltar to miss

familia f [fameel-ya] family

famoso famous

fardo m (Cu) trousers, (US) pants

farmacia f [farmas-ya] chemist's, pharmacy

farmacia de turno [deh toorno] emergency chemist's/pharmacy, duty chemist

faro m light; headlight; lighthouse

faro antiniebla [anteen-yebla] fog lamp

farra f partying

nos vamos de farra el viernes we are going out partying on Friday

faso m (Rpl) fag, cigarette

faul f [fowl] foul

favor: a favor de [fabor deh] in favour of

por favor please

si hace el favor [aseh] if you don't mind

fayuca f [fa-yooka] (Mex) contraband goods

fayuquero m [fa-yookairo] (Mex) seller of contraband goods

febrero m [febrairo] February

fecha f date

fecha de caducación, fecha de caducidad expiry date

fecha de nacimiento [deh naseem-yento] date of birth

fecha límite de venta sell-by date

¡Felices Pascuas y Próspero Año Nuevo! [felees-es paskwas ee prospairo an-yo nwebo] Merry Christmas and a Happy New Year!

felicidad f [feleeseeda] happiness

¡felicidades! [feleeseedad-es] happy birthday!; congratulations!

felicitar [feleeseetar] to congratulate

feliz [felees] happy

¡feliz cumpleaños! [koompleh-an-yos] happy birthday!

feo [feh-o] ugly

feria f [fair-ya] fair; loose change; (CSur, Pe) market

feriado: días feriados [fair-yados] public holidays

Fe

ferretería f [fairretairee-a] hardware store

ferrocarril m railway, railroad

festividad f [festeebeeda] celebration

festivos bank holidays, public holidays

fiaca f [f-yaka] (Andes, CSur) laziness

me da fiaca I can't be bothered

fiambrería f (CSur) delicatessen

fibras naturales natural fibres

fiebre f [f-yebreh] fever; high temperature

fiebre del heno [eno] hay fever

fierro m [f-yairro] iron; (SAm) gun

fiesta f public holiday; party

fiesta de ... [deh] feast of ...

fifar [feefar] (Rpl) to screw

fila f row

fila india single file

filmar [feelmar] to film

filo: tengo filo I'm hungry

filtro m filter

filtro solar sunblock

fin m [feen] end; purpose

por fin at last, finally

a fin de que [deh keh] so that

fin de semana [deh] weekend

fin de serie discontinued articles

final m [feenal] end

final de autopista end of motorway/highway

financiamiento m [feenans-yam-yento] funding

fingir [feenHeer] to pretend

fino fine; delicate

firma f signature; company

firmar to sign

flaco thin, skinny

flequillo m [flekee-yo] fringe

flete m [fleteh] carriage, transport cost

flojera: me da flojera [floHaira] I can't be bothered

flojo [floHo] lazy

flor f flower

florería f [florairee-a] florist
florero m [florairo] vase
floristería f (Col, Ven) florist
flotadores mpl lifebelts
flotar to float
FMT [efemeteh] (Mex) tourist card
foco m light bulb
folleto m [fo-yeto] pamphlet
Folleto de Migración Turística [deh meegras-yon] (Mex) tourist card
fonda f simple restaurant; boarding house
fondo m bottom; background
  al fondo (de) at the bottom (of)
fondos mpl funds, money
fontanero m [fontanairo] plumber
footing m jogging
forma f form
  en forma fit
forro m (Rpl) condom
fósforo m match
foto f photograph
  sacar fotos to take photographs
fotografía f photograph; photography
fotografiar [fotograf-yar] to photograph
fotógrafo m photographer
fotómetro m light meter
fracatán (RD) a lot of
fraccionamiento m [fraks-yonam-yento] (Mex) housing estate
francamente [–menteh] frankly
francés [frans-es] French

Francia f [frans-ya] France
franela f (Rpl) duster
franqueado [frankeh-ado] franked
franqueo m [frankeh-o] postage
frazada f [frasada] blanket, rug
frecuencia: con frecuencia [frekwens-ya] often
fregadero m [fregadairo] (Mex) sink
fregar to keep on at; to annoy
  fregar los platos (Mex) to do the washing up
  fregarlo to screw up
freír [freh-eer] to fry
frenar to brake
freno m brake
freno de mano [deh] handbrake, parking brake
frente f [frenteh] forehead
  hacer frente a ... [asair] to face up to ...
fresa (Mex) posh
fresco fresh
friforol m (Pan) chaos
frigorífico m (Mex) fridge
frío [free-o] cold
  hace frío [aseh] it's cold
frontera f [frontaira] border
frutería f [frootairee-a] fruit shop; greengrocer's
fue [fweh] he/she/it went; he/she/it was; you went; you were
fuego m [fwego] fire
  ¿tiene fuego? do you have a light?
fuegos artificiales [arteefees-yal-es] fireworks

Fu

fuente f [fwenteh] fountain; source; font

fuera [fwaira] outside; he/she/ it was; he/she/it went; you were; you went

fuera de [deh] apart from

fuera de horas pico off-peak hours

fuera de servicio [deh sairbees-yo] out of order

fuéramos [fwairamos] we were; we went

fueran [fwairan] they were; they went; you were; you went

fueron [fwairon] they were; they went; you were; you went

fuerte [fwairteh] strong; loud

fuerza f [fwairsa] force; strength

fuetazo m [fwetaso] lash

fui [fwee] I was; I went

fuimos [fweemos] we were; we went

fuiste [fweesteh] you were; you went

fulo (Pan) blond

fumadores [foomador-es] smoking

fumar to smoke

función de noche late showing

función de tarde early showing

funcionar [foons-yonar] to work

funcionario m [foons-yonar-yo] civil servant; employee

funda f [foonda] (Mex) crown

(on tooth); pillow case

funeraria f [foonairar-ya] undertaker's

funicular m [fooneekoolar] cable car

furioso [foor-yoso] furious

furúnculo m abscess; boil

fusible m [fooseebleh] fuse

fútbol m football

futuro (m) [footooro] future

G

gachupín m [gachoopeen] (Mex) Spaniard

gafas fpl glasses, (US) eyeglasses

gafas de bucear [deh booseh-ar] goggles

gafas de sol sunglasses

gafo (Ven) stupid, dumb

galería f [galairee-a] gallery; enclosed balcony

galería de arte [deh arteh] art gallery

Gales m [gal-es] Wales

galés [gal-es] Welsh

gallo [ga-yo] (Hond) skillful

gama: toda la gama the whole range

gamulán m (Rpl) sheepskin coat

gamuza f [gamoosa] suede

ganadería f [–dairee-a] cattle farming

ganadero m [–dairo] (cattle) rancher

ganado m cattle

ganar to win; to earn
gancho m hanger; (Rpl) staple
ganga f bargain
ganso m goose
garaje m [garaHeh] garage
garantía f guarantee
garantizar [–teesar] to guarantee
garganta f throat
garoso [garoso] (Col) greedy
garrón: de garrón (Rpl) free
gásfiter m [gasfeetair] (Ch) plumber
gasfitero m [gasfeetairo] (Pe) plumber
gasolina f petrol, (US) gas
gasolina normal two-star petrol, (US) regular (gas)
gasolina super [soopair] (Mex) four-star petrol, (US) premium (gas)
gasolinera f [gasoleenaira] petrol/gas station, filling station
gastar to spend
gata f (Ch) jack
gatillero m [gateeyairo] (Mex) gunman
gato m cat; jack
gayola f [ga-yola] (Rpl) slammer
gemelos mpl [Hemelos] twins; cufflinks
general: por lo general [Henairal] usually
en general generally, in general
genio m [Hen-yo] genius
gente f [Henteh] people
una gente a person

gerente m/f [Hairenteh] manager; manageress
gestionar [Hest-yonar] to negotiate
gimnasia f [Heemnas-ya] gymnastics
gimnasio m gymnasium
ginecólogo m [Heenekologo] gynaecologist
gira f [Heera] tour
girar [Heerar] to turn
gire a la izquierda [Heereh] turn left
giro [Heero] money order
gis m [Hees] (Mex) chalk
gitano m [Heetano] gypsy
globo m balloon
glorieta f [glor-yeta] roundabout, (US) traffic circle
gobierno m [gob-yairno] government
gobilote m [gobeeloteh] (Hond) turkey
gol m goal
golero m (Rpl) goalkeeper
golfito m mini-golf
Golfo (de México) m Gulf of Mexico
golpe m [golpeh] blow
de golpe all of a sudden
golpear [golpeh-ar] to hit; to beat up
golpiza f [golpeesa] beating
goma f glue; elastic band, rubber band; (CSur) tyre
gomelo (Col) posh
gomita f rubber band; (Rpl) elastic band

gordo fat

gorra f cap

gorrero m scrounger, free-loader

gorro m bonnet, cap

gorro de baño [deh ban-yo] bathing cap

gorro de ducha shower cap

gota f drop

gotera f [gotaira] leak

gozar [gosar] to enjoy

grabadora f tape recorder

gracias [gras-yas] thank you

gracias a usted [oosteh] thank you (more emphatic)

gracioso [gras-yoso] funny

grado m degree

grafitos mpl graffiti

grama f lawn

gramática f grammar

gramo m gramme

Gran Bretaña f [bretan-ya] Great Britain

grande [grandeh] big, large; old

grandes almacenes mpl [grand-es almasen-es] large department store

granizo m [graneeso] hail

granja f [granHa] farm

granjero m [granHairo] farmer

grano m grain; spot

grapa f paper clip

grasa f fat

grasiento [gras-yento] greasy

grasoso greasy

gratis free

grave [grabeh] serious; very ill/sick

gravilla f (Mex) loose chippings; gravel

gremio m trade union

grifo m tap, (US) faucet; (Pe) petrol/gas station, filling station

gringo m gringo, foreigner

gripa f (Col, Mex) flu

gripe f [greepeh] flu

gris grey

gritar to shout

grosería [grosairee-a] swearword, oath

decir groserías [deseer] to swear

grosero [grosairo] rude

grúa f [groo-a] tow truck, breakdown lorry; crane

grueso [grweso] thick

grupo m group

grupo sanguíneo [sangeeneh-o] blood group

guacamayo m [gwakama-yo] parrot

guacarear [gwakareh-ar] (Mex) to throw up

guachimán m [gwacheeman] (SAm) watchman

guagua f [gwagwa] (Cu) bus; (Ec) mf kid

guajiro m [gwaHeero] (Cu) peasant

guajolote m [gwaHoloteh] (Mex) turkey

guambra m/f [gwambra] (Ec) teenager

guanaco [gwanako] (Nic) stupid

guanajo [gwanaHo] (Cu) stupid

guante m [gwanteh] glove

guapo [gwapo] handsome

guaraches mpl [gwarach-es] (Mex) sandals

guardacostas m/f [gwardakostas] coastguard

guardafango m mudguard

guardar [gwardar] to keep; to put away

guardarropa m [gwardarropa] cloakroom, (US) checkroom

guardería (infantil) f [gwardairee-a (eenfanteel)] crèche; nursery school

guárdese en lugar fresco keep in a cool place

guardia m/f [gward-ya] guard

guarura m/f [gwaroora] (Mex) thug, hood

guata f [gwata] (Mex) belly

guatemalteco (m) [gwatemalteko] Guatemalan

guayabera f [gwa-yabaira] embroidered shirt

guayabo m [gwa-yabo] (Col) hangover

güero [gwairo] blond, light skinned

guerra f [gairra] war

guerra civil civil war

guía m/f [gee-a] guide

guía telefónica f phone book, telephone directory

guía turístico m tourist guide

güila mf [gweela] (CR) kid

güirro m [gweerro] (Hond) kid

guisar [geesar] to cook

guita f [geeta] (Arg) money

guitarra f [geetarra] guitar

guloso greedy

gusano m worm

gustar to please

me gusta ... [meh] I like ..

(si) gusta pasar would you like to go in?

me gustaría ... I'd like to ...

gusto: mucho gusto [moocho] pleased to meet you

con mucho gusto certainly, with great pleasure

el gusto es mío how do you do; it is a pleasure

¡qué gusto de verte! [keh – deh bairteh] it's good to see you!

H

h is not pronounced in Spanish

ha he/she/it has; you have

habichuelas fpl [abeechwelas] runner beans

hábil [abeel] skilful

días hábiles working days

habitante m/f [abeetanteh] inhabitant

habitar to live

hablador talkative

hablar to speak

hable aquí speak here

habrá there will be; he/she/it will have; you will have

habrán they will have; you will have

habrás you will have

habré [abreh] I will have

habremos we will have

h is not pronounced in Spanish

habría [ab**ree**-a] I would have; he/she/it would have; you would have

habríamos [ab**ree**-amos] we would have

habrían [ab**ree**-an] they would have; you would have

habrías [ab**ree**-as] you would have

hacer [a**sair**] to make; to do

hace tres días [**a**seh] three days ago

hace calor/sol it is hot/ sunny

se me hace que ... [seh meh – keh] I believe that ...

no le hace [leh] (Mex) don't worry about it

¿cuánto se hace de México a Veracruz? how long does it take from Mexico City to Veracruz?

hacerse [a**sair**seh] to become

hacia [**as**-ya] towards

haga: ¡hágalo ahora! do it now!

hago I do; I make

hallar [a-**yar**] to find

hamaca f [a**maka**] hammock

hambre: tengo hambre [**ambreh**] I'm hungry

han they have; you have

haré [a**reh**] I will do

harto full, stuffed

estar harto (de) [deh] to be fed up (with)

es harto difícil [deefee**seel**] it's

very difficult

has you have

hasta even; until

hasta que [keh] until

hasta luego [**lwego**] goodbye, cheerio, see you later

¡hasta mañana! [man-**yana**] see you tomorrow!

¡hasta pronto! see you soon!

hawaiana f [Hawa-**yana**] (Rpl) flip-flop

hay [i] there is; there are

haz [as] do; make

¡hazlo tú! you do it!

he [eh] I have

hecho (m) made; done; fact

hecho a la medida made-to- measure

helada f frost

heladera f [elad**aira**] (Rpl) fridge

heladería f [eladair**ee**-a] ice- cream parlour

helado m ice cream

helar to freeze

hembra f female

hemos we have

henequén m [ene**ken**] (Mex) sisal-type fibre from the henequen plant, used for making rope and fabrics

herida f [ai**reeda**] wound

herido injured

hermana f [air**mana**] sister

hermano m [air**mano**] brother

hermoso [air**moso**] beautiful

herramientas fpl [airram-**yentas**] tools

hervir [air**beer**] to boil

hice [**eeseh**] I made; I did

hidratante: crema hidratante f [eedra**tan**teh] moisturizer
hielo m [**ye**lo] ice
hierba f [**yair**ba] grass
hierro m [**yai**rro] iron
hija f [**ee**Ha] daughter
hijo m [**ee**Ho] son
¡hijo de la chingada! son of a bitch!
¡híjole! [**ee**Holeh] (Mex) hell!, damn!
hilo m thread
hipermercado [eepairmair**ka**do] hypermarket
hipo m hiccups
hipódromo m horse-racing track
historia f [ees**tor**-ya] history; story
hizo [**ee**so] he/she made; he/she did; you made; you did
hogar m home; household goods
hoja f [**o**Ha] leaf; sheet of paper
hoja de afeitar [deh afay**tar**] razor blade
hojalata f [oHa**la**ta] tin plate
¡hola! hello!, hi!
hombre m [**om**breh] man
hombre de negocios [deh ne**gos**-yos] businessman
hombro m shoulder
hondo deep
hondureño (m) [ondoo**ren**-yo] Honduran
honrado honest
hora f hour
 ¿qué hora es/qué hora tiene/

me da su hora? what time is it?
hora local local time
horario m [o**rar**-yo] timetable, (US) schedule
horario de autobuses [deh owto**boo**s-es] bus timetable/schedule
horario de invierno [eemb**yair**no] winter timetable/schedule
horario de recogidas [reko**Hee**das] collection times
horario de trenes [**tren**-es] train timetable/schedule
horario de verano [**bai**rano] summer timetable/schedule
horas de consulta surgery hours, (US) office hours
horas de oficina [ofee**see**na] opening hours
horas de visita [bee**see**ta] visiting hours
horas pico rush hour
horma de queso f (Arg) a cheese
hormiga f ant
horno m oven
horquilla m [or**kee**-ya] hairslide, hairpin
hospedarse [ospe**dar**seh] to stay
hotel-garaje m [–gara**Heh**] (Mex) hotel where rooms are rented by the hour
hoy [oy] today
hoyo m [**o**-yo] hole
huaraches mpl [wa**rach**-es] (Mex) leather sandals

h is not pronounced in Spanish

hube [**oo**beh] I had

hubieron [oob-**yai**ron] they had; you had

hubimos [oob**ee**mos] we had

hubiste [oob**ee**steh] you had

hubo [**oo**bo] he/she/it had; you had; there was/were

húbole: ¿qué húbole? [keh **oo**boleh] (Mex) how's it going?

hueco m [**we**ko] (Guat) poof; hole

huele: huele a ... [**we**leh] it smells of ...

huelga f [**wel**ga] strike

huella f [**we**ya] print; trace

huellas digitales [dee**Hee**tal-es] fingerprints

hueso m [**we**so] bone; stone (of fruit etc)

huésped m/f [**we**sped] guest

huevo poché m (Rpl) poached egg

huillo [**wee**-yo] (Salv) weird

huipil m [wee**pee**l] (Mex) short, embroidered blouse

huiuncha f [wee-**oo**ncha] (Bol, Ch, Pe) hair band

hule m [**oo**leh] (Mex) rubber

humedad f [**oo**me**da**] humidity, dampness

húmedo damp

humo m smoke

humor m humour

hundirse [**oo**nd**eer**seh] to sink

huracán m hurricane

Hu

I

idéntico (a/que) [keh] identical (to)

idioma m [eed-**yo**ma] language

idiota m/f [eed-**yo**ta] idiot

iglesia f [ee**gles**-ya] church

ignorar: ignoro si ... I don't know whether ...

igual [ee**gwal**] equal; like

me da igual [meh] it's all the same to me

imbécil (m) [eemb**eseel**] idiot; stupid

impaciente [eempas-**yen**teh] impatient

impactante [eempakt**an**teh] striking; shocking

impermeable (m) [eempairmeh-**ableh**] waterproof; raincoat

importación f [eemportas-**yon**] import; importing

artículos de importación imported goods

importante [eemport**an**teh] important

importar: no importa it doesn't matter

¿le importa si ...? [leh] do you mind if ...?

importe m [eem**por**teh] amount, sum

importe total total due

imposible [eempos**ee**bleh] impossible

impreso m [eem**pre**so] form

impuesto m [eem**pwe**sto] tax

incendiar [eensend-**yar**] to set

fire to

incendio m [eensend-yo] fire
(blaze)

incluido [eenkloo-**ee**do]
included

incluso even

inconsciente [eenkons-**y**enteh]
unconscious; unaware

increíble [eenkreh-**ee**bleh]
incredible

indemnizar [eendemneesar] to
compensate

independiente [eendepend-
yenteh] independent

indicaciones fpl [eendeekas-yon-
es] instructions

indicador m indicator

indicador de nivel [deh neebel]
gauge

indicar to indicate

indígena (m/f) [eendee**H**ena]
Indian; native inhabitant

indignado indignant

indispuesto [eendeespwesto]
unwell

industria f industry; factory

infantil children's

infarto m heart attack

infección f [eenfeks-yon]
infection

infectarse [eenfektarseh] to
become infected

inflamado swollen

inflamarse [eenflamarseh] to
swell

influenciar [eenflwens-yar] to
influence

información f [eenformas-yon]
information

información de vuelos flight
information

información turística tourist
information

información y turismo tourist
information office

informar to inform

informarse (de/sobre)
[–marseh (deh/sobreh)] to get
information (on/about)

informe m [in**f**ormeh] report

infracción f [eenfraks-yon]
offence

ingeniero m [eenHen-ya**i**ro]
engineer

Inglaterra f [eenglata**i**rra]
England

inglés (m) [eeng-les] English;
Englishman

inglesa f Englishwoman

ingresar to enter

ingreso m [eengreso] income;
entry

ingresos mpl income;
deposits

ingüeroviable [eengwairob-
yableh] (Parag) incredible

iniciales fpl [eenees-yal-es]
initials

inmediatamente [eenmed-
yatamenteh] immediately

inocente [eenosenteh] innocent

inscribirse [–be**e**rseh] to
register, to enrol

insistir to insist

insolación f [eensolas-yon]
sunstroke

instrucciones fpl [eenstrooks-
yon-es] instructions

In

instrucciones de lavado
washing instructions
íntegro [**ee**ntegro] complete;
intact
inteligente [eenteleeHenteh]
intelligent
intentar to try
interés m [eentair-es] interest
interesante [eentairesanteh]
interesting
intereses mpl [eentaires-es]
interest
interino: en el interino
[eentair**ee**no] meanwhile
interior (m) [eentairee-**or**]
interior, inner; domestic,
home
interiores mpl [eentairee-or-es]
(Col, Ven) underpants
intermedio (m) [eentairmed-
yo] intermission, interval;
intermediate
intermitente m [eentairmeetenteh]
indicator
interno m (Rpl) extension
intérprete m/f [eentairpreteh]
interpreter
interruptor m [eentairrooptor]
switch
interurbano long-distance
intoxicación alimenticia f
[eentokseekas-yon aleementees-
ya] food poisoning
introduzca el dinero exacto
insert exact amount
introduzca la tarjeta y marque
insert card and dial
introduzca moneda insert
coin

inundación f [eenoondas-yon]
flood
inundar to flood
inútil useless, pointless
inversión f [eenbairs-yon]
investment
invierno m [eemb-yairno] winter
invitada f [eembeetada], **invitado
m** guest
invitar [eembeetar] to invite
inyección f [een-yeks-yon]
injection
ir [eer] to go
ir de paseo [deh paseh-o] to go
for a walk
Irlanda f [eerlanda] Ireland
Irlanda del Norte [norteh]
Northern Ireland
irlandés (m) [eerland-es] Irish;
Irishman
irlandesa f Irishwoman
irse [**ee**rseh] to leave, to go
away
isla f [**ee**sla] island
itinerario m [eeteenairar-yo]
itinerary
**IVA (impuesto sobre el valor
añadido)** [**ee**ba] VAT
izq. (izquierda) left
izquierda f [eesk-y**ai**rda] left
a la izquierda (de) [deh] on
the left (of)

J

jabón m [Habon] soap
jabón de afeitar [deh afaytar]
shaving soap

jacal m [Hakal] (Mex) straw hut; shack

jacha f [Hacha] (CR) face

jaiba f [Hiba] crab

jalar [Halar] to pull

jama f [Hama] (Cu) food

jamaiquino [Hamī-keeno] Jamaican

jamás [Hamas] ever; never

jardín m [Hardeen] garden

jardín de niños [deh neen-yos] kindergarten

jardines públicos mpl [Hardeenes] park, public gardens

jarra f [Harra] jug

jarrón m [Harron] vase

jayán [Ha-yan] (Nic) rude

jeba f [Heba] (Ven) girl

jebo m [Hebo] (Arg) boyfriend

jefe m [Hefeh] boss; chief

jefe de tren [deh] guard

jején m [HeHen] mosquito

jícara f [Heekara] (Mex) gourd

jinetera f [Heenetaira] (Cu) prostitute

jocho [Hocho] (Hond) toothless

joder [Hodair] to irritate, to annoy; to mess about; to screw up

¡lo jodiste! [Hodeesteh] you screwed up!

jodido [Hodeedo] annoying, a nuisance; knackered

jogging m [yogeen] (Rpl) tracksuit, (US) sweats

jojote m [HoHoto] (Ven) sweetcorn

jornada f [Hornada] working day

jorongo m [Horongo] (Mex) poncho

joven (m/f) [Hoben] young; young man; young woman

joyas fpl [Hoyas] jewellery

joyería f [Hoyairee-a] jewellery; jeweller's

jubilación f [Hoobeelas-yon] pension

jubilada f [Hoobeelada], **jubilado m** retired person, pensioner

jubilarse [Hoobeelarseh] to retire

juca f [Hooka] (Hond) beer

juda m [Hooda] (Ec) plainclothes policeman

judío [Hoodee-o] Jewish

juego (m) [Hwego] game; I play

el juego gambling

juerga f [Hwairga] partying

jueves m [Hweb-es] Thursday

jugar [Hoogar] to play

juguera f [Hoogaira] (Ch, Rpl) juicer; blender

juguete m [Hoogeteh] toy

juguetería f [Hoogetairee-a] toyshop

juicio m [Hwees-yo] judgement; opinion; trial

llevar una persona a juicio to take someone to court

julepe m [Hoolepeh] (Parag) fright

julio m [Hool-yo] July

jumarse [Hoomarseh] (CR) to get drunk

junio m [Hoon-yo] June

juntar [Hoontar] to collect, to gather

junto (a) [Hoonto] next (to)

juntos together

justo [Hoosto] just; exact, precise

juventud f [Hoobentoo] youth; the young

juzgar [Hoosgar] to judge

K

kínder m [keendair] kindergarten

klaxon m [klakson] (Mex) horn

L

la the; her; it

labios mpl [lab-yos] lips

laborables weekdays, working days

laburante m [labooranteh] (Rpl) worker

laburo m (CSur) work

laca f hair spray

Ladatel (Mex) long-distance phone

lado m side

al lado de [deh] beside, next to

ladrar to bark

ladridos mpl barking

ladrillo m [ladree-yo] tile; brick; (Salv) thief

ladrón m thief

lagartija f [lagarteeHa] lizard

lagarto m alligator; (Cu) litre of beer

lago m lake

lágrimas fpl tears

lama f (Mex) moth

lámpara f lamp

lamparoso (Ec) lying

lana f wool; (CAm, Mex) money

lana pura pure wool

lanzar [lansar] to throw

lapicera fuente f (CSur) fountain pen

lápiz de ojos [deh oHos] eyeliner

lápiz de pasta m (Ch) biro®, ball point

lápiz m [lapees] pencil

lapizlabios m [lapees-lab-yos] (Mex) lipstick

larga distancia [deestans-ya] long-distance

largavistas m [largabeestas] (Rpl) binoculars

largo (m) length; long

a lo largo de [deh] along

¡lárguese! [largeseh] go away!

las the; them; you

las que ... the ones that ...

lata f tin; can

dar lata to be a nuisance

latinoamericana (f), latinoamericano (m) Latin American

latón m brass

lavabo m [lababo] washbasin

lavado m [labado] washing

lavado de carros [deh] carwash

lavadora f [labadora] washing machine

lavandería f [labandairee-a]
laundry
lavandería automática
[owtomateeka] launderette,
(US) laundromat
lavandina f (Arg) bleach
lavaplatos mpl (Andes, Mex) sink
lavar [labar] to wash
lavar a mano wash by hand
lavar en seco dry clean
lavar la ropa to do the
washing
lavar separado wash
separately
lavarse [labarseh] to wash
  lavarse la cara to wash one's
  face
lavavajillas m [lababaнee-yas]
dishwasher
laxante m [laksanteh] laxative
le [leh] him; her; you
lección f [leks-yon] lesson
leche limpiadora f [leemp-
yadora] skin cleanser
lechería f [lechairee-a] (Mex)
dairy; dairy shop
lechero m (Col, Pe) lucky so-
and-so, lucky bastard
lectura f [lektoora] reading
leer [leh-air] to read
lejano [leh-нano] distant,
faraway
lejía f [leнee-a] (Mex) bleach
lejos [leнos] far away
  lejos de [deh] far from
lengua f [lengwa] tongue;
language
lenguaje m [lengwaнeh]
language

lentes de contacto fpl [lent-es
deh] contact lenses
lentillas fpl [lentee-yas] (Mex)
contact lenses
lento slow
les them; you
letra f letter; banker's draft
levantar [lebantar] to raise, to
lift; to pick up, to pull
levantarse [lebantarseh] to
get up
ley f [lay] law
libra f pound
libre [leebreh] free; vacant
libre de impuestos [deh
eempwestos] duty-free
librería f [leebrairee-a]
bookshop, bookstore
librero m [leebrairo] (Mex)
bookshelves; bookseller
libreta f [leebreta] (Rpl) cheque-
book; (Urug) driving licence
libreta de ahorros f [deh a-orros]
savings account book
libreta de direcciones [deereeks-
yon-es] address book
libretista m scriptwriter
libreto m script
libro m book
libro de bolsillo [deh bolsee-yo]
paperback
libro de frases [fras-es]
phrasebook
lica f (Salv) movie
licencia f driving licence
licenciado m [leesens-yado]
graduate
líder m [leedair] leader
liga f elastic band; suspender

ligero [leeHairo] light

lima de uñas f [deh oon-yas] nailfile

límite f [leemeeteh] limit

límite de altura maximum height

límite de peso weight limit

límite de velocidad [deh beloseedad] speed limit

limpiaparabrisas m [–breeas] windscreen wiper, (US) windshield wiper

limpiar [leemp-yar] to clean

limpieza f [leemp-yesa] cleanliness; cleaning

limpieza en seco dry-cleaning

limpio [leemp-yo] clean

limpión m (Col) dishcloth, tea towel

lindo [leendo] beautiful, lovely

línea f [leeneh-a] line

linterna f [leentairna] torch, (US) flashlight

lío m [lee-o] mess

liquidación f [leekeedas-yon] sale; redundancy pay

liquidación total clearance sale

liso flat; plain; straight; (Hond) penniless

lista f list

lista de correos [deh korreh-os] poste restante, (US) general delivery

lista de espera [espaira] standby; waiting list

listo clever; ready

litera f [leetaira] (Mex) couchette

litro m litre

llamada f [yamada] call

llamada por cobrar reverse charge call

llamar [yamar] to call; to name

llamar por teléfono to call, to phone

llamarse [yamarseh] to be called

¿cómo te llamas? [teh yamas] what's your name?

llame a la puerta please knock

llame al timbre please ring

llame antes de entrar knock before entering

llamo: me llamo ... [meh yamo] my name is ...

llanos mpl [yanos] plains

llanta f [yanta] tyre, (US) tire

llantero m [yantairo] (Mex) tyre repairs

llave f [yabeh] key; spanner, (US) wrench; tap, (US) faucet

llave inglesa [eenglesa] spanner, (US) wrench

llegada f [yegada] arrival

llegadas internacionales [eentairnas-yonal-es] international arrivals

llegadas nacionales [nas-yonal-es] domestic arrivals

llegar [yegar] to arrive; to get to

llegué [yegeh] I arrived

llenar [yenar] to fill

llenar el depósito to fill up

lleno [yeno] full

llevar [yebar] to carry; to take; to bring

llevo dos años trabajando aquí I've been working here for two years

llevar a juicio [Hwees-yo] to take to court

llevarse [yebarseh] to take away; to remove

llorar [yorar] to cry

llover [yobair] to rain

lloviendo: está lloviendo [yob-yendo] it's raining

llovizna f [yobeesna] drizzle

llueve [yweh-beh] it's raining

lluvia f [yoob-ya] rain

lo it; the

en lo de Juan at Juan's (place)

localidad f [lokaleeda] place; seat

localidades fpl [lokaleedad-es] ticket office

localizador m pager

loción antimosquitos f [los-yon anteemoskeetos] insect repellent

loción bronceadora [bronseh-adora] suntan lotion

loción para después del afeitado [despwes del afaytado] aftershave

loco (m) mad; madman

locomotora f engine

locutor m [lokootor]**, locutora f** television presenter

lodo m mud

loma f hill

lonchería f (Mex) lunch counter

Londres [lond-res] London

longitud f [lonHeetoo] length

los the

los que ... the ones that ...

loza f [losa] crockery

luces de cruce [loos-es deh krooseh] dipped headlights

prender luces de cruce switch headlights on

luces de posición fpl [posees-yon] sidelights

luces traseras [trasairas] rear lights

lucha f [loocha] fight, struggle

lucha libre [leebreh] all-in wrestling

luchar to fight

luego [lwego] then; afterwards; soon

luego luego right away, immediately

lugar m place

en lugar de [deh] instead of

lugar de veraneo [bairaneh-o] summer resort

lugares de interés [loogar-es deh eentair-es] places of interest

lujo m [looHo] luxury

lujoso [looHoso] luxurious

luna f moon

lunes m [loon-es] Monday

luto m mourning

luz f [loos] light

luz de carretera full beam

M

M.N. (moneda nacional) f national currency

macanudo (CSur) great

machista m male chauvinist, sexist

macho m male; large banana**

macizo [maseeso] solid; (Hond) great

madera f [madaira] wood

madrazo m [madraso] beating

madre f [madreh] mother
  dar en la madre a uno to give someone a good beating
  ¡me vale madre! [meh baleh] I don't give a shit!

madrear [madreh-ar] (Mex) to beat up; (Col) to swear

madrina f [madreena] godmother

madrugada f small hours
  las cuatro de la madrugada four o'clock in the morning

madrugador m someone who stays up very late/gets up very early, early riser

madrugar to stay up very late; to get up very early

madurar to mature, to ripen; to come to term

maduro ripe

maestra f [ma-estra], **maestro** m teacher; primary school teacher

magna sin [seen] (Mex) unleaded

maguey m [magay] (Mex) agave cactus

maíz m [ma-ees] maize, (US) corn

maje [maHeh] (Salv) stupid

mal (m) wrong; evil; bad; badly

mal de alturas altitude sickness

mal genio m [Hen-yo] bad temper

mal humor m [oomor] bad mood; bad temper; anger

malagua f [malagwa] (Pe) jellyfish

malandro m (Ven) criminal

maleado [maleh-ado] (Hond) furious

maleducado rude

malentendido m misunderstanding

maleta f suitcase; (Ch, Pe) boot, (US) trunk
  hacer las maletas to pack

maletero m [maletairo] boot (of car), (US) trunk

malinchismo m (Mex) betrayal of one's country

malo bad; sick, ill, unwell

maluco (Col, Cu, Ven) to be poorly

mamá f mum

mamadera f (CSur, Pe) baby's bottle

mameluco m (CSur) overalls

mamera: tengo una mamera horrible (Col) I feel terribly lazy

mamila f (Mex) baby's bottle

mamo m (Hond) jail

mamón! (Mex) idiot!

mamplora (Nic) poofy

manantial m [manant-yal] spring

mancha f stain

manchar to stain, to dirty

mandadero m [mandadairo] (Rpl) errand boy

mandar to send; to order

mandatario: el primer mandatario [mandatar-yo] leader; President; Prime Minister

mandato m period in government

¿mande? [mandeh] (Mex) sorry?, pardon (me)?

mandíbula f jaw

manejar [maneHar] to drive

maneje con cuidado drive with care

manejo [maneHo] I drive

manera: de esta manera [deh – manaira] in this way

de manera que so (that)

manga f sleeve

sin manga sleeveless

manglar m mangrove swamp

mango m handle; mango

manifestación f [maneefestas-yon] demonstration; manifestation

manija f [maneeHa] crank

dar manija (Rpl) to encourage

mano f hand; pal, mate, buddy

manopla f flannel

manoplas fpl (Mex) mittens

manta f blanket, rug

mantel m tablecloth

mantelerías fpl [mantelairee-as] table linen

mantenga limpia la ciudad keep our city tidy

manténgase en lugar fresco store in a cool place

manténgase fuera del alcance de los niños keep out of the reach of children

mantenimiento m [manteneem-yento] maintenance

manubrio m [manoobr-yo] handlebars

manzana f [mansana] apple; city block

mañana (f) [man-yana] morning; tomorrow

por la mañana/de mañana in the morning

¡hasta mañana! see you tomorrow!

pasado mañana the day after tomorrow

mañana por la mañana tomorrow morning

mañana por la tarde [tardeh] tomorrow afternoon; tomorrow evening

mañanitas: cantar las mañanitas a alguien [man-yaneetas] (Mex) to serenade someone on his/her birthday

mapa m map

mapa de carreteras [deh karretairas] road map

mapa de recorrido network map

maquillaje m [makee-yaHeh] make-up

maquillarse [makee-yarseh] to put one's make-up on

máquina de afeitar eléctrica f [makeena deh afaytar] electric shaver

máquina de escribir typewriter

Ma

Ma

máquina de fotos camera

máquina tragaperras slot machine

maquinaria f [makeenar-ya] machinery

maquinilla de afeitar f [makeenee-ya deh afaytar] electric shaver

mar m sea

maravilloso [marabee-yoso] marvellous

marca registrada f [reHeestrada] registered trade mark

marcador m (SAm) felt-tip pen

marcar to dial; to mark

marcar el número dial the number

marcha f gear

marcha atrás reverse gear

marcharse [marcharseh] to go away

marea f [mareh-a] tide

mareado [mareh-ado] dizzy; sick; drunk

mareo m [mareh-o] sickness; faintness

marica m gay

marica m, maricón m poof

marido m husband

marina f navy

mariposa f butterfly; fairy, pansy

mariposo m gay

marisquería f [mareeskairee-a] shellfish restaurant

marque ... dial ...

martes m [mart-es] Tuesday

martes de carnaval [deh karnabal] Shrove Tuesday, (US) Mardi Gras

martillo m [martee-yo] hammer

marzo m [marso] March

más more

más de/que [deh/keh] more than

más pequeño smaller

el más caro the most expensive

ya no más that's enough

más o menos more or less

matar to kill

mate m [mateh] (Rpl) bitter tea

matraca f (Ven) bribe

matrícula f licence plate; registration; registration fees

maule [mowleh] (Hond) clumsy

máximo personas maximum number of people

maya (m/f) [ma-ya] Maya; Mayan

mayo m [ma-yo] May

mayor [ma-yor] adult; bigger; older; biggest; oldest

la mayor parte (de) [parteh (deh)] most (of)

mayor de edad of age, adult

mayoría: la mayoría [ma-yoree-a] most; the majority

mazucho [masoocho] (Salv) skilful

me me; myself

me duele aquí [dweleh] I have a pain here

mecánico m mechanic

mecate m [mekateh] (Mex) string; rope; cord

media docena (de) f [med-ya dosena (deh)] half a dozen

media hora f [**o**ra] half an hour

media pensión f [pens-**yon**] half board

mediano [med-**ya**no] medium; average

medianoche f [med-yan**o**cheh] midnight

medias fpl [med-yas] stockings; tights, pantyhose

  ir/pagar a medias to go Dutch, to share the costs

medias bombacha fpl (Rpl) pantyhose, tights

medias pantalón fpl (Col) pantyhose, tights

medias panty fpl (Ven) pantyhose, tights

medicina f [medee**see**na] medicine

médico m [**me**deeko] doctor

médico general [Hen**ai**ral] GP

medida f size; measure

medida del cuello f [kw**eh**-yo] collar size

medio m [med-yo] middle

  por medio de [deh] by (means of)

  de tamaño medio [tam**a**n-yo] medium-sized

medio boleto m half fare

medio litro m half a litre

mediodía m [med-yod**ee**-a] midday

medir to measure

medusa f jellyfish

mejor [me**Hor**] better; best

mejorar [me**Hor**ar] to improve

  se está mejorando [seh] he's getting better

mencionar [mens-yon**ar**] to mention

menor smaller; younger; smallest; youngest

menor de edad minor, under-age

menos less; least; fewer; fewest

  a menos que [keh] unless

  echo de menos a mi ... [deh] I miss my ...

mensual [mens**wal**] monthly

mentar: mentarle la madre a alguien [ment**ar**leh la m**a**dreh] to insult someone, to swear at someone

menú turístico m set menu

menudo (Mex) tiny, minute

  a menudo often

mercado m [mair**ka**do] market

mercado cubierto [koob-**yair**to] indoor market

mercado de divisas [deh deeb**ee**sas] exchange rates

mercería f [mairsair**ee**-a] haberdashery; (Ch) hardware store

merendar (Mex) to have an afternoon snack

merendero m [mairend**air**o] (Mex) open-air café

merienda f [mair-**yen**da] (Mex) tea, afternoon snack

mero [m**ai**ro] (Mex) exact; almost, nearly

  ya mero (Mex) any minute now, right away

el mero mero (Mex) the big cheese

está aquí mero (Mex) it's just near here

mersa (Rpl) tacky

mes m month

mesa f table

mesera f [mesaira] waitress; chambermaid

mesero m waiter

mesón m restaurant specializing in regional dishes; (Andes) worktop

mesonera f (Ven) waitress

mestizo [mesteeso] mixed race, interracial

meta f goal

metate m [metateh] (Mex) mortar and pestle

metiche [meteecheh] nosy

metro m metre; underground, (US) subway

mexicana (f), [meнeekana] **mexicano** (m) Mexican

México m [meнeeko] Mexico; Mexico City

mezquita f [meskeeta] mosque

mi my

mí me

mía [mee-a] mine

micro m (Ch) bus

microondas: horno microondas [orno meekro-ondas] microwave oven

miedo m [m-yedo] fear

tengo miedo (de/a) [deh] I'm afraid (of)

miel f [m-yel] honey

mientras [m-yentras] while

mientras que [keh] whereas

mientras tanto meanwhile

miércoles m [m-yairkol-es] Wednesday

miércoles de ceniza [deh seneesa] Ash Wednesday

¡mierda! [m-yairda] shit!

migra f (Mex) immigration police

mil [meel] thousand

militar m soldier, serviceman

millón m [mee-yon] million

un millón de ... [deh] a million ...

milpa f (Mex) maize field

mina f mine; (Arg) girl

minifalda f mini-skirt

minúsculo tiny

minusválido (m) [meenoosbaleedo] disabled; disabled person

minuto m minute

mío [mee-o] mine

miope [m-yopeh] short-sighted

mirador m scenic view; vantage point

mirar to look (at); to see

mis my

misa f mass

mismo same

mitad f [meeta] half

mitad de precio [deh pres-yo] half price

mochila f rucksack, backpack

mochilero m backpacker

moda f fashion

de moda fashionable

moda juvenil [Hoobeneel] young fashions

modas caballeros fpl [kaba-yairos] men's fashions

modas niños/niñas [neen-yos] children's fashions

modas pre-mamá (Mex) maternity fashions

modas señora [sen-yora] ladies' fashions

modelo m model; design; style

moderno [modairno] modern

modista f dressmaker; fashion designer

modisto m fashion designer

modo: de modo que [deh – keh] so (that)

ni modo that's how it is, what can you do?

modo de empleo instructions for use

mofle m [mofleh] (CAm) exhaust

mojado [moHado] wet

molcajete m [molkaHeteh] (Mex) mortar and pestle

molestar to disturb; to bother

molesto annoying

monasterio m [monastair-yo] monastery

moneda nacional f [nas-yonal] national currency

monedas fpl coins

monedero m [monedairo] purse

monitorear [moneetoreh-ar] to monitor

monitoreo m monitoring

mono (m) (Col) blond; monkey

monoambiente m [mono-amb-yenteh] (Arg) studio flat

monopatín m (Rpl) scooter

montacargas m service lift, service elevator

montaje m [montaHeh] assembly

montaña f [montan-ya] mountain

montaña rusa f big dipper, roller coaster

montañismo m [montan-yeesmo] climbing

montar to get in; to ride; to assemble

montar a caballo [kaba-yo] to go horse-riding

montar en bicicleta [beeseekleta] to cycle

morado purple; (Ven) bruise

morbo m morbid interest

mordedura f bite

morder [mordair] to bite

mordida f bribe

moreno dark-haired; dark-skinned

moretón m bruise

morfar (Rpl) eat

morir to die

moropo m (Cu) head

morral m (Col, Ven) rucksack

mosca f fly; (Andes) alert

mostrador m counter; check-in desk; (Rpl) worktop

mostrar to show

motel-garaje m [garaHeh] (Mex) hotel where rooms are rented by the hour

moto f motorbike

motora f motorboat

mover [mobair] to move

mucha [**moo**cha] much; a lot;
a lot of

muchacha f girl

muchacho m boy

muchas a lot; a lot of; many
muchas gracias [gras-yas]
thank you very much
muchísimas gracias thank
you very much indeed

muchísimo enormously, a
great deal

mucho [**moo**cho] much; a lot;
a lot of
mucho más a lot more
mucho menos a lot less
mucho gusto a pleasure to
meet you
muchos a lot; a lot of; many

muebles mpl [**mwebl**-es]
furniture

muela f [**mwela**] tooth
sacarse una muela [sa**karseh**]
to have a tooth out

muela del juicio [Hwees-yo]
wisdom tooth

muelle m [**mweh**-yeh] spring;
quay

muerte f [**mwairteh**] death

muerto (m) [**mwairto**] dead;
dead person

mugriento [moogr-**yento**] filthy

mujer f [moo**Hair**] woman; wife

mula f drug courier

muletas fpl crutches

mulita f (Rpl) armadillo

multa f fine; parking ticket
multa por uso indebido
penalty for misuse

multifamiliar m block of flats,

apartment block

mundo m world

muñeca f [moon-**yeka**] wrist;
doll

muro m wall

músculo m muscle

museo m [moo**seh**-o] museum

museo de arte [deh **arteh**] art
gallery

música f music

muslo m thigh

musulmán Muslim

muy [mwee] very
muy bien [b-yen] very well

N

N$ m (Mex) new peso

na (Parag) please

nabo (Rpl) stupid, dumb

nácar m mother-of-pearl

nacer [na**sair**] to be born

nacido [na**seedo**] born

nacimiento m [naseem-**yento**]
birth; Nativity

nacional [nas-yo**nal**] domestic
el turismo nacional local
tourism

nacionalidad f [nas-yonal**eeda**]
nationality

nacionalismo m [nas-
yonal**eesmo**] nationalism

nacionalización f [nas-
yonaleesas-**yon**] nationalization

nada nothing
de nada [deh] you're
welcome, don't mention it
antes que nada [ant-es keh]

first of all
nada que declarar nothing to declare
nadar to swim
nadie [nad-yeh] nobody
nafta f (Rpl) petrol, (US) gasoline
nagüilón [nagweelon] (Guat) cowardly
náhuatl (m) [nawatl] Aztec; language of the Aztecs
narcotraficante m/f [–kanteh] drug trafficker
narcotráfico m drug trade, drug traffic
nariz f [narees] nose
natación f [natas-yon] swimming
natural [natooral] natural
al natural at room temperature
naturaleza f [natooralesa] nature
naturalmente [–menteh] naturally; of course
náusea: siento náuseas [s-yento nowseh-as] I feel sick
navaja f [nabaHa] penknife; flick knife
Navidad f [nabeeda] Christmas
¡feliz Navidad! [felees] merry Christmas!
neblina f mist
necesario [nesesar-yo] necessary
necesitar [neseseetar] to need
negar to deny
negativa f [negateeba] denial; refusal
negativo m negative

negocio m [negos-yo] business
negro (m) black; furious; black man
nena f baby girl; little girl; (Col) bird, chick
nene m [neneh] baby boy; little boy
nervioso [nairb-yoso] nervous
me pone nervioso [meh poneh] it makes me nervous
neurótico [neh-ooroteeko] neurotic
nevar [nebar] to snow
nevera f [nebaira] (SAm) fridge
nevería f [neberee-a] (Mex) ice cream parlour
ni neither; nor
ni ... ni ... neither ... nor ...
nica m/f Nigaraguan
nicaragüense (m/f) [neekaragwenseh] Nicaraguan
niebla f [n-yebla] fog
nieta f [n-yeta] granddaughter
nieto m [n-yeto] grandson
nieva [n-yeba] it's snowing
nieve f [n-yebeh] snow; ice cream; sorbet
ningún none; not one; no ...
en ningún sitio [seet-yo] nowhere
ninguno nobody; none; not one
niña f [neen-ya] child
niñera f [neen-yaira] nanny
niño m [neen-yo] child
nítido [neeteedo] (Pan) fun, enjoyable
nivel del aceite m [neebel del asayteh] oil level

no no; not
no contiene alcohol does not contain alcohol
no estacionarse no parking
no estacionarse, se usa grúa illegally parked vehicles will be towed away
no exceda la dosis indicada do not exceed the stated dose
no fumadores [foomador-es] no smoking
no fumar no smoking
no funciona [foons-yona] out of order
no hay de qué [ī deh keh] you are welcome
no hay localidades sold out
no molestar do not disturb
no para en ... does not stop in ...
no pisar el pasto keep off the grass
no rebasar no overtaking, no passing
no recomendada para menores de 18 años not recommended for those under 18 years of age
no se admiten devoluciones no refunds given
no se admiten perros no dogs allowed
no ... sino ... not ... but ...
no tocar please do not touch
no utilizar lejía do not bleach
noche f [nocheh] night
de noche at night
buenas noches [bwenas noch-es] good night

esta noche tonight
por la noche at night
pasar la noche to spend the night
Nochebuena f [nocheh-bwena] Christmas Eve
Nochevieja f [nocheh-b-yeHa] New Year's Eve
nocturno [noktoorno] night
nomás just, only
díselo nomás [deeselo] just tell him/her
nombre m [nombreh] name
nombre de pila [deh] first name
nombre de soltera [soltaira] maiden name
nopal m (Mex) cactus leaf
nordeste m [nordesteh] north-east
normal (m) [nor-mal] normal; lower grade petrol, (US) regular (gas)
normalmente [–menteh] usually
noroeste m [noro-esteh] north-west
norte m [norteh] north
al norte de la ciudad [deh la s-yooda] north of the city
norteamericana (f) [norteh-amaireekana], norteamericano (m) North American
norteño [norten-yo] from the north of Mexico
nos us; ourselves
nosotras, nosotros we; us
nota f note
nota de consumo [deh] receipt
noticias fpl [notees-yas] news

noticiero m [notees-**yai**ro] news bulletin

nova f [**no**ba] two-star petrol, (US) regular gas

nova plus four-star petrol, (US) premium gas

novecientos [nobes-**yen**tos] nine hundred

novecito [nobes**ee**to] (Mex) very new

novela f [no**be**la] novel

noveno [no**be**no] ninth

noventa [no**ben**ta] ninety

novia f [**nob**-ya] girlfriend; fiancée; bride

noviembre m [nob-**yem**breh] November

novillada f [nobee-**ya**da] bullfight featuring young bulls

novio m [**nob**-yo] boyfriend; fiancé; groom

Nte. north

nube f [**noo**beh] cloud

nublado cloudy

nuboso cloudy

nuera f [**nwai**ra] daughter-in-law

nuestra [**nwes**tra], **nuestras, nuestro, nuestros** our

Nueva York [**nwe**ba] New York

nueve [**nwe**beh] nine

nuevo [**nwe**bo] new

nuevón (Andes) inexperienced

número m [**noo**mairo] number; size

número de calzado [deh kal**sa**do] shoe size

número de teléfono phone number

nunca never

nutritivo [nootree**tee**bo] nutritious

Ñ

ñampearse [n-yam**peh-ar**seh] (Cu) to die

ñata f nose

ñembotavy: ¡no te hagas el ñembotavy! [n-yembota**bee**] (Parag) don't pretend it's nothing to do with you!

O

o or

o ... o ... either ... or ...

obispo m [o**bees**po] bishop

objeción f [obHes-**yon**] objection

objetar [obHe**tar**] to object

objetivo m [obHe**tee**bo] lens; objective

objetos de escritorio [ob**He**tos deh eskree**tor**-yo] office supplies

objetos perdidos lost property, (US) lost and found

obra f [**ob**ra] work; play

obras fpl roadworks

obrero m [o**brai**ro] worker

obsequio m [ob**sek**-yo] gift

obstruido [obstroo-**ee**do] blocked

obturador m shutter

ocambo m (Cu) elderly person

ocasión f [okas-yon] occasion; opportunity; bargain
de ocasión [deh] second hand
occidental [okseedental] Western
occidente m [okseedenteh] West
Océano Pacífico m [oseh-ano] Pacific Ocean
ochenta eighty
ocho eight
ocho días mpl [dee-as] week
ochocientos [ochos-yentos] eight hundred
ocote m [okoteh] (Mex) resinous pine used for burning
octavo [oktabo] eighth
octubre m [oktoobreh] October
oculista m/f optician
ocultar to hide
oculto hidden
ocupado engaged; occupied; busy
ocupar to occupy
ocurrir [okooreer] to occur, happen
ocurre que [okoorreh keh] it so happens that
odiar [od-yar] to hate
odio (m) [od-yo] hate, hatred; I hate
odioso odious, revolting; horrible
oeste m [o-esteh] west
al oeste de la ciudad [deh la s-yooda] west of the city
ofender [ofendair] to offend
oferta f [ofairta] special offer
oficial (m/f) [ofees-yal] officer; official

oficina f [ofeeseena] office
oficina de correo [deh korreh-os] post office
oficina de correos y telégrafos (Mex) post office and telegrams
oficina de información y turismo [eenformas-yon] tourist information office
oficina de objetos perdidos [obHetos] lost property office, (US) lost and found
oficina de reclamaciones [reklamas-yon-es] (Mex) complaints department
oficina de registros [reHeestros] registrar's office
oficina de turismo tourist information office
oficinista m/f [ofeeseeneesta] office worker
oficio m [ofees-yo] job; trade
ofrecer [ofresair] to offer
oído (m) [o-eedo] ear; hearing; heard
¡oiga! [oyga] listen here!; excuse me!
oigo I am listening
oír [o-eer] to listen
ojo m [oHo] eye
¡ojo! watch out!
ojota f [oHota] (Rpl) flip-flop
ola f wave
ola de calor [deh] heatwave
oler [olair] to smell
olfato m sense of smell
olla: en la olla [oya] (Col) broke, skint
olor m smell

olvidar [olbeedar] to forget
ómnibus m (Cu, Pe, Urug) bus
once [onseh] eleven
ONU f [o eneh oo] UN
operación f [opairas-yon] operation
operadora f operator
operarse [opairarseh] to have an operation
oportunidad f [oportooneeda] chance, opportunity
oposición f [oposees-yon] opposition
óptica f optician's
óptico m optician
optimista optimistic
¡órale! [oraleh] (Mex) go on then!, get on with it!
orden f order, instruction
  a sus órdenes at your service
orden m order
  en orden in order
organización f [organeesas-yon] organization
organizar [organeesar] to organize
orgulloso [orgoo-yoso] proud
oriental east, eastern
orientar to direct, to guide
oriente m [or-yenteh] east
orilla f [oree-ya] shore; side
orita (CAm, Mex) right away
oro m gold
orquesta f [orkesta] orchestra
oscuro dark
oso: hacer el oso to play the fool
Ote. east

otoño m [oton-yo] autumn, (US) fall
otorrinolaringólogo m ear, nose and throat specialist
otra vez [bes] again
otro another (one); other
óvalo m (Pe) roundabout, (US) traffic circle
oveja f [obeHa] sheep
overol m [obairol] overall
oye [o-yeh] he/she listens; you listen; he/she hears; you hear

P

pabellón m [pabeh-yon] (hospital) ward
paca f (CR) police
pacha f (CAm) baby's bottle
pachamanca f (Pe) meat barbecued between two hot stones
pachanga f (Mex) party; partying
paciente m/f [pas-yenteh] patient
paco m (Ch, Col) policeman
padecer [padesair] to suffer
  padecer del corazón [korason] to have a heart condition
padre m [padreh] father
  ¡está padre! (Mex) it's great!
padres mpl [pad-res] parents
padrino m [padreeno] godfather
pagadero [pagadairo] payable
pagar to pay
página f [paHeena] page

páginas amarillas [amaree-yas] yellow pages

pago m payment

país m [pa-ees] country

paisaje m [pīsaнeh] landscape; scenery

paja f [paнa] (CAm) tap, (US) faucet

pájaro m [paнaro] bird; (Cu) gay

pajuerano m [paнwairano] (Rpl) hick

pala f spade

palabra f word

palacio m [palas-yo] palace

Palacio de Justicia [deh ноostees-ya] Law Courts

paladar m (Cu) small restaurant in a private house

palanca f influence

  necesitas tener palanca you need to know an influential person

  palanca de velocidades [beloseedad-es] gear lever, gear shift

palco m box (at theatre)

paleta f ice lolly

paliacate m [pal-yakateh] (Mex) headscarf

palmera f [palmaira] palm tree

palo m stick; tree

paloma (Salv) difficult

palomitas (de maíz) fpl popcorn

palos de golf mpl [deh] golf clubs

pálpito m (SAm) hunch, feeling

palta f [palta] (Bol, CSur, Pe) avocado

paluchero [paloochairo] (Cu) show-off

paludismo m [paloodeesmo] malaria

pana m (Ven) friend, pal

panadería f [panadairee-a] baker's

panal m honeycomb

panameño (m) [panamen-yo] Panamanian

panceta f (Rpl) bacon

pancho m (Rpl) hot dog

pantaletas fpl (Mex, Ven) knickers, panties

pantalla f [panta-ya] screen

pantalón corto m shorts

pantalones mpl [pantalon-es] trousers, (US) pants

patantaco (Guat) clumsy

panteón m [panteh-on] cemetery

pantimedias fpl (Mex) tights, pantyhose

pantis mpl knickers, panties

pants mpl (Mex) tracksuit, (US) sweats

pantufla f slipper

panza f [pansa] belly

pañal m [pan-yal] nappy, (US) diaper

pañuelo m [panwelo] handkerchief; scarf

papa f [papa] potato

papá m dad

papalote m [–loteh] (Mex) kite

Papanicolau m [papaneekolow] smear test

papas chips fpl (Urug) crisps, (US) potato chips

papaya: darle papaya a alguien [papa-ya] (Col) to give someone the opportunity to take advantage of you

ser papaya (Ch) to be a piece of cake

papel m [papel] paper; rôle; (Ch) toilet paper

papel de envolver [deh embolbair] wrapping paper

papel de escribir writing paper

papel de plata (Mex) silver foil

papel sanitario [saneetar-yo] toilet paper

papel tapiz [tapees] wallpaper

papelera f [papelaira] litter; litter bin

papelería f [papelairee-a] stationery, stationer's

paquete m [paketeh] packet; package holiday

paquetería f [paketairee-a] left luggage office, baggage check

par m pair

para for; in order to

cuarto para las tres quarter to three, (US) quarter of three

para que [keh] in order that

para uso del personal staff only

para uso externo not to be taken internally

parabrisas m windscreen, (US) windshield

paracaidismo m [parakïdeesmo] parachuting; squatting

paracaidista m/f parachutist; squatter

parachoques m [parachok-es] bumper, (US) fender

parada f stop

parada de autobús [deh] bus stop

paradero f [paradairo] stop

paraguas m [paragwas] umbrella

parar to stop

pararse to stand (up)

parcela f [parsela] plot (of land)

parcero m [parsairo] (Col) friend, pal

parecer [paresair] to seem; to resemble

parece que sí/no it seems so/not

me parece (que) ... I think (that) ...

parecido [pareseedo] similar

pared f [pareh] wall

pareja f [pareHa] pair; couple; partner

parezco [paresko] I am like

pari f (RD) party

pariente m/f [par-yenteh] relative

parir to give birth

parque m [parkeh] park

parque de atracciones [deh atraks-yon-es] amusement park

parque de bomberos [bombairos] fire station

parque de recreo [rekr**eh**-o] amusement park

parque infantil [eenfant**eel**] children's park

parrilla f [parr**ee**-ya] grill

párroco m parish priest

parte f [p**a**rteh] part

en todas partes [p**a**rt-es] everywhere

en otra parte elsewhere

en alguna parte somewhere

¿de parte de quién? [deh – k-yen] who's calling?

parte m [p**a**rteh] report

participar [parteese**ep**ar] to take part; to inform

particular [parteekool**a**r] private

un particular a private individual

partida f game

partido m match, game; bout; (political) party

partir to cut (into pieces); to leave, to go

a partir de mañana as from tomorrow

parto m birth

parvulario m [parbool**a**ree-o] (Mex) nursery school

pasado last

la semana pasada last week

pasado mañana [man-y**a**na] the day after tomorrow

pasado de moda [deh] out of fashion

pasadores mp (Pe) shoelaces

pasaje m [pas**a**Heh] ticket; fare

pasajero m [pasa**Ha**iro] passenger

pasajeros de tránsito transit passengers

pasaporte m [pasap**o**rteh] passport

pasaportes passport control

pasar to pass; to overtake; to happen

pasar la aduana [ad**wa**na] to go through Customs

pasarlo bien [b-yen] to enjoy oneself

pasatiempo m [pasat-y**e**mpo] hobby

Pascua [p**a**skwa] Easter

pase [p**a**seh] come in

pase m (Col) driving licence

pasear [paseh-**a**r] to go for a walk; to take for a walk

paseo m [pas**eh**-o] walk; drive; ride

paseo de ... ... avenue

pasillo m [pas**ee**-yo] corridor

paso m passage; pass; step

estar de paso [deh] to be passing through

paso a desnivel underpass

paso a nivel level crossing, (US) grade crossing

paso de contador [deh] (metered) unit

paso de peatones [peh-at**o**n-es] pedestrian crossing

paso prohibido no admittance, no entry

paso subterráneo pedestrian underpass

pasó: ¿qué pasó? how's it going?, what's happening?

pasta f (Ch) shoe polish

pasta de dientes f [deh d-yent-es] toothpaste

pastel de queso m (Arg) cheesecake

pastelería f [pastelairee-a] cake shop

pastilla f [pastee-ya] pill, tablet

pastillas para la garganta throat pastilles

pata m (Pe) friend, pal

patatas fritas crisps, (US) potato chips

patente f [patenteh] (CSur) number plate, (US) license plate

patinaje m [pateenaнeh] skating

patinar to skid; to skate

patria f [patree-a] motherland, home country

las fiestas patrias celebration of national independence

patrulla f [patroo-ya] (Andes, Mex) patrol car

patrullero m [patroo-yairo] (Rpl) patrol car

pavada f (Rpl) silly thing to say/do

paz f [pas] peace

PB ground floor, (US) first floor

peatón m [peh-aton] pedestrian

peatón, circula por tu izquierda pedestrians keep to the left

peatonal pedestrian

peatones [peh-aton-es] pedestrians

pebre m [pebreh] (Pan) food

pecado m sin

pecho m chest; breast

pechú [pechoo] (RD) brave

pécora f (Pe) stink of smelly feet

pecoso freckly

pedazo m [pedaso] piece

pediatra m/f [pedee-atra] pediatrician

pedir to order; to ask for

pedir disculpas to apologize

pedir la hora [ora] to ask the time

pedo m trouble

pegar to hit; to stick

no me pega la gana I don't feel like it

pegue m [pegeh] (Nic) work

peinar [paynar] to comb

peinarse [paynarseh] to comb one's hair

peine m [payneh] comb

peineta f (Ch) comb

peinilla f [paynee-ya] comb

pelado (m) cropped; bare, barren; skint, penniless; (CSur) bald guy, baldie

pelapapas m potato peeler

pelea f [peleh-a] fight

peletería f [peletairee-a] furs, furrier

película f film, movie

película de color [deh] colour film

película en versión original [bairs-yon oreeнeenal] film/movie in the original language

peligro m danger

Pe

peligro de incendio danger: fire hazard

peligro deslizamientos slippery road surface

peligroso dangerous

es peligroso asomarse do not lean out

es peligroso bañarse danger: no swimming

pelirrojo [peleerroHo] redheaded

pelo m [peneh] hair

pelón (CAm, Mex) bald

pelota f ball

peluca f wig

peluquera f [pelookaira], **peluquero m** hairdresser

peluquería f [pelookairee-a] hairdresser's

peluquería de caballeros [deh kaba-yairos] gents' hairdresser's

peluquería de señoras [sen-yoras] ladies' salon

pena f sadness, sorrow; (Andes, CAm, Cu, Mex) embarrassment

¡qué pena! [keh] what a pity!

me da mucha pena [meh] I'm very sorry

tener pena [tenair] to be shy, to be embarrassed

penca f (Mex) cactus leaf

pendejada f [pendeHada] (piece of) stupidity

pendejo m [pendeHo] bloody idiot, (US) jerk

pendiente m [pend-yenteh] slope

estar pendiente de [deh] to be waiting for

estar al pendiente de to watch out for

pene m [peneh] penis

penetrar [penetrar] to enter

penicilina f [peneeseeleena] penicillin

penoso (Andes, CAm, Cu, Mex) embarrassing; shy

pensamiento m [pensam-yento] thought

pensar to think

pensión f [pens-yon] guesthouse, boarding house; pension

pensión completa [kompleta] full board

pensionista m [pens-yoneesta] (Mex) old-age pensioner

peña f [pen-ya] rock, boulder; singing club

peón m [peh-on] labourer; pawn

peor [peh-or] worse; worst

pepenar (Mex) to scavenge, to scour rubbish tips

pequeño (m) [peken-yo] small; child

perder [pairdair] to lose

echar a perder to miss

perderse [pairdairseh] to get lost

pérdida f [pairdeeda] loss

perdón [pairdon] sorry, excuse me; pardon, pardon me

perezosa f (Col, Pe) deckchair

perezoso (m) lazy; (Urug) deckchair

perfecto [pairfekto] perfect

perfumería f [pairfoomairee-a]
perfume shop

perilla f [pairee-ya] doorknob

periódico m [pair-yodeeko]
newspaper

periodista m/f [pair-yodeesta]
journalist

período m [pairee-odo] period

perla f [pairla] pearl

permanente m [pairmanenteh]
perm

permiso m [pairmeeso] licence;
permit

 con permiso excuse me, may
I pass?

permitir [pairmeeteer] to allow

pero [pairo] but

perol m (Cu) car

perro m [pairro] dog

perro caliente m [kal-yenteh]
hot dog

persona f [pairsona] person

persona mayor [ma-yor]
elderly person, senior
citizen

pesadilla f [pesadee-ya]
nightmare

pesado heavy; boring,
tedious

pésame: dar el pésame
[pesameh] to offer one's
condolences

pesar: a pesar de que [deh keh]
despite the fact that

 a pesar de in spite of

pesca f fishing

 ir a pescar to go fishing

pescadería f [peskadairee-a]
fishmonger's

pescar to fish; to catch out

pesero m [pesairo] (Mex)
minibus

peso m weight; peso (currency)

peso máximo maximum
weight

peso neto net weight

pestañas fpl [pestan-yas]
eyelashes

pestañina f [pestan-yina] (Col)
mascara

petaca f (Mex) suitcase

petate m [petateh] (Mex) straw
mat

petróleo para lámparas m
[petroleh-o] paraffin oil,
kerosene oil

pez m [pes] fish

pibe m [peebeh] (Rpl) boy

picadura f bite

picante [peekanteh] hot, spicy

picar to sting; to itch

pico: horas pico fpl rush hour

picor m itch

picoso [peekoso] (Mex) hot

pidió [peed-yo] he/she asked
for; you asked for

pie m [p-yeh] foot

 a pie on foot

piedra f [p-yedra] stone

piedra preciosa [pres-yosa]
precious stone

piel f [p-yel] skin

pienso [p-yenso] I think

pierna f [p-yairna] leg

pijalío m [peeHalee-o] (Hond)
remote place, back of
beyond

pijama m [peeHama] pyjamas

pijinear [peeHeeneh-**ar**] (Hond) to party

pila f battery

píldora f pill

pileta f (Rpl) swimming pool; sink

pileta cubierta f (Rpl) indoor swimming pool

pileta infantil f (Rpl) children's pool

pilinqui [peel**een**kee] (Pan) stingy

pilocho (Salv) naked

piloto m pilot

pilotos mpl rear lights

pimentón m [peement**on**] (SAm not Rpl) pepper

pincel m [peen**sel**] paint brush

pinchar puncture; (Cu) to work

pinchazo m [peen**cha**so] puncture

pinche [**peen**cheh] (Mex) bloody; lousy

pintada f graffiti

pintar to paint

pintura f painting; paint

pinzas fpl [**peen**sas] tweezers

piña f [**peen**-ya] pineapple

piola (Rpl) great, fun

pipa f pipe

piquete [peek**eteh**] (Col) picnic

piragua f [peer**agwa**] canoe

piragüismo m [peeragw**eesmo**] canoeing

pirámide f [peer**ameedeh**] pyramid

pirulo m (Parag) year

piscina f [pees**eena**] swimming pool

piscina cubierta [koob-y**airta**] indoor swimming pool

piscina infantil children's pool

piso m floor

pista f track; clue

pista de baile [deh b**īleh**] dance floor

pista de tenis tennis court

pisto m (Salv) money

pistola f gun

pituco (CSur) posh

placa f [**plaka**] number plate, (US) license plate

placa de dientes (Ch) dentures

plancha f iron

planchado (Ch) broke, skint; (Rpl) shattered

planchar to iron

planear [plan**eh-ar**], planificar [planeefeek**ar**] to plan

planilla f [plan**ee**-ya] form

plano (m) flat; map

planta f plant; floor

planta baja [b**aHa**] ground floor, (US) first floor

plástico (m) plastic

plata f silver; money, (US) dough

plateado [plateh-**ado**] silver

plática [plat**eeka**] (Mex) conversation; talk

platicar [plateek**ar**] (Mex) to talk, to converse

platillo m [plat**ee**-yo] saucer

plato m plate; dish, course

playa f [pl**a-ya**] beach

playa de estacionamiento (CSur, Pe) car park, (US) parking lot

playera f [pla-**ya**ira] (Mex) T-shirt

playeras fpl [pla-**ya**iras] (Mex) trainers, (US) sneakers

playo m (CR) poof

playo f (Nic) prostitute

plaza f [pl**a**sa] square; seat

plaza de mercado (Col) market

plaza de toros [deh] bullring

plazas libres [**lee**b-res] seats available

plomero m [plom**ai**ro] plumber

pluma f pen; feather

pluma atómica (Mex) biro®, ball point

plumón m [ploom**on**] (Ch, Mex) felt-tip pen

población f [poblas-y**on**] village; town; population

población callampa [ka-**ya**mpa] (Ch) shanty town

pobre [p**o**breh] poor

pobreza f [pobr**e**sa] poverty

pocho (Mex) Americanized

pochoclo m (Arg) popcorn

poco little; rarely

poco profundo shallow

pocos few

  unos pocos a few

poder (m) [pod**ai**r] to be able to; power

podrido rotten

policía f [polees**ee**-a] police

policía m/f policeman; policewoman

política f politics

político (m) politician; political

póliza de seguros f [p**o**leesa deh] insurance policy

pollera f [po-y**ai**ra] (Arg, Bol) skirt

polvo m [p**o**lbo] powder; dust

polvo de hornear baking powder

pólvora f [p**o**lbora] gunpowder

pomada f ointment; (Rpl) shoe polish

pomelo m (CSur) grapefruit

pon put

ponchadura f (Mex) puncture

ponchar (Mex) to puncture

poner [pon**ai**r] to put

ponerle el gorro a alguien (Ch) to two-time someone

ponerle los cuernos a alguien [kw**ai**rnos] to two-time someone

ponerse de pie [pon**ai**rseh deh p-yeh] to stand up

ponerse en marcha to set off

pongo I put

poniente m [pon-y**e**nteh] west

popote m [pop**o**teh] (Mex) (drinking) straw

poquito: un poquito [pok**ee**to] a little bit

por by; through; for

  por allí [a-y**ee**] over there

  por fin [feen] at last

  por lo menos at least

  por semana per week

  por ciento [s-y**e**nto] per cent

  por favor [fab**o**r] please

  por qué [keh] why

porcentaje m [porsentaHeh] percentage

porotos mpl (CSur) beans

porotos verdes mpl (Ch) runner beans

porque [porkeh] because

portada f cover

portaequipajes m [porta-ekeepaH-es] luggage rack

portátil [portateel] portable

portero m [portairo] porter; doorman; goalkeeper

portugués [portoog-es] Portuguese

posada f hotel, inn; restaurant; hospitality

posible [poseebleh] possible

postal f [pos-tal] postcard

posudo (Col) posh

precaución f [prekows-yon] caution

precio m [pres-yo] price

precio unidad [ooneeda] price per unit, price per item

precios fijos [feeHos] fixed prices

precioso [pres-yoso] beautiful; precious

predio m [pred-yo] building

preferencia f [prefairens-ya] right of way; preference

preferir [prefaireer] to prefer

prefijo m [prefeeHo] dialling code, area code

pregunta f question

preguntar to ask

premio m [prem-yo] prize

prenda las luces switch on your lights

prendas fpl clothing

prender [prendair] to light; to switch on

prensa f press; newspapers

preocupado [preh-okoopado] worried

preocuparse [preh-okooparseh] to worry (about)

¡no te preocupes! [teh preh-okoop-es] don't worry!

prepa(ratoria) f (Mex) pre-university level school

preparar to prepare

prepararse [prepararseh] to get ready

prepotente [prepotenteh] arrogant

presentar to introduce

preservativo m [presairbateebo] condom

presidencia f [preseedens-ya] presidency

presión f [pres-yon] pressure

presión de las llantas [deh las yantas] tyre pressure

prestado: pedir prestado to borrow

prestar to lend

prieto [pree-yeto] (Mex) dark-skinned; black

prima f cousin

primavera f [preemabaira] spring

primer piso first floor, (US) second floor

primer plato m first course

primera (clase) f [klaseh] first class

primera especial [espes-yal] deluxe first-class

primero first

primeros auxilios [owseel-yos] first-aid post

primo m cousin

principal [preenseepal] main

principiante m/f [preenseep-yanteh] beginner

principio m [preenseep-yo] beginning

prioridad a la derecha give way/yield to vehicles coming from the right

prisa: tener prisa to be in a hurry

privado (m) [preebado] private; cul-de-sac

privatización f [preebateesas-yon] privatization

probablemente [probableh-menteh] probably

probador m fitting room

probarse [probarseh] to try on

problema m problem

producto preparado con ingredientes naturales product prepared using natural ingredients

productos alimenticios [prodooktos aleementees-yos] foodstuffs

productos de belleza [deh beh-yesa] beauty products

profesor m, profesora f teacher; lecturer

profundidad f [profoondeeda] depth

profundo deep

prohibida la entrada no entry, no admission

prohibida la entrada a menores de ... no admission for those under ... years of age

prohibida la vuelta en U no U-turns

prohibida su reproducción copyright reserved

prohibida su venta not for sale

prohibido [pro-eebeedo] prohibited, forbidden; no

prohibido asomarse do not lean out of the window

prohibido bañarse no swimming

prohibido cantar no singing

prohibido echar basura no litter

prohibido el paso no entry; no trespassing

prohibido escupir no spitting

prohibido estacionarse no parking

prohibido estacionarse excepto carga y descarga no parking except for loading and unloading

prohibido fijar carteles stick no bills

prohibido fumar no smoking

prohibido girar a la izquierda no left turn

prohibido hablar con el chofer do not speak to the driver

prohibido hacer auto-stop no hitch-hiking

prohibido pescar no fishing

prohibido pisar el pasto keep off the grass

prohibido prender fuego no campfires

prohibido sacar fotografías no photographs

prohibido tocar el claxon (Mex) do not sound your horn

prolijo [proleeHo] (Rpl) tidy

prometer [prometair] to promise

prometida f fiancée

prometido (m) engaged; fiancé

pronóstico del tiempo m [t-yempo] weather forecast

pronto early; soon
  de pronto suddenly
  ¡hasta pronto! [asta] see you soon!
  llegar pronto [yegar] to be early

pronunciar [pronoons-yar] to pronounce

propaganda f advertising; publicity; propaganda

propiedad privada [prop-yeda preebada] private property

propietario m [prop-yetar-yo] owner

propina f tip

propósito: a propósito deliberately

proteger [proteHair] to protect

provecho: ¡buen provecho! [bwen probecho] enjoy your meal!

provincia f [probeens-ya] province
  en provincia in the country, in the provinces

provocar [probokar] to cause

¿te provoca un café? [teh] do you feel like a coffee?

próximo next
  la semana próxima next week

prudente [proodenteh] careful

prueba de alcoholemia f [prweba deh alko-olem-ya] breath test

prueba de embarazo [embaraso] pregnancy test

público (m) public; audience

pueblo m [pweblo] village; people; nation; ordinary people

puede [pwedeh] he/she can; you can

puede ser [sair] maybe

puedo [pwedo] I can

puente m [pwenteh] bridge

puente aéreo [a-aireh-o] shuttle flight

puente colgante [kolganteh] rope bridge

puente de cuota [kwota] (Mex) toll bridge

puerta f [pwairta] door; gate
  por la otra puerta use other door

puerta de embarque [embarkeh] gate

puerto m [pwairto] harbour, port

puerto de montaña [deh montan-ya] mountain pass

puerto deportivo marina

pues [pwes] since; so

puesta de sol f [pwesta deh] sunset

puesto de periódicos m [pair-yodeekos] newspaper kiosk

puesto de socorro first-aid post

puesto que [keh] since

pulga f flea

pullman m luxury bus

pulmones mpl [poolmon-es] lungs

pulmonía f [poolmonee-a] pneumonia

pulque m [poolkeh] (Mex) drink made from fermented agave cactus sap

pulquería f [poolkairee-a] (Mex) bar specializing in pulque

pulsera f [poolsaira] bracelet

pulso m pulse

puna f (Ch) altitude sickness

punto m dot; spot; point
hacer punto [asair] to knit

punto de vista [deh beesta] point of view

puntual: llegar puntual [yegar poontwal] to arrive on time

pura lana virgen pure new wool

puro (m) [pooro] cigar; pure
es la pura verdad [bairda] it's the absolute truth

puse [pooseh] I put

Q

que [keh] who; that; which; than

¿qué? what?; which?

¿qué hubo? [oobo] what's happening?; how's things?

¿qué tal? how do you do?

¡qué va! [ba] no way!

quedar [kedar] to stay; to remain
quédate con él [kedateh] keep it
no me queda otra [meh keda] I've no choice
¿dónde queda? [dondeh] where is it?
queda muy cerca it's very near

quedarse [kedarseh] to stay
quedarse con to keep
quedarse sin gasolina to run out of petrol/gas

quejarse [keh-Harseh] to complain

quemadura f [kemadoora] burn

quemadura de sol [deh] sunburn

quemar [kemar] to burn

quemarse [kemarseh] to burn oneself

queque m [kekeh] (Ch, Pe) cake

querer [kerair] to love; to want

querido [kaireedo] dear

queso m [keso] cheese

¿quién? [k-yen] who?

quiero [k-yairo] I want; I love
no quiero I don't want to

¿quihubo? [k-yoobo] how's it going?

quilombo m [keelombo] (Bol, Rpl) mess

quince [keenseh] fifteen

quince días [dee-as] fortnight, two weeks

quinientos [keen-yentos] five hundred

quinto [keento] fifth

quiño m [keen-yo] (Ec) punch

quiosco m [k-yosko] kiosk

quisiera [kees-yaira] I would like; he/she would like; you would like

quiso [keeso] he/she wanted; you wanted

quitaesmalte m [keeta-esmalteh] nail polish remover

quitar [keetar] to remove

quiubo [kee-oobo] (Andes, Mex) how's it going?

quizá(s) [keesa(s)] maybe

R

rabia f [rab-ya] rage; rabies
me da rabia it makes me mad

rabioso [rab-yoso] furious

rabona: hacerse la rabona (Rpl) to play truant

raca (Bol) stingy

ración f [ras-yon] portion

radiador m [rad-yador] radiator

radio f radio

radio m [rad-yo] spoke

radiografía f [rad-yografee-a] X-ray

ráid: pedir ráid [rīd] (Mex) to hitch-hike

rajarse [raHarseh] to back down, to run away

ranchero m [ranchairo] small farmer

rancho m small farm, smallholding

ranchos mpl (Ven) shanty town

rápidamente [–menteh] quickly

rápido fast

raponero m (Col) bag-snatcher

raro rare; strange

rascar to scratch

rasgar to tear

rasgo m feature

rasuradora f shaver

rasurarse [rasoorarseh] to shave

rata f rat

rato: espera un rato wait a minute, wait a bit
pasar buen/mal rato to have a good/bad time
cada rato every now and then

ratón m mouse; (Ven) hangover

rayas: de rayas [deh ra-yas] striped

razón f [rason] reason; rate
tiene razón [t-yeneh] you're right
con razón ... so that's why ...

razonable [rasonableh] reasonable

realizar [reh-aleesar] to carry out

realmente [reh-almenteh] really; in fact

rebajado [rebaHado] reduced

rebajas fpl [rebaHas] reductions, sale

rebajas de verano [deh bairano]

summer sale

rebasar to overtake, to pass

rebozo m [reboso] shawl

recado m message
¿quiere dejar recado? would you like to leave a message?

recámara f (Mex) bedroom

recepción f [reseps-yon] reception

recepcionista m/f [resepsyoneesta] receptionist

receta f [reseta] recipe; prescription
con receta médica only available on prescription

recetar [resetar] to prescribe

recetario m cookbook

recibir [reseebeer] to receive

recibo m [reseebo] receipt

recién [res-yen] recently
recién salía de casa cuando ... I'd just left home when ...

recién pintado wet paint

reclamación de equipajes f [reklamas-yon deh ekeepaH-es] baggage claim

reclamaciones fpl [reklamasyon-es] complaints

reclamo m complaint

recoger [rekoHair] to collect; to pick up

recogida de equipajes f [rekoHeeda deh ekeepaH-es] baggage claim

recoja su boleto take your ticket

recomendar to recommend

reconocer [rekonosair] to recognize; to examine

reconocimiento m [rekonoseem-yento] examination
reconocimiento médico medical examination

recordar to remember

recorrer [rekorrair] to travel; to travel through; to move along

recorrido m journey

recreo m [recreh-o] playtime, break

recto straight
todo recto straight ahead

recuerdo (m) [rekwairdo] memory; souvenir; I remember

red f [reh] network; net

redondo round

reduzca la velocidad reduce speed now

reembolsar [reh-embolsar] to refund

reembolsos refunds

reestreno m [reh-estreno] re-release (of a classic movie)

refacciones fpl [refaks-yon-es] (Mex) spare parts, spares; (SAm) refurbishment

refrigerador m [refreeHairador] fridge

refrigeradora f [refreeHairadora] (Col, Pe) fridge

regadera f [regadaira] shower

regalo m present

regalón (Mex) spoiled

regatear [regateh-ar] to haggle

regenta f [reHenta], **regente** m [reHenteh] (Mex) mayor régimen m [reHeemen] diet; regime

registrar [reHeestrar] to search; to register, to certify

registro m (Arg) driving licence

registro de equipajes m [reHeestro deh ekeepaH-es] check-in

regla f rule; period

reglamento m rule

regresar to return

regresar a casa to go home

regreso m return

reina f [rayna] queen

Reino Unido m United Kingdom

reír [reh-eer] to laugh

relajarse [relaHarseh] to relax

relajo m [relaHo] disorder; noise, hubbub

rellenar [reh-yenar] to fill in; to fill

reloj m [reloH] watch; clock

reloj de pulsera [deh poolsaira] watch, wristwatch

relojería f [reloHairee-a] watches and clocks; watchmaker's shop

remar to row

remate m [remateh] sale, auction sale; the final detail

remera f (Rpl) T-shirt

remitente m/f [remeetenteh] sender

remo m oar

remolque m [remolkeh] trailer

renguera f [rengaira] (SAm) limp

renta f rent; rental

rentado rented

rentar to rent; to hire

se renta to rent, for hire

renunciar [renoons-yar] to resign

reparación f [reparas-yon] repair(s)

reparación de calzado [deh kalsado] shoe repairs

reparaciones [reparas-yon-es] faults service

reparar to repair

repasador m (Rpl) dishcloth, tea towel

repelente de mosquitos m [repelenteh deh] mosquito repellent

repente: de repente [deh repenteh] suddenly

repetir to repeat; to have a second helping

reponerse [reponairseh] to recover

reposera f (Rpl) deckchair

representante m/f [representanteh] representative, agent

repuestos mpl [repwestos] spare parts

repugnante [repoognanteh] disgusting

requisito m [rekeeseeto] requirement, condition

res m cow, bull

resaca f hangover

resbaladizo [resbaladeeso] slippery

resbalar to slip

rescatar to rescue

reserva f [resairba] reservation

reserva de asientos [deh as-yentos] seat reservation

reservado [resairbado] reserved

reservado el derecho de admisión the management reserve the right to refuse admission

reservar [resairbar] to reserve; to book

reservas fpl reservations

resfriado m [resfree-ado] cold

respeto m respect

respirar to breathe

responder [respondair] to answer, to reply

responsable (m/f) [responsableh] the person in charge; responsible

respuesta f [respwesta] answer

restaurante m [restowranteh] restaurant

resto m rest

retar to challenge; (CSur) to tell off

rete: está rete lindo [reteh] (Mex) it's really beautiful

retrato hablado m identikit

reumatismo m [reh-oomateesmo] rheumatism

reunión f [reh-oon-yon] meeting

revelado m [rebelado] film processing

revelar [rebelar] to develop; to reveal

reversa f reverse (gear)

revisar [rebeesar] to check

revisor m [rebeesor] conductor; guard

revista m [rebeesta] magazine

revolución f [reboloos-yon] revolution

rey m [ray] king

Reyes: día de los Reyes m [dee-a deh los reh-yes] 6th of January, Epiphany

rico rich

ridículo ridiculous

riego: tierras de riego fpl irrigated land

rímel m mascara

rin: a puro rin (Hond) naked

rincón m corner

riñón m [reen-yon] kidney

río m [ree-o] river

risa f laughter
  me da risa [meh] it makes me laugh

rizado [reesado] curly

robar to steal

robo m theft

roca f rock

roco (CR) old

rodilla f [rodee-ya] knee

rogar to beg

rojo [roHo] red

rómpase en caso de emergencia break in case of emergency

romper to break

ropa f clothes

ropa de caballeros [deh kaba-yairos] men's clothes

ropa de cama bed linen

ropa de señoras [sen-yoras] ladies' clothes

ropa infantil [eenfanteel] children's clothes

ropa interior [eentair-**yor**] underwear

ropa sucia [**soo**s-ya] laundry

rosa (f) pink; rose

roto broken

rubeola f [roobeh-**o**la] German measles

rubí m [roo**bee**] ruby

rubio [**roo**b-yo] blond

rubor m (Mex, Rpl) blusher

rueda f [r**we**da] wheel; (Rpl) spare wheel

rueda de repuesto f [deh rep**we**sto] spare wheel

ruega: se ruega ... [seh r**we**ga] please ...

ruego I request

rufa f (Cu) bicycle

ruido m [r**wee**do] noise

ruidoso [r**wee**doso] noisy

ruinas fpl [r**wee**nas] ruins

rumba f (Col, Ven) party

rural [roo**ral**] rural, country

ruta f route

S

S.A. (Sociedad Anónima) PLC, Inc

sábado m Saturday

sábana f sheet

saber [sa**bair**] to know

saber a to taste of

sabor m taste

sabroso tasty, delicious

sacacorchos m corkscrew

sacar to take out; to get out

sacar un boleto to buy a ticket

sacar una foto to take a photo

saco m jacket

saco tejido m [te**Hee**do] (Rpl) cardigan

sal (f) salt; leave

sala f room; lounge; hall

sala climatizada [kleematee**sa**da] air-conditioned

sala de belleza [beh-**ye**sa] beauty salon

sala de cine [deh **see**neh] cinema, movie theater

sala de conciertos [kons-**yair**tos] concert hall

sala de embarque [em**bar**keh] departure lounge

sala de espera [es**pai**ra] waiting room

sala de exposiciones [esposees-**yon**-es] exhibition hall

sala de tránsito transit lounge

sala X X-rated cinema, adult movie theater

salado salty; jinxed

salchichonería f [salcheechonai-**ree**-a] (Mex) delicatessen

saldar to sell at a reduced price; to pay off

saldo m clearance; balance

sales de baño fpl [sal-es deh ban-yo] bath salts

salgo I'm leaving, I'm going out

salida f exit; departure

salida ciudad take this direction to leave the city

salida de ambulancias

ambulance exit

salida de autopista end of motorway/highway; motorway/highway exit

salida de camiones heavy goods vehicle exit, works exit

salida de emergencia [deh emairiens-ya] emergency exit

salida de incendios [eensend-yos] fire exit

salida de socorro f (Mex) emergency exit

salidas fpl departures

salidas internacionales [eentairnas-yonal-es] international departures

salidas nacionales [nas-yonal-es] domestic departures

salir to go out; to leave

salivar [saleebar] to spit

salón de baile m [deh bīleh] dance hall

salón de belleza [beh-yesa] beauty salon

salón de demostraciones [demostras-yon-es] exhibition hall

salón de peluquería [pelookairee-a] hairdressing salon

salpicadera f [salpeekadaira] (Mex) mudguard

salsamentaria f (Col) delicatessen

saltar to jump

Salubridad f (Mex) Ministry of Health

salud f [saloo] health

saludar to greet

saludos best wishes

salvadoreño (m) [salbadoren-yo] Salvadorean

salvavidas m/f lifeguard

salvo que [keh] except that

sandalias fpl sandals

sangrar to bleed

sangre f [sangreh] blood

sanitarios mpl [saneetar-yos] toilets, rest rooms

sano healthy

sarampión m [saramp-yon] measles

sarape m [sarapeh] (Mex) woven blanket

sartén f frying pan

sastre m [sastreh] tailor

scotch® m Sellotape®, Scotch tape®

se [seh] himself; herself; itself; yourself; themselves; yourselves; oneself

se aceptan tarjetas de crédito we accept credit cards

se habla inglés English spoken

se hacen fotocopias photocopying service

se necesita ... ... needed, required

se precisa ... ... needed

se prohíbe ... ... forbidden

se prohíbe echar basura no litter

se prohíbe fumar no smoking

se prohíbe hablar con el chofer do not speak to the driver

se prohíbe la entrada no
  entry, no admittance
se prohíbe la entrada a
  mujeres, uniformados e
  integrantes de la fuerzas
  armadas no admittance to
  women, members of the
  armed forces and anyone in
  uniform
se renta for hire, to rent
se renta departamento flat to
  let, apartment for rent
se rentan cuartos rooms to
  rent
se ruega please ...
se ruega desalojen su cuarto
  antes de las doce please
  vacate your room by twelve
  noon
se ruega no ... please do
  not ...
se ruega no estacionarse no
  parking please
se ruega no molestar please
  do not disturb
se ruega pagar en caja please
  pay at the desk
se vende for sale
sé I know
  no sé I don't know
secador de pelo m [deh] hair
  dryer
secar to dry
secarse el pelo [sekarseh] to
  dry one's hair, to have a
  blow-dry
sección f [seks-yon]
  department
seco dry

secretaria f, secretario m
  secretary
secretaría f (Mex) Ministry
secreto secret
Sectur (Mex) tourist office
sed: tengo sed [seh] I'm
  thirsty
seda f silk
seda natural pure silk
sede f [sedeh] head office,
  headquarters
seguida: en seguida [segeeda]
  immediately, right away
seguido [segeedo] often
seguir [segeer] to follow
según according to
segunda (clase) f [klaseh]
  second class
segundo (m) second
  de segunda mano second-
  hand
segundo piso second floor,
  (US) third floor
seguridad f [segooreeda] safety;
  security
seguro (m) safe; sure;
  insurance; safety pin
seguro de viaje [deh b-yaHeh]
  travel insurance
seis [says] six
seiscientos [says-yentos] six
  hundred
selva f [selba] jungle; rain
  forest
semáforo m traffic lights
semana f week
Semana Santa Holy Week
semanal weekly
semiñoca [semeen-yoka] (Cu)

stupid
senador m Senator
sencillo [sensee-yo] simple
sensible [senseebleh] sensitive
sentar: sentar bien (a) [b-yen] to suit
sentarse [sentarseh] to sit down
sentido m direction; sense; meaning
sentir to feel; to hear
señalizador m [sen-yaleesador] (Ch) indicator
señas fpl [sen-yas] address
señor [sen-yor] gentleman, man; sir
  el señor López Mr López
señora f [sen-yora] lady, woman; madam
  la señora López Mrs López
señoras fpl ladies; ladies' toilet, ladies' room; ladies' department
señores mpl [sen-yor-es] men; gents' toilet, men's room
señorita f [sen-yoreeta] young lady, young woman; miss
  la señorita López Miss López
separado separate; separated
  por separado separately
septiembre m [sept-yembreh] September
séptimo [septeemo] seventh
sequía f [sekee-a] drought
ser [sair] to be
  a no ser que [keh] unless
serio [sair-yo] serious
  en serio seriously
serpiente f [sairp-yenteh] snake

serranía f mountains
serrucho m handsaw; (RD) whip-round
servicio a través de operadora operator-connected calls
servicio automático direct dialling
servicio de cuarto [sairbees-yo deh kwarto] room service
servicio de fotocopias photocopying service
servicio estrella [estreh-ya] first class (coach) service
servicios mpl [sairbees-yos] toilets, rest rooms
servicios de rescate [deh reskateh] mountain rescue
servicios de socorro emergency services
servilleta f [sairbee-yeta] serviette, napkin
servir [sairbeer] to serve
sesenta [sesenta] sixty
sesión continua continuous showing
setecientos [setes-yentos] seven hundred
setenta seventy
sexo m sex
sexto [sesto] sixth
si [see] if
si no otherwise
sí yes; oneself; herself; itself; yourself; themselves; yourselves; each other
sicario m (SAm) gunman
sida m [seeda] Aids
sido been
siempre [s-yempreh] always

siempre que [keh] whenever; as long as
siento [s-yento] I sit down; I feel
  lo siento I'm sorry
sierra f [s-yairra] mountain range
siesta f siesta, nap
siete [s-yeteh] seven
sifrino (Ven) posh
siga recto straight ahead
siglo m century
significado m meaning
significar to mean
siguiente [seeg-yenteh] next
  al día siguiente the day after
silencio m [seelens-yo] silence
silla f [see-ya] chair
silla de playa f deckchair
silla de ruedas [deh rwedas] wheelchair
sillita de ruedas [see-yeeta] pushchair, buggy
sillón m [see-yon] armchair
simpático nice
sin [seen] without
sin duda undoubtedly
sin embargo however, nevertheless
sin plomo unleaded
sinagoga f synagogue
sincero [seensairo] sincere
sindicalista m/f trade unionist
sindicato m trade union, (US) labor union
singado (Cu) mean
singuangua [seengwangwa] (Cu) tasteless
sino: no ... sino ... not ...

but ...
sino que [keh] but
siquiera [seek-yaira] even if; at least
sírvase [seerbaseh] please
sírvase frío serve cold
sírvase usted mismo help yourself
sitio m [seet-yo] place
  en ningún sitio [neen-goon] nowhere
smoking m [esmokeen] dinner jacket
soborno m bribe
sobrar to be left over; to be too many
sobre (m) [sobreh] envelope; on; above
sobrecarga [sobrekarga] excess weight; extra charge
sobrevivir [sobrebeebeer] to survive
sobrina f niece
sobrino m nephew
sobrio [sobr-yo] sober
sobros leftovers
socado (CR) drunk; (Salv) difficult
sociedad f [sos-yeda] society; company
socio m [sos-yo] associate; member
socorrer [sokorair] to help
socorrista m/f lifeguard
¡socorro! help!
sol m sun
  al sol in the sun
solamente [solamenteh] only
soleado [soleh-ado] sunny

solera f (Ch) kerb

solo lonely

sólo only

no sólo ... sino también ... [tamb-yen] not only ... but also ...

sólo autobuses buses only

sólo carga y descarga loading and unloading only

sólo laborables weekdays only

sólo motos motorcycles only

sólo para residentes (del hotel) hotel patrons only

soltera (f) [soltaira] single; single woman

soltero (m) [soltairo] single; bachelor

solterón m [soltairon] bachelor

solterona f [soltairona] spinster

sombra f shade; shadow

sombra de ojos [deh oHos] eyeshadow

sombrero m [sombrairo] hat

sombrilla f [sombree-ya] parasol

somnífero m [somneefairo] sleeping pill

somos we are

son they are; you are

sonreír [sonreh-eer] to smile

sonrisa f smile

sordo deaf

soroche m [sorocheh] (Andes) altitude sickness

sorprendente [sorprendenteh] surprising

sorpresa f surprise

sostén m bra

sótano m lower floor; basement

soutien m [soot-yen] (Urug) bra

soy I am

sport: de sport [deh] casual

Sr. (Señor) Mr

Sra. (Señora) Mrs

Sres. (Señores) Messrs

Srta. (Señorita) Miss

su [soo] his; her; its; their; your

suave [swabeh] soft; quiet

subido (Hond) arrogant

subir to go up; to get on; to get in; to take up

subsuelo m [soobs-welo] (Rpl) basement

subtitulado sub-titled

subtítulos mpl subtitles

suburbios mpl [sooboorb-yos] suburbs; poor quarters

suceder [soosedair] to happen

sucio [soos-yo] dirty

sucursal f branch

sudadera f (Col) tracksuit, (US) sweats

sudamericana (f) [soodamaireekana], sudamericano (m) South American

sudar to sweat

Suecia f [swes-ya] Sweden

sueco [sweko] Swedish

suegra f [swegra] mother-in-law

suegro m [swegro] father-in-law

suela f [swela] sole

suelo (m) floor; I am used to
suelto [swelto] small change
sueño (m) [swen-yo] dream; I dream
tener sueño [tenair] to be tired/sleepy
suerte f [swairteh] luck
por suerte luckily, fortunately
¡buena suerte! [bwena] good luck!
suéter m [swetair] sweater
suficiente: es suficiente [soofees-yenteh] that's enough
sufragio efectivo, no reelección effective suffrage, no re-election (slogan on many official documents)
suicidarse [sweeseedarseh] to commit suicide
Suiza f [sweesa] Switzerland
sumar to add; to add up to
supe [soopeh] I knew
súper [soopair] (Mex) four-star petrol, (US) premium (gas); supermarket
supermercado m [soopairmairkado] supermarket
supuesto: por supuesto [soopwesto] of course
sur m south
al sur de [deh] south of
sureste m [sooresteh] south-east
suroeste m [sooro-esteh] south-west
surtido m assortment
sus [soos] his; her; its; their;

your
susto m shock
susurrar to whisper
sutil subtle
suya [soo-ya], **suyas, suyo, suyos** his; hers; its; theirs; yours

T

tabaco m tobacco; cigarettes
tabique m [tabeekeh] (Mex) brick
tabla de surf f [deh soorf] surfboard
tabla de windsurf sailboard
tablero de instrumentos m [tablairo deh eenstroomentos] dashboard
tablón de anuncios m [anoons-yos] notice board, bulletin board
tablón de información [deh eenformas-yon] indicator board
tabo m (CR) jail
tachero m (Rpl) taxi driver
tacho m (Rpl) taxi
tacho de la basura (Mex) bin, dustbin, trashcan
tacón m heel
tacones altos [takon-es] high heels
tacones planos flat heels
taguara [tagwara] (Ven) cheap restaurant
tal such
con tal (de) que provided that

tal vez [bes] maybe
talco m talcum powder
talla f [**ta**-ya] size
 ¿**qué número talla?** what size are you?
tallador m [ta-ya**dor**] banker
tallas grandes [gr**a**nd-es] large sizes
tallas sueltas [sw**e**ltas] odd sizes
taller mecánico m [ta-y**air** mek**a**neeko] garage
talón m heel
talón de equipajes [ekeepa**H**-es] baggage slip
talonario (de cheques) m [talon**ar**-yo (deh chek-es)] cheque book, checkbook
tamaño m [tam**a**n-yo] size
tamarindo m (Mex) traffic cop
también [tamb-y**en**] also
 yo también me too
tampoco neither, nor
 yo tampoco me neither
tan: tan bonito so beautiful
 tan pronto como as soon as
tanque m [t**a**nkeh] tank
tantito: espere tantito wait a moment
tanto (m) so much; point
tanto ... como ... both ... and ...
tantos so many
tapa f lid
tapabarros m (Andes) mud-guard
tapadora f (Rpl) bulldozer
tapadura f [tapad**oo**ra] (Ch) filling (in tooth)

tapar to cover
tapas fpl savoury snacks, tapas
tapete m [tap**e**teh] rug, carpet
tapón m plug; (CSur) fuse
taquería f [takair**ee**-a] (Mex) taco restaurant, taco stall
taquilla f [tak**ee**-ya] ticket office
tardar: ¿cuánto tarda? [kw**a**nto] how long does it take?
 no tarda he/she won't be long
 no tardes [t**a**rd-es] don't be long
tarde (f) [t**a**rdeh] afternoon; evening; late
 a las tres de la tarde [deh] at 3 p.m.
 esta tarde this afternoon, this evening
 por la tarde in the evening
 llegar tarde [yeg**a**r] to be late
tarifa f charge, charges
tarifa especial estudiante [espes-y**a**l estood-y**a**nteh] student reduced rate
tarifa normal standard rate
tarifa reducida [redoos**ee**da] reduced rate
tarjeta f [tar**H**eta] card
tarjeta bancaria [bank**a**r-ya] cheque card
tarjeta de crédito [deh kr**e**deeto] credit card
tarjeta de embarque [emb**a**rkeh] boarding pass
tarjeta postal postcard

tarjeta telefónica phonecard
tarjeta verde Green Card (tourist permit in Mexico)
tarro de la basura m (Ch) bin, dustbin, trashcan
tatú f (Bol, Parag, Rpl) armadillo
tauromaquia f [towromak-ya] bullfighting
taxista m/f taxi driver
taza f [tasa] cup
te [teh] you; yourself
té m tea
té de hierbas m [teh deh yairbas] herbal tea
té de yuyos m [teh deh yoo-yos] (Pe, Rpl) herbal tea
teatro m [teh-atro] theatre
techo m ceiling
teclado m keyboard
técnica f technique; technology
técnico technical
tecnología f [teknoloнee-a] technology
tecolote m [–loteh] (Mex) owl
tejado m [teнado] roof
tejanos mpl [teнanos] jeans
tejidos mpl [teнeedos] materials, fabrics
tela f material
teleférico m cable car
teléfono m telephone
teléfono interurbano long-distance phone
teléfonos de emergencia emergency telephone numbers
telesilla m [telesee-ya] chairlift
televisión f [telebees-yon] television

televisor m television (set)
temblor m earthquake
temer [temair] to fear
temor m fear
tempestad f [tempesta] storm
templo m temple; church
temporada f season
temporariamente [–menteh] temporarily
ten hold
tender to make; to set
tenedor m fork
tener [tenair] to have
tener derecho to have the right
tener prioridad [pree-oreeda] to have right of way
tener prisa to be in a hurry
tener que [keh] to have to
¡tenga cuidado! [kweedado] be careful!
tengo I have
tengo que I have to, I must
tenis m trainers, (US) sneakers; tennis
tensión f [tens-yon] blood pressure
teñirse el pelo [ten-yeerseh] to dye one's hair, to have one's hair dyed
tepetate m [tepetateh] (Mex) type of soft stone used for building
terapia f [terap-ya] intensive care
tercer piso m [tairsair] third floor, (US) fourth floor

tercera edad f [eda] old age
tercero third
tercio m [tairs-yo] third
terciopelo m [tairs-yopelo] velvet
terco [tairko] stubborn
terminal f [tairmeenal] terminus; terminal
terminal de transportes m [deh transport-es] (Col) bus station
terminar to finish
termo m Thermos® flask
termómetro m thermometer
terrateniente m/f [tairra-ten-yenteh] large landowner
terreno m [tairreno] piece/plot of land
testigo m witness
testimonio m [testeemon-yo] evidence; statement
tetera f [tetaira] teapot
tetero m (Col) baby´s bottle
tetunta f (Hond) head
Teuacán ® [teh-wakan] (Mex) mineral water
tezontle m [tesontleh] (Mex) volcanic marble-like rock
ti [tee] you
tía f [tee-a] aunt
tianguis m [t-yangees] (Mex) market
tibio [teeb-yo] lukewarm
tiburón m shark
tico Costa Rican
tiempo m [t-yempo] time; weather
  a tiempo on time
  al tiempo at room temperature

tiempo de recreo [deh rekreh-o] leisure
tiempo libre [leebreh] free time
tienda f [t-yenda] shop, store; tent
  esta tienda se traslada a ... this business is transferred to ...
tienda de abarrotes [deh abarrot-es] (Andes, CAm, Mex) grocer's, dry goods store
tienda de artículos de piel [p-yel] leather goods shop
tienda de campaña tent
tienda de comestibles [komesteebl-es] grocer's
tienda de deportes [deport-es] sports shop
tienda de electrodomésticos electrical goods shop
tienda de muebles [mwebl-es] furniture shop
tienda de regalos gift shop
tienda de ultramarinos grocer's
tienda de vinos y licores [beenos ee leekor-es] off-licence, (US) liquor store
tienda libre de impuestos [leebreh deh eempwestos] duty-free shop
tiene: ¿tiene ...? [t-yeneh] have you got ...?, do you have ...?; do you sell ...?
  tiene que [keh] he/she has to; you have to
tierra f [t-yairra] earth; land
tifo m typhus
tijeras fpl [teeHairas] scissors

tiliches mpl [teel**eech**-es] (Mex) bits and pieces

timbre m [t**ee**mbreh] bell; stamp

timbre de alarma [deh] alarm bell

tímido shy

timón m (Andes) steering wheel

tina f bath(tub)

tintorería f [teentorair**ee**-a] dry-cleaner's

tío m [t**ee**-o] uncle

tipo de cambio m [deh k**a**mb-yo] exchange rate

tira m (Mex) policeman

tirar to throw; to shoot; to waste; to fuck

tirita f Elastoplast®, (US) Bandaid®

tiro m shot

tlapalería f [tlapalair**ee**-a] (Mex) hardware store

toalla f [to-**a**-ya] towel

toalla de baño [deh b**a**n-yo] bath towel

toalla sanitaria [saneet**a**r-ya] (SAm) sanitary napkin/towel

toallita f [to-a-y**ee**ta] (SAm) flannel

tobillo m [tob**ee**-yo] ankle

tobo m (Ven) bucket

tobo de la basura m (Ven) bin, dustbin, (US) trashcan

tocadiscos m record player

tocar to touch; to play

tocayo m [tok**a**-yo] namesake

todavía [todab**ee**-a] still; yet

todavía no not yet

todo all, every; everything

todos los días every day

todo derecho straight on

todo recto straight ahead

todos everyone

tomado drunk

tomar to take; to drink

tomar el sol to sunbathe

tomate m [tom**a**teh] tomato

tomavistas m (Mex) cine-camera

tome usted [t**o**meh oost**eh**] take

tómese antes de las comidas to be taken before meals

tómese después de las comidas to be taken after meals

tómese ... veces al día to be taken ... times per day

tonelada f tonne

tongo m (Pan) police officer

tono m dialling tone; shade

tonto silly

topes mpl (Mex) speed bumps, 'sleeping policemen'

torcer [tors**air**] to twist; to sprain; to turn

torcerse el tobillo [tob**ee**-yo] to twist one's ankle

torero m [tor**ai**ro] bullfighter

tormenta f storm

tormentoso stormy

tornillo m [torn**ee**-yo] screw

toro m bull

toros mpl bullfighting

torpe [t**o**rpeh] clumsy

torre f [t**o**rreh] tower

tortillera f [tortee-y**ai**ra] lesbian

tos f cough

toscano m (Rpl) cigar
toser [tos**air**] to cough
tosferina f [tosfair**eena**] whooping cough
total: en total [tot-**al**] altogether
totalmente [total**menteh**] absolutely
tóxico [t**o**kseeko] poisonous
toxicómano m [tokseek**o**mano] drug addict
trabajador (m) [trabaHa**dor**], **trabajadora** (f) worker; industrious
trabajar [trabaH**ar**] to work
trabajo m [trab**a**Ho] work; job
traducir [trad**oo**seer] to translate
traer [tra-**air**] to bring
tráfico: tráfico de drogas drug traffic; drug-trafficking
tragamonedas fpl slot machine
tragar to swallow
tragarse [trag**a**rseh] to swallow; to put up with; to fall for; (Col) to fall in love
trago m drinking
traigo [tr**i**go] I bring
tráiler m [tr**i**lair] large truck; caravan, (US) trailer
tráiners mpl [tr**i**nairs] trainers, (US) sneakers
traje (m) [tr**a**Heh] I brought; suit; clothes
traje de baño [deh b**a**n-yo] swimming costume
traje de noche [n**o**cheh] evening dress

traje de señora [sen-y**o**ra] lady's suit
traje típico traditional regional costume
trámites mpl [tra-m**ee**t-es] bureaucracy, paperwork
tranquilizante [trankeelees**a**nteh] tranquillizer
tranquilizarse [trankeelees**a**rseh] to calm down
tranquilo [trank**ee**lo] quiet
transar (Mex) to sell out, to compromise
tránsito m traffic
trapear [trapeh-**ar**] to mop
trapo de cocina m dishcloth
tras after
trasbordo m transfer; change **hacer trasbordo en ...** change at ...
trasero (m) [tras**i**ro] bottom; back; rear
trasladar to move **se traslada** under new management
trasnochar to spend the night
traste m [tr**a**steh] (CSur) bottom; back; rear
tratamiento m [–m-y**e**nto] treatment
tratar to treat; to try
trato m way of treating people
través: a través de [trab-**e**s deh] across, through
travieso [trab-y**e**so] mischievous
trece [tr**e**seh] thirteen
treinta [tr**i**nta] thirty

tren m train

tren de carga [deh] goods train

tren de lavado automático [labado owtomateeko] carwash

tren de pasajeros [pasaHairos] passenger train

tren directo through train

tren tranvía [tranbee-a] stopping train

tres three

tres cuartos de hora mpl [kwartos deh ora] three quarters of an hour

trescientos [tres-yentos] three hundred

tribunal m [treeboonal] court; tribunal

tripulación f [treepoolas-yon] crew

triste [treesteh] sad

tristeza f [treestesa] sadness

trompudo (Guat) angry

tronco m body; buddy

tropezar [tropesar] to trip

trueno m [trweno] thunder

tu [too] your

tú you

tú mismo yourself

tuanis [twanees] (Salv) cool, great

tubo de escape m [deh eskapeh] (Mex) exhaust

tubo de respirar snorkel

tuerce a la izquierda turn left

tuerza [twairsa] turn

tumbona f deckchair

túnel m [too-nel] tunnel

turismo m tourism; luxury

bus; tourist office

turista m/f tourist

turístico [tooreesteeko] tourist

turno m [toorno] turn; round; shift

es mi turno it's my turn/ round

tus [toos] your

tuya [too-ya], tuyas, tuyo, tuyos yours

U

u [oo] or

ubicarse [oobeekarseh] to be located

¿lo ubicas? do you know the one I mean?

Ud. (usted) [oosteh] you

Uds. (ustedes) [oostedes] you

úlcera (de estómago) f [oolsaira] (stomach) ulcer

últimamente [oolteemamenteh] recently, lately

último last; latest

últimos días [dee-as] last days; last few days

ultramarinos m grocer's

un [oon] a

una [oona] a

unas some

universidad f [ooneebairseeda] university

uno one; someone

unos some; a few

uña f [oon-ya] fingernail

urbanización f [oorbaneesas-yon] housing estate

urbano urban, city
urgencias [oorHens-yas] casualty (department); emergencies
uruguayo [ooroogwa-yo] Uruguayan
usado used; secondhand
usar to use
 no se usa [seh] it isn't done
uso use
uso externo not to be taken internally
uso obligatorio cinturón de seguridad seatbelts must be worn
 el uso del tabaco es perjudicial para su salud smoking can damage your health
usted [oosteh] you
ustedes [oosted-es] you
útil useful
utilidades fpl profits

V

v is pronounced more like a b than an English v

v.o. subtitulada version in the original language with subtitles
va he/she/it goes; you go
vaca f cow; (Col) whip-round
vacacionar [bakas-yo-nar] go on holiday
vacaciones fpl [bakas-yon-es] holiday, vacation

vacacionista m/f holiday maker
vacilar [baseelar] to party, to have a good time
vacilón [baseelon] fun-loving
vacío [basee-o] empty
vacuna f vaccination
vacunarse [bakoonarseh] to be vaccinated
vagón m carriage, coach
vagón de literas [deh leetairas] sleeping car
vagón restaurante [restowranteh] restaurant car
vainitas fpl [bineetas] (Ven) runner beans
vajilla f [baHee-ya] dinner service, set of crockery
vale: ¿cuánto vale? [kwanto baleh] how much is it?
 me vale (madre) [madreh] (Mex) I don't give a shit
valer [balair] to be worth
valiente [bal-yenteh] brave
valija f [baleeHa] (Rpl) suitcase
valla f [ba-ya] fence
valle m [ba-yeh] valley
valores mpl [balor-es] securities
válvula f valve
vamos we go
van they go; you go
vapor m steam
vaquero m [bakairo] cowboy
vaqueros mpl jeans
vaquita f [bakeeta] (CSur, Mex) whip-round
vara f pole; (CR) excuse
variar [bar-yar] to vary
 para variar for a change

v is pronounced more like a b than an English v

varicela f [bareesela] chickenpox

varios [bar-yos] several; different

varón m male

varonil manly

vas you go

vasco Basque

vaso m glass

vatio m [bat-yo] watt

vaya [ba-ya] go; I/he/she/you should go; I/he/she/you might go

Vd. (usted) you

Vds. (ustedes) you

ve [beh] go; he/she sees; you see

veces: a veces [bes-es] sometimes

vecindad f [beseenda] (Mex) inner city slum

vecino m [beseeno] neighbour

vehículos pesados heavy vehicles

veinte [baynteh] twenty

vejez f [beн-es] old age

vela f candle; sail

velero m [belairo] sailing boat

velocidad f [beloseeda] speed

velocidad controlada por radar radar speed checks

velocidad limitada speed limits apply

velocidades fpl [beloseedad-es] gears

velocímetro m [beloseemetro] speedometer

ven [ben] come; they see; you see

vena f vein

venda f bandage

vendar to dress (wound)

vendemos a ... selling rate

vender [bendair] to sell

veneno m poison

venezolano [benesolano] Venezuelan

vengo I come

venir to come

venta f sale

de venta aquí on sale here

venta de estampillas stamps sold here

venta de localidades tickets (on sale)

ventana f window

ventanilla f [bentanee-ya] window; ticket office

ventas a crédito credit terms available

ventas a plazos hire purchase, (US) installment plan

ventas al contado cash sales

ventilador m fan

ver [bair] to see; to watch

veraneante m/f [bairaneh-anteh] holiday-maker, vacationer

veranear [bairaneh-ar] to holiday, to take a vacation

veraneo: centro de veraneo [sentro deh bairaneh-o] holiday resort

verano m [bairano] summer

veras: de veras [deh bairas] really, honestly

verdad f [bairda] truth
¿verdad? don't you?; do you?; isn't it?; isn't he?; is he? etc
verdadero [bairdadairo] true
verde (m) [bairdeh] green
vereda f (CSur, Pe) pavement, sidewalk
vergüenza f [bairgwensa] shame
verraco (Col) fantastic; gutsy
versión f [bairs-yon] version
en versión original [oreegeenal] in the original language
vestido m dress
vestir to dress
vestirse [besteerseh] to get dressed; to dress
vestuarios mpl [bestwar-yos] fitting rooms; changing rooms
vez f [bes] time
una vez once
en vez de [deh] instead of
vi [bee] I saw
vía f [bee-a] platform, (US) track
vía aérea: por vía aérea [a-aireh-a] by air mail
vía oral orally
vía rectal per rectum
viajar [b-yaHar] to travel
viaje m [b-yaHeh] journey
¡buen viaje! [bwen] have a good trip!
viaje de negocios [deh negos-yos] business trip
viaje de novios [nob-yos] honeymoon
viaje organizado [organeesado]

package tour
viajero m [b-yaHairo] traveller
víbora f [beebora] snake
vida f life
vidriera f [beedree-aira] (Rpl) shop window
vidrio m [beedr-yo] glass; window
viejo (m) [b-yeHo] old; mate, buddy
mi viejo my old man, my father
mis viejos my parents
viene: la semana que viene [keh b-yeneh] next week
viento m [b-yento] wind
vientre m [b-yentreh] stomach
viernes m [b-yairn-es] Friday
Viernes Santo Good Friday
villa miseria f [bee-ya meesair-ya] (Arg) shanty town
vincha f [beencha] (Parag) hair-band
vine [beeneh] I came
viñedo [been-yedo] vineyard
vinos y licores wines and spirits
violación f [b-yolas-yon] rape
violar [b-yolar] to rape
violencia f [b-yolensee-a] violence
violento [b-yolento] violent
visita f visit
visita con guía [gee-a] guided tour
visitante m/f [beeseetanteh] visitor
visitar to visit
visor m viewfinder

v is pronounced more like a b than an English v

víspera f [**bee**spaira] the day before

vista f view

visto seen

dar el visto bueno a [**bweno**] to approve

vitrina f [beet**ree**na] (Ch, Col, Ven) shop window

viuda f [b-**yoo**da] widow

viudo m widower

vivir to live

vivo alive; I live

VO (versión original) original language

voceador m [bosea**dor**] newspaper seller

vocero m [bos**airo**] spokesman

volante m [bo**lanteh**] steering wheel

volantín m (Ch) kite

volar to fly

volcán m [bol**kan**] volcano

volibol m [bolee**bol**] volleyball

voltaje m [bolta**Heh**] voltage

voltear [bolteh-**ar**] to turn over; to knock over

volver [bol**bair**] to come back

volver a hacer algo to do something again

vomitar to vomit

voy I go

voz f [bos] voice

vuelo m [**bwelo**] flight

vuelo nacional [nas-yo**nal**] domestic flight

vuelo regular scheduled flight

vuelta f [**bwelta**] tour, trip

a la vuelta around the corner

dar una vuelta to go for a walk

vuelto m [**bwelto**] change

vuelvo [**bwelbo**] I return

vulcanizadora f [boolkaneesa**dora**] vulcanizer, tyre repairs

Y

y [ee] and

ya already; now

ya está there you are

ya mero [**mairo**] (Mex) right here, right now

ya que [keh] since

yace [ya-**seh**] lies

yanqui m/f [**yankee**] Yankee, North American

yatismo m (CSur) yachting

yéneca (Cu) pally

yerba f [**yairba**] herb

yerbero m (Mex) healer

yerno m [**yairno**] son-in-law

yeso m [**yeso**] (SAm) plaster cast

yeta f (Rpl) jinx

yo I; me

yo mismo myself

yuca (CAm) difficult

yunta m (Ec) friend, pal

yuyos mpl [**yoo**-yos] (Pe, Rpl) herbs

Z

zafarse [safarseh] to get away,
to escape
zafra f (CAm, Cu, Mex) (sugar
cane) harvest
zamuro m (Ven) buzzard,
vulture
zancudo m [sankoodo]
mosquito
zapallito m (Rpl) zucchini,
courgette
zapallo m (CSur, Pe) pumpkin
zapatería f [sapatairee-a] shoe
shop/store
zapatero m [sapatairo] cobbler;
shoe repairer
zapatos mpl [sapatos] shoes
zaperoco m (Ven) chaos
zenzontle m [sensontleh] (Mex)
mockingbird
zócalo m [sokalo] (Mex) central
square
zoco (Ec) blond
zona f [sona] area
zona arqueológica [arkeh-
ologeeka] archaeological site
zona de servicios [deh sairbees-
yos] service area
zona industrial [eendoostree-al]
industrial estate
zona monumental historic
monuments
zona postal [pos-tal] postcode,
(US) zip code
zona (reservada) para
peatones pedestrian precinct
zona roja [roHa] red light

district
zopilote m [sopeeloteh] (Mex)
vulture
zorrillo m [sorree-yo] (Andes,
CAm, Cu, Mex) skunk
zorrino m [sorreeno] (Rpl) skunk
zurdo [soordo] left-handed

Menu
Reader:
Food

Essential Terms

bread el pan
butter la mantequilla [mantek**ee**-ya]
cup la taza [**ta**sa]
dessert el postre [**po**streh]
fish el pescado
fork el tenedor
glass (tumbler) el vaso [**ba**so]
  (wine glass) la copa
knife el cuchillo [koo**chee**-yo]
main course el plato principal
meat la carne [**ka**rneh]
menu la carta
pepper (spice) la pimienta [peem-**ye**nta]
plate el plato
salad la ensalada
salt la sal
set menu el menú, la comida corrida, la comida corriente [korr-**ye**nteh]
soup la sopa
spoon la cuchara
starter la entrada
table la mesa

another ..., please otro/otra ..., por favor [fa**bo**r]
waiter! ¡señor! [sen-**yo**r]
waitress! ¡señorita! [sen-yor**ee**ta]
could I have the bill, please? me pasa la cuenta, por favor [meh pasa la kw**e**nta]

abrebocas (Col) appetizers

acaramelado [akaramelado] toffee-coated

aceite [asayteh] oil

aceite de oliva [deh oleeba] olive oil

aceitunas [asaytoonas] olives

aceitunas aliñadas [aleen-yadas] olives with salad dressing

aceitunas negras [neh-gras] black olives

aceitunas rellenas [reh-yenas] stuffed olives

acelgas [aselgas] spinach beet

achicoria [acheekor-ya] chicory, endive

achiote [ach-yoteh] (Mex) spicy seasoning from Yucatán

acocil [akoseel] freshwater shrimp

acompañamiento ... [akompan-yamyento] served with ...

adobado tossed in adobo seasoning

adobo red chilli paste used for cooking, in marinades etc

aguacate [agwakateh] avocado

ahumado [owmado] smoked

ají [aHee] chilli

ajiaco [aHyako] (Col) stew of chicken, potatoes, vegetables and corn on the cob

ajo [aHo] garlic

a la brasa barbecued

a la crema creamed

a la criolla [kree-o-ya] in hot, spicy sauce

a la marinera [mareenaira] in white wine sauce with garlic

a la mexicana [meHeekana] (Mex) with chilli peppers, onions and garlic

a la parrilla [parree-ya] grilled

a la plancha grilled

a la romana fried in batter

a la tampiqueña [tampeeken-ya] (Mex) with chilli sauce and black refried beans

a la veracruzana [bairakroosana] (Mex) in a tomato-based sauce with olives, capers and chillies

al carbón grilled

al clima at room temperature

al horno [orno] baked

al mojo de ajo [moHo deh aHo] in a garlic sauce

al natural [natooral] plain

al tiempo at room temperature

al vapor steamed

albahaca [albaka] basil

albacora [albakora] (Ch) swordfish

albaricoques [albareekokes] apricots

albóndigas meatballs

albóndigas de lomo [deh] pork meatballs

alcachofas artichokes

alcachofas a la romana artichokes in batter

alcaparras capers

aliñado [aleen-yado] with salad dressing

alioli garlic mayonnaise

almejas [almeh-Has] clams

almejas a la marinera [mareenaira] clams stewed in white wine

almejas al natural [natooral] live clams

almendras almonds

almuerzo [almwairso] set menu; lunch

ambrosía [ambrosee-a] (Rpl) type of sweet custard

ananás pineapple

anchoas [ancho-as] anchovies

anchoas a la barquera [barkaira] marinated anchovies with capers

anguila [angeela] eel

angulas [angoolas] baby eels

ante [anteh] (Mex) dish made with sweet potato and pineapple

anticucho [anteekoocho] (Bol, Ch, Pe) kebab

antojitos [antoHeetos] snacks

apanado (Andes) coated in breadcrumbs

apio [ap-yo] celery

arenque [arenkeh] herring

arenque ahumado kipper

arepa corn meal pancake

arequipe [arekeepeh] (Col) fudge

arroz [arros] rice

arroz a la cubana boiled rice with fried eggs and either bananas or chillies

arroz a la mexicana [meHeekana] rice with garlic, tomato and coriander

arroz a la valenciana rice with seafood

arroz blanco boiled white rice

arroz con leche [lecheh] rice pudding

arroz con mariscos rice with seafood

arroz integral brown rice

arroz verde [bairdeh] rice with olives and green peppers

asado roast; roast meat

ate [ateh] (Mex) quince jelly

atún tuna

avellanas [abeh-yanas] hazelnuts

aves [ab-es] poultry

azafrán [asafran] saffron

azúcar [asookar] sugar

babilla [babee-ya] flank, thigh

bacalao a la vizcaína [bakala-o – beeska-eena] cod served with ham, peppers and onions

bacalao al pil pil [peel] cod cooked in olive oil

bagre [bagreh] catfish

baleada [baleh-ada] corn meal pancake filled with beans, cheese and eggs

banana, banano banana

bandeja [bandeHa] main dish

bandeja paisa (Col) beef, beans, eggs, rice and vegetables

barbacoa barbecued meat

barbecú [barbek**oo**] (Ch) barbecue

berenjena [bairen**H**ena] aubergine, eggplant

berlín [bairl**een**] (Ch) type of doughnut or sweet roll

berlina [bairl**ee**na] (Col) jam

besugo sea bream

besugo al horno [**o**rno] baked sea bream

besugo asado baked sea bream

besugo mechado sea bream stuffed with ham and bacon

betabel (Mex) beetroot

betún [bet**oon**] (Ch, Mex) icing, topping

bien hecho [b-yen **e**cho] well-done

bife [b**ee**feh] steak

birria [b**ee**rr-ya] (Mex) mutton stew

bistec steak

bistec alemán (Ch) steak tartare

bistec de ternera [deh tair**nai**ra] veal steak

bizcocho [beesk**o**cho] sponge finger

bizcochuelo [beesk**o**chwelo] (CSur) sponge cake

blanquillo [blank**ee**-yo] (Mex) egg

bocadillo [bokad**ee**-yo] (Col, Ven) guava jelly

bocado [bok**a**do] (Ch) vanilla ice cream

bolillo [bol**ee**-yo] (Mex) bread roll

bollo [b**o**-yo] roll

bomba (Rpl) éclair

bomba de chocolate (Rpl) chocolate éclair

bomba de crema (Rpl) cream puff

bomba helada [el**a**da] baked Alaska

bonito tuna

bonito al horno [**o**rno] baked tuna

bonito con jitomate [**H**itom**a**teh] tuna with tomato

boquerones fritos [bokair**o**n-es] fried fresh anchovies

borgoña [borg**o**n-ya] (Ch) strawberries in red wine

borracho cake soaked in rum

botanas snacks

brazo de gitano [br**a**so deh **H**eet**a**no] swiss roll

brevas [br**e**bas] figs

brochetas kebabs

budín bread pudding

budín inglés trifle

buey [bw**e**h-ee] beef

bufet frío cold buffet

bufet libre set price buffet

buñuelos [boon-yw**e**los] light fried pastries; doughnuts

burritos stuffed tortilla parcels

buseca [boos**e**ka] oxtail soup with peas and beans

butifarra [booteef**a**rra] spicy blood sausage

cabeza [kab**e**sa] pig's head (brains, cheeks etc)

cabrilla [kabr**ee**-ya] sea bass

cabritas [kabreetas] (Ch) popcorn

cabrito kid

cabrito al pastor grilled kid

cabrito asado roast kid

cacahuates [kakawat-es] peanuts

cachelada [kachelada] pork stew with tomatoes, onions and garlic

cachito [kacheeto] (Ven) croissant

caguama [kagwama] (Mex) turtle

cajeta [kaнeta] (Mex) fudge

calabacines [kalabaseen-es] courgettes, zucchini; marrow, squash

calabacitas courgettes, zucchini

calabaza [kalabasa] pumpkin, squash

calamares a la romana [kalamar-es] squid rings fried in batter

calamares en su tinta squid cooked in their ink

calamares fritos fried squid

caldeirada [kaldayrada] fish soup

caldillo [kaldee-yo] stew

caldo de ... [deh] ... soup

caldo de gallina chicken soup

caldo de perdiz [pairdees] partridge soup

caldo de pescado clear fish soup

caldo de pollo [po-yo] chicken soup

caldo gallego [ga-yego] clear soup with green vegetables, beans

caldo tlalpeño [tlalpen-yo] (Mex) chicken broth with vegetables, chicken strips and coriander

caldo Xóchitl [socheetl] (Mex) chicken broth with pumpkin blossoms

callampas [kayampas] (Ch) mushrooms

callos [ka-yos] tripe

callos a la madrileña [madreelen-ya] tripe cooked with chillis

caluga [kalooga] (Ch) toffee

camarones [kamaron-es] prawns

camarones al mojo de ajo [moнo deh aнo] garlic prawns

cambur [kamboor] (Ven) banana

camote [kamoteh] (Mex) sweet potato

campechana de camarón [deh] spicy prawn cocktail

canela cinnamon

canelones [kanelon-es] cannelloni

cangrejos de río [kan-greнos] river crabs

capirotada (Mex) bread pudding

caracoles [karakol-es] sea snails

caramelo: a punto de caramelized

caraotas [kara-otas] (Ven) beans

carne [karneh] meat

carne a la cacerola pot roast
carne de chancho (Ch, Pe) pork
carne de cochino (Ven) pork
carne de marrano [karn-eh deh marrano] (Col) pork
carne de puerco [pwairko] pork
carne de res beef
carne desmechada (Col, Ven) shredded meat
carne de venado venison
carne magra lean meat
carne picada minced meat, (US) ground beef
carne roja [roHa] red meat
carnero [karnairo] mutton
carnes [karn-es] meat; meat dishes
carnitas barbecued pork
carta menu
casero [kasairo] home-made
castañas [kastan-yas] chestnuts
catalina [kataleena] (Ven) type of cookie
causa [kowsa] (Pe) potato salad
causeo [kowseh-o] (Ch) dish made with cold meat, tomato and onion
caza [kasa] game
cazuela [kaswela] casserole, stew
cazuela de ave [aveh] (Ch) soup made with chicken and vegetables
cazuela de hígado [deh eegado] liver casserole
cazuela de mariscos seafood stew

cazuela de pescado fish casserole
cazuela de vacuno (Ch) soup made with meat and vegetables
cebada perlada [sebada] pearl barley
cebolla [sebo-ya] onion
cebolla de verdeo (Arg) spring onion
cebollitas [sebo-yeetas] spring onions
cecina [seseena] cured beef or pork; (Ch) pork sausage
cena [sena] dinner, evening meal
centollo [sento-yo] spider crab
cerdo [sairdo] pork, pig
cereza [sairesa] cherry
ceviche [sebeecheh] marinated raw seafood cocktail
chabacano (Mex) apricot
chairo [chīro] mutton and potato broth
chalupa fried tortilla with filling
champiñones [champeen-yon-es] mushrooms
chancada [chankada] (Pe) maize cake
chancho pork, pig
chanquetes [chanketes] fish similar to whitebait
charamusca [charamooska] (Mex) candy twist
charcha [charcha] (Ch) scrag end

239

charqui [charkee] (SAm) jerked beef, spicy beef

charquicán [charkeekan] (Bol, Ch) stew made with charqui and vegetables

chauchas [chowchas] (Rpl) green beans

chayote [cha-yoteh] vegetable similar to marrow or squash

chícharos (Mex) peas

chicharrón pork crackling

chifa [cheefa] (Pe) Chinese food

chilaquiles [cheelakeel-es] (Mex) fried tortillas in hot chilli sauce

chile [cheeleh] chilli pepper

chile de árbol [deh] dried reddish chilli pepper

chile güero [gwairo] (Mex) very hot, white chilli pepper

chile habanero [abanairo] (Mex) very hot red or green chilli

chile jalapeño [Halapen-yo] (Mex) green chilli pepper, usually in vinegar with onions and carrots

chile Pekín (Mex) small, green, very hot chilli pepper

chile poblano (Mex) large green bell pepper, usually stuffed

chile rubio (Mex) very hot, white chilli pepper

chile serrano [sairrano] (Mex) very hot, thin green chilli pepper

chiles en nogada [cheel-es] (Mex) stuffed peppers with a sauce made from walnuts and pomegranate seeds

chiles rellenos [reh-yenos] (Mex) stuffed green peppers

chiltoma [cheeltoma] (CAm) sweet pepper

chimichanga (Mex) stuffed, fried tortilla

china [cheena] orange

chinchulines [cheenchooleenes] (Bol, Rpl) chitterlings

chip (Arg) bread roll, bridge roll

chipichipi [cheepeecheepee] (Col, Ven) baby clam

chipirones [cheepeeron-es] baby squid

chiporro [cheeporro] (Ch) lamb

chipotle [cheepotleh] (Mex) dark chilli sauce

chirimoya soursop (a tart-flavoured fruit)

chirla [cheerla] baby clam

chirmol [cheermol] hot sauce made from tomatoes, onion and mint

chivito [cheebeeto] (Arg) goat's meat; (Urug) steak sandwich

choclo (SAm) maize, corn on the cob, sweet corn

chocos squid

cholga (Ch) mussel

chompique [chompeekeh] (CAm, Mex) turkey

chongo (Mex) dessert made of fried bread, topped with cheese or cinnamon

chongos zamoranos

[samor**anos**] (Mex) curds in syrup

chorizo [chor**eeso**] spicy red sausage

choro (Chi, Pe) mussel

chotos (Rpl) chitterlings

chuchoca [chooch**oka**] (Ch) dried maize flour

chuleta chop, cutlet

chuleta de cerdo [deh s**airdo**] pork chop

chuleta de cerdo empanizada [empanees**ada**] breaded pork chop

chuleta de chancho pork chop

chuleta de cordero [kord**airo**] lamb chop

chuleta de lomo ahumado [ow**mado**] smoked pork chop

chuleta de ternera [tairn**aira**] veal chop

chuleta de ternera empanizada [empanees**ada**] breaded veal chop

chuleta de venado [b**enado**] venison chop

chumpique [choomp**eekeh**] (CAm) turkey

chuños [ch**oo**n-yos] freeze-dried potatoes

chupe [ch**oopeh**] (Andes) chowder

chupete [ch**oopeteh**] lollipop

chupete helado (Andes) ice lolly, (US) Popsicle®

churrasco roast or grilled meat

churros [ch**oo**rros] long fritters

cigalas [s**eegalas**] crayfish

cigalas a la parrilla [parr**ee**-ya] grilled crayfish

cilantro [s**eelantro**] coriander

ciruela [s**eerwela**] plum, greengage

ciruela pasa prune

clavos [k**labos**] cloves

cobertura [kobairt**oora**] icing, (US) frosting

cocaleca [kok**aleka**] popcorn

cochinillo asado [kocheen**ee**-yo] roast sucking pig

cochinita pibil [peeb**eel**] barbecued pork

cocido [kos**eedo**] stew made from meat, chickpeas and vegetables

coco coconut

coctel de frutas fruit cocktail

coctel de gambas prawn cocktail

coctel de langostinos king prawn cocktail

coctel de mariscos seafood cocktail

codornices [kodorn**ees**-es] quails

codornices estofadas braised quails

col cabbage

coles de Bruselas [k**ol**-es deh] Brussels sprouts

corvina bass

coliflor cauliflower

coliflor con bechamel [bech**amel**] cauliflower in white sauce

comal (Mex) griddle

comida set menu; meal; food
comida corrida set menu
comida corriente set menu
comidas para llevar [yebar]
take-away meals
comino cumin
completo (Ch) hot-dog
conejo [koneHo] rabbit
conejo asado roast rabbit
congrio [kon-gryo] conger eel
conservas [konsairbas] jams,
preserves
consomé de pollo [deh po-yo]
chicken consommé
copa de helado [Helado]
assorted ice creams
corazón [korason] (Col) palmier,
a biscuit/cookie made of
layers of puff pastry rolled
in sugar
cordero [kordairo] lamb
cordero asado roast lamb
coriandro [kor-yandro] (Arg)
coriander
corteza de pan crust
costillas [kostee-yas] ribs
costillas de cerdo [deh sairdo]
pork rib
cotufa [kotoofa] (Ven) popcorn
coyotas (Mex) biscuits,
cookies
crema cream
crema ácida soured cream
crema batida whipped cream
crema de espárragos cream
of asparagus soup
crema de espinacas cream of
spinach soup
crema doble [dobleh] double

cream
crema líquida single cream
cremada dessert made from
egg, sugar and milk
crepa sweet pancake
crep(e) pancake
crepes imperiales [krep-es
eempair-yal-es] crêpes suzette
criadillas [kree-adee-yas] bull's
testicles
crocante [krokanteh] ice cream
with chopped nuts
croquetas [kroketas] croquettes
croquetas de pescado [deh]
fish croquettes
crudo raw
cuajada [kwaHada] milk curds
cubierto menu
cuchuco [koochooko] wheat
and pork soup
cuerno [kwairno] (Mex)
croissant
cuitlacoche [kweetlakocheh]
(Mex) type of edible
mushroom which grows on
the maize/corn plant
curanto [kooranto] dish of
various meats, seafood and
vegetables
curvina [koorbeena] sea bass
cuy [koo-ee] guinea pig

damascos [damaskos] (CSur)
apricots
dátiles [dateel-es] dates
de fabricación casera [deh
fabreekas-yon kasaira] home-
made
desayuno [desa-yoono]

breakfast

dorado type of fish

dulce de leche [doolseh deh lecheh] (Rpl) fudge

dulce de membrillo [membree-yo] quince jelly

dulces [dools-es] sweets, candies

durazno [doorasno] peach

ejotes [eнot-es] (Mex) green beans, runner beans

elote [eloteh] (Mex) maize, corn on the cob, corncob

embutidos cured pork sausages

empanada pasty filled with meat or fish

empanadillas de queso [empanadee-yas deh keso] cheese pasties

empanizado [empaneesado] in breadcrumbs

en escabeche [eskabecheh] pickled

enchilada (Mex) fried corn meal pancake filled with meat, vegetables and cheese

enchiladas rojas [roнas] (Mex) stuffed tortillas in red chilli sauce

enchilada suiza [sweesa] (Mex) stuffed tortilla with soured cream

enchiladas verdes [baird-es] (Mex) stuffed tortillas in green chilli sauce

endivias [endeeb-yas] endive, chicory

endulzante [endoolsanteh] sweetener

ensalada salad

ensalada de frutas [deh] fruit salad

ensalada de pollo [po-yo] chicken salad

ensalada mixta [meesta] mixed salad

ensalada rusa Russian salad – cold diced potatoes and other vegetables in mayonnaise

ensalada verde [bairdeh] green salad

ensaladilla [ensaladee-ya] vegetables and chicken in mayonnaise

ensaladilla rusa Russian salad

entrada starter

entrante [entranteh] starter

entraña [entran-ya] (Rpl) skirt (cut of beef)

entrecot de ternera [deh tairnaira] veal entrecôte

entremeses [entremes-es] hors d'oeuvres

entremeses variados [bar-yados] assorted hors d'œuvres

epazote [epasoteh] (Mex) commonly used Mexican herb

escabeche de ... [eskabecheh deh] pickled ...

escalope de ternera veal escalope

escamoles [eskamol-es] (Mex) ants' eggs

escarola curly endive
esencia de café [esens-ya] coffee essence
esencia de vainilla [binee-ya] vanilla essence
espada ahumado [owmado] smoked swordfish
espaguetis [espagetees] spaghetti
espaldar loin
espárragos asparagus
espárragos con mayonesa [ma-yonesa] asparagus with mayonnaise
espárragos dos salsas asparagus with mayonnaise and vinaigrette dressing
espárragos en vinagreta [beenagreta] asparagus in vinaigrette dressing
especia [espes-ya] spice
especialidad [espes-yaleeda] speciality
espinacas spinach
espinacas a la crema creamed spinach
espinazo de cerdo con papas stew of pork ribs with potatoes
estofado de... ... stew
estofado de liebre [l-yebreh] hare stew
estragón tarragon

fabada (asturiana) [astoor-yana] bean stew with red sausage
factura [faktoora] (Rpl) rolls, croissants, cookies etc
fajitas [faHeetas] (Mex) soft wheat tortillas stuffed with chicken or beef, peppers and onion
faisán [fisan] pheasant
faisán con castañas [kastan-yas] pheasant with chestnuts
faisán estofado stewed pheasant
faisán trufado pheasant with truffles
falda brisket
fiambres [f-yambres] cold meats, cold cuts
fideos [feedeh-os] thin pasta; noodles; vermicelli
filete [feeleteh] meat or fish steak
filete a la parrilla [parree-ya] grilled beef steak
filete a la plancha grilled beef steak
filete de puerco [deh pwairko] pork fillet
filete de res beef steak
filete de ternera [tairnaira] veal steak
flan crème caramel
flan con nata crème caramel with whipped cream
flan de café [deh kafeh] coffee-flavoured crème caramel
flan de caramelo crème caramel
flan (quemado) al ron [kemado] crème caramel with rum
flautas [flowtas] (Mex) fried tacos
flor de calabaza [deh kalabasa] pumpkin flower

frambuesas [frambwesas] raspberries

fresas strawberries

fresas con nata strawberries and cream/whipped cream

frijol [freeHol] bean

frijoles [freeHol-es] kidney beans

frijoles blancos white beans

frijoles borrachos (Mex) beans cooked with beer

frijoles de olla [deh o-ya] boiled beans in gravy-type sauce

frijoles en salsa de tomate baked beans

frijoles negros [neh-gros] black beans

frijoles refritos (Mex) refried beans

fritada [freetada] fried fish

fritanga [freetanga] (Andes, CAm, Mex) fried meal, consisting of pork, beef, plantain, black pudding, sausage, giblets, potato and cassava

fruta fruit

fruta variada [bar-yada] selection of fresh fruit

frutas en almíbar fruit in syrup

frutillas [frootee-yas] strawberries

galleta [ga-yeta] biscuit, cookie

galleta de campaña [kampan-ya] (CSur) type of bread

galleta de champaña [champan-ya] (Ch) sponge finger

galleta de soda (Andes) cracker

gallina [ga-yeena] chicken

gallina con pepitoria chicken stewed with peppers

gallopinto (CAm) re-fried rice and beans

gallos [ga-yos] cornmeal pancakes filled with meat or chicken in sauce

gamba large prawn

garbanzos [garbansos] chickpeas

garnachas (Mex) tortillas with garlic sauce, typical of Veracruz

garobo iguana

gazpacho andaluz [gaspacho andaloos] cold soup made from tomatoes, onions, garlic, peppers and cucumber

gelatina [Helateena] gelatine; jelly, (US) jello

glaseado glazed

gomita [gomeeta] (Ven) marshmallow

gorditas (Mex) stuffed tortillas

granada pomegranate

granadilla [granadee-ya] passion fruit

gratén de... ... au gratin, baked in a cream and cheese sauce

gratinado au gratin – baked in a cream and cheese sauce

greifrú [grayfroo] (CAm, Ven) grapefruit

grosellas [groseh-yas] redcurrants

guacamole [gwakamoleh] avocado dip

guachalomo [gwachalomo] (Ch) sirloin

guanábana [gwanabana] soursop (a tart-flavoured fruit)

guapote [gwapoteh] (CAm) freshwater fish

guayaba [gwa-yaba] guava

guargüero [gwargwairo] (Pe) sweet fritter filled with fudge

guasacaca [gwasakaka] (Ven) avocado sauce similar to guacamole

guasca [gwaska] (Col) frenchweed, aromatic herb used for seasoning

guatita [gwateeta] (Ch) tripe

guinda [geenda] black cherry; alcoholic drink made from black cherries

guineo [geeneh-o] small banana

güirila [gweereela] (CAm) maize pancake

guisado [geesado] stew

guiso [geeso] stew

gusanos de maguey [deh magay] (Mex) maguey worms

habanitos [abaneetos] (Arg) chocolate fingers

habas [abas] broad beans

habichuelas [abeechwelas] runner beans

hallaquita [a-yakeeta] (Ven)

ground corn wrapped in leaves for cooking

hallulla [a-yoo-ya] (Ch) type of white bread

hamburguesa [amboorgesa] hamburger

harina [areena] flour

harina de maíz [ma-ees] cornflour

hayaca [a-yaka] (Col, Ven) cornmeal, meat and vegetables wrapped in banana leaves

helado [elado] ice cream

helado de chocolate [deh chokolateh] chocolate ice cream

helado de fresa strawberry ice cream

helado de nata dairy ice cream

helado de vainilla [bīnee-ya] vanilla ice cream

hierbas [yairbas] herbs

hígado [eegado] liver

hígado con cebolla [sebo-ya] liver cooked with onion

hígado de ternera estofado [deh tairnaira] braised calves' liver

hígado encebollado [ensebo-yado] liver in an onion sauce

hígado estofado braised liver

higos [eegos] figs

higos con miel y nueces [m-yel ee nwes-es] figs with honey and nuts

higos secos dried figs

hongos [ongos] mushrooms

hormigas culonas [ormeegas koolonas] (Col) large fried ants

huachinango [wacheenango] (Mex) red snapper

huachinango al ajo [aHo] (Mex) red snapper with garlic butter

huevo [webo] egg

huevo duro [dooro] hard-boiled egg

huevo pasado por agua [agwa] boiled egg

huevo tibio [teeb-yo] soft-boiled egg

huevos a la copa boiled eggs

huevos a la mexicana [meHeekana] (Mex) scrambled eggs with peppers, onions and garlic

huevos a la oaxaqueña [waHaken-ya] (Mex) eggs in chilli and tomato sauce

huevos chimbos dessert made with eggs, cognac and syrup

huevos cocidos [koseedos] hard-boiled eggs

huevos con jamón [Hamon] ham and eggs

huevos con papas fritas fried eggs and chips/French fries

huevos con picadillo [peekadee-yo] eggs with minced sausage

huevos con salchichas eggs and sausages

huevos con tocino [toseeno] eggs and bacon

huevos duros hard-boiled eggs

huevos escalfados poached eggs

huevos estrellados [estrehyados] fried eggs

huevos fritos fried eggs

huevos fritos con chorizo [choreeso] fried eggs with Spanish sausage

huevos hilados [eelados] sweetened strands of egg yolk

huevos motuleños [motoolen-yos] (Mex) eggs cooked in chillis and tomatoes, served on a fried tortilla and garnished with cheese, ham and chillis

huevos pasados por agua soft-boiled eggs

huevos pericos (Col) scrambled eggs

huevos poché [pocheh] (Rpl) poached eggs

huevos rancheros [ranchairos] (Mex) fried eggs with hot tomato sauce and tortilla

huevos rellenos [reh-yenos] stuffed eggs

huevos revueltos [rebweltos] scrambled eggs

huevos sancochados hard-boiled eggs

humita [oomeeta] (SAm) flavored corn paste wrapped in corn leaves

incluye pan, postre y vino includes bread, dessert and wine

247

jaiba [Hība] crab

jalapeños [Halapen-yos] (Mex) hot green chilli peppers

jalea [Haleh-a] gelatine; jelly, (US) jello

jamón [Hamon] ham

jamón serrano [sairrano] cured ham, similar to Parma ham

jamón York boiled ham

jarabe [Harabeh] syrup

jeta [Heta] pigs' cheeks

jícama [Heekama] sweet turnip-like fruit eaten with lemon juice or chilli

jitomate [Heetomateh] (Mex) tomato

jojote [HoHoteh] sweetcorn

jojoto [HoHoto] (Ven) maize

lagarto (Ven) cheap cut of meat

langosta lobster

langosta a la americana [amaireekana] lobster with brandy and garlic

langosta fría con mayonesa [free-a kon mī-yonesa] cold lobster with mayonnaise

langosta gratinada lobster au gratin

langostinos a la plancha grilled king prawns

langostinos con mayonesa [mī-yonesa] king prawns with mayonnaise

langostinos dos salsas king prawns cooked in two sauces

laurel [lowrel] bay leaves

leche frita [lecheh] pudding

made from milk, eggs and semolina

lechona [lechona] sucking pig

lechosa [lechosa] papaya

lechuga [lechooga] lettuce

lengua [lengwa] tongue

lengua de cordero estofada [deh kordairo] stewed lambs' tongue

lengua de res ox tongue

lenguado a la plancha [lengwado] grilled sole

lenguado a la romana sole in batter

lenguado frito fried sole

lentejas [lenteHas] lentils

liebre estofada [l-yebreh] stewed hare

lima [leema] lime

limón lemon; lime

llapingachos [yapeengachos] potato and cheese pancakes

lobina sea bass

lobina a la marinera sea bass in a parsley sauce

lobina al horno baked sea bass

locro maize and meat soup

lombarda rellena [reh-yena] stuffed red cabbage

lombarda salteada sautéed red cabbage

lomo pork fillet, pork loin, tenderloin

lomo curado pork-loin sausage

lomo saltado stir-fried pork with vegetables

lonchas de jamón [Hamon] sliced, cured ham

longaniza [longan**ee**sa] cooked spicy sausage

lulo [**loo**lo] (Col) a tomato-like fruit

macarrones [makarr**on**-es] macaroni

macarrones gratinados macaroni cheese

macedonia de fruta [mased**on**-ya] fruit salad

machaca (Mex) shredded meat

macho large green banana

maduro ripe; (Col) plantain

magdalena sponge cake, (US) muffin

maíz [ma-**ees**] sweetcorn, maize, (US) corn

majarete [ma**H**ar**e**teh] (Ven) corn pudding

malaya [mala-ya] (Ch) skirt (cut of beef)

malojo [malo**Ho**] (Ven) maize

mamey [mam**ay**] round, apple-sized tropical fruit

mandarina tangerine

mandioca [mand-y**o**ka] cassava

maní [man**ee**] peanuts

manitas de cerdo [deh s**ai**rdo] pig's trotters

manitas de cordero [kord**ai**ro] leg of lamb

manjar blanco [man**H**ar] (Andes) fudge dessert

mantecadas [mante**ka**das] small sponge cakes

mantequilla [mantek**ee**-ya] butter

manzana [man**sa**na] apple

manzanas acarameladas toffee apples

manzanas asadas baked apples

mañoco [man-y**o**ko] (Ven) cassava flour

maracuyá [marakoo-y**a**] passion fruit

mariscada cold mixed shellfish

mariscal (Ch) mixed seafood dish

mariscos shellfish

mariscos de temporada seasonal shellfish

mariscos del día fresh shellfish

marrano (Col) pork

marraqueta [marrak**e**ta] (Ch) bread roll

masa dough

matambre [mat**a**mbreh] (Rpl) skirt (cut of beef)

matambre arrollado rolled beef stuffed with spinach, onion, carrots and eggs

mazamorra [masam**o**rra] (SAm) milky pudding; (Pe) pudding made with corn starch, sugar and honey; (Col) maize soup

mayonesa [mī-yon**e**sa] mayonnaise

mazapán [masap**a**n] marzipan

mazorca [mas**o**rka] corn on the cob, (US) corncob

medallones de anguila [meda-y**o**n-es deh ang**ee**la] eel steaks

medallones de merluza
[mairl**oo**sa] hake steaks

medialuna [med-yal**oo**na] (Rpl)
croissant

mejillones [meHee-y**o**n-es]
mussels

mejillones a la marinera
[mareen**ai**ra] mussels in wine
sauce with garlic

mejillones con salsa mussels
with tomato and herb sauce

melcocha [melk**o**cha] candy
made with molasses

melocotón peach

melocotones en almíbar
peaches in syrup

melón melon

membrillo [membr**ee**-yo]
quince; quince jelly

menestra de verduras [deh
baird**oo**ras] vegetable stew

menú [men**oo**] set menu

menú de la casa [deh] fixed-
price menu

menú del día today's set menu

menudencias [menood**e**ns-yas]
giblets

menudo tripe; sweetbreads

menú turístico set menu

merluza a la parrilla [mairl**oo**sa a
la parr**ee**-ya] grilled hake

merluza a la plancha grilled
hake

merluza a la riojana [r-yo**Ha**na]
(Mex) hake with chillies

merluza a la romana hake
steaks in batter

merluza en salsa hake in
sauce

merluza en salsa verde hake
in a parsley and wine sauce

merluza fría cold hake

merluza frita fried hake

mermelada [mairmel**a**da] jam;
marmalade

mermelada de ciruelas [deh
seersw**e**las] plum jam

mermelada de damasco
apricot jam

mermelada de durazno
[door**a**sno] peach jam

mermelada de frambuesas
[frambw**e**sas] raspberry jam

mermelada de fresas
strawberry jam

mermelada de limón lemon
marmalade

mermelada de naranja
[naran**Ha**] orange
marmalade

miel [m-yel] honey

milanesa breaded chop or
escalope

milanesa de ternera [deh
tairn**ai**ra] breaded veal
escalope

milhojas [meelo**Ha**s]
millefeuille

minuta [meen**oo**ta] (Rpl) quick
meal

mojarro [mo**Ha**rro] type of fish

mojicón [moHeek**o**n] sponge
finger

mole [m**o**leh] (Mex) sauce
made with chilli peppers,
chocolate and spices

mole de olla [deh **o**-ya] (Mex)
spicy meat stew

mole oaxaqueño [waHak**en**-yo] (Mex) type of black or green mole sauce

mole poblano (Mex) rich mole sauce made from nuts, prunes and bananas, a Puebla speciality

mollejas de ternera [mo-ye**H**as deh tairn**ai**ra] calves' sweetbreads

molletes [mo-ye-tes] toasted roll with refried beans and cheese

mondongo tripe

mora blackberry

morcilla [mors**ee**-ya] black pudding, blood sausage

morcilla de ternera [deh tairn**ai**ra] black pudding made from calves' blood

moronga (CAm, Mex) black pudding

morrocoy (Col, Ven) tortoise

mortadela salami-type sausage

mosh (Guat) oats with cinammon and honey

mostaza [mostasa] mustard

mote [m**o**teh] (Andes) boiled wheat

mousse de limón [deh] lemon mousse

nabo turnip

naco (Col) purée

nacatamales [nakatamal-es] corn meal dough filled with meat in sauce and steamed in banana leaves

nachos tortilla chips with cheese

naiboa [nib**o**-a] (Ven) cassava bread filled with brown sugar

nalga (Rpl) rump steak

naranja [naranHa] orange

nata cream

natilla [natee-ya] custard

natillas [natee-yas] cold custard with cinnamon

natillas de chocolate [deh chokolateh] cold custard with chocolate

nieve [n-yebeh] (Mex) sorbet; ice cream

níscalos wild mushrooms

nísperos [neespairos] medlars – fruit like crab apples

nixtamal [neestamal] (Mex) maize dough, (US) corn dough

nopalitos (Mex) chopped cactus-leaf salad

nueces [nwes-es] walnuts

nuez [nwes] nut

nuez de Castilla [kastee-ya] (Mex) walnut

nuez moscada nutmeg

ñoquis [n-yokees] gnocchi

ñoquis a la romana gnocchi in batter

ñoquis de sémola semolina gnocchi

oblea wafer

onces [onses] (Andes) (afternoon) tea

ostión [ost-yon] oyster; (Ch) scallop

ostras oysters

pabellón [pabeh-yon] minced meat/ground beef, beans, rice and banana

pachamanca (Pe) meat barbecued between two hot stones

pacumutu [pakoomootoo] beef kebabs

paella [pa-eh-ya] fried rice with seafood and chicken

paella valenciana [balens-yana] paella with assorted shellfish

paila [pīla] fried or poached eggs with bread

paleta ice lolly

pallar [pa-yar] (Pe) butter bean

palmita [palmeeta] (Rpl) palmier, a biscuit/cookie made of layers of puff pastry rolled in sugar

palmito palm heart

palomitas popcorn

palta (Bol, CSur, Pe) avocado

pan bread

pan blanco white bread

pan de azúcar [asookar] sugarloaf

pan de carne [karneh] meat loaf

pan de cazón [kason] (Mex) layered dish of tortillas, beans and dogfish with a hot sauce

pan de centeno [senteno] brown bread

pan de higos [eegos] dried fig cake with cinnamon

pan de huevo [Hwevo] (Ch) bun, sweet roll

pan de molde [moldeh] pan loaf

pan de Pascua (Ch) panettone

pan de Viena (Rpl) bridge roll

pan dulce [doolseh] buns and cakes, sweet pastries; (Rpl) panettone

pan francés (Rpl) French bread

pan integral [eentegral] wholemeal bread

pan lactal (Rpl) type of white bread

pan molido (Mex) breadcrumbs

pan rallado [ra-yado] breadcrumbs

pana (Ch) liver

panceta [panseta] (Rpl) bacon

pancho (Rpl) hot dog

pancita [panseeta] tripe

pantruca [pantrooka] (Ch) dumpling

papa potato

papa rellena [reh-yena] stuffed potato

papadzules [papadsul-es] (Mex) tortillas stuffed with hard-boiled eggs from Yucatán

papas a la huancaína [wanka-eena] (Arg) stuffed potato

papas a la criolla [cree-o-ya] potatoes in hot, spicy sauce

papas asadas baked potatoes

papas bravas potatoes in cayenne pepper

papas chips (Urug) crisps, (US) potato chips

papas fritas chips, French fries

papaya papaya, pawpaw

papelón (Ven) sugarloaf

pargo red snapper

parrillada de caza [parree-yada deh kasa] mixed grilled game

parrillada de mariscos mixed grilled shellfish

pasas raisins

pasta biscuit, cookie; pastry; pasta

pasta de hojaldre [oHaldreh] puff pastry

pastel cake; pie

pastel de carne [karneh] brawn, jellied meat

pastel de queso [keso] cheesecake

pasticho [pasteecho] lasagna

pata foot, trotter

patacones [patakon-es] banana chips

patatas (fritas) crisps, (US) potato chips

patilla [patee-ya] (Col) watermelon

pato duck

pato a la naranja [naranHa] duck à l'orange

pato asado roast duck

pavo [pabo] turkey

pavo relleno [reh-yeno] stuffed turkey

pay [pi] pie with a sweet filling

pay de queso [deh keso] cheesecake

pebre [pebreh] (Ch) dressing made with onion, chili, coriander, parsley and tomato

pechuga de pollo [deh po-yo] breast of chicken

pepián meat stew

pepinillos [pepeenee-yos] gherkins

pepinillos en vinagreta [beenagreta] gherkins in vinaigrette dressing

pepino cucumber

pera [paira] pear

perdices [pairdees-es] partridges

perdices a la campesina partridges with vegetables

perdices asadas roast partridges

perdices con chocolate [chokolateh] partridges with chocolate

perdices encebolladas [ensebo-yadas] partridge with onion

perejil [paireh-Heel] parsley

perro caliente [pairro kal-yenteh] hot dog

pescaditos fritos fried sprats

pescado fish

pescado a la veracruzana [bairakroosana] (Mex) seasoned sea bass or red snapper fillets fried and served with tomato sauce on top

peto (Col) corn/maize soup

pez espada ahumado [owmado] smoked swordfish

píbil (Mex) cooked in a pit

picadillo [peekadee-yo] minced meat, (US) ground beef

picadillo de pollo [deh po-yo] minced chicken

picadillo de ternera [tairnaira] minced veal

picante [peekanteh] hot, spicy; (Chi, Pe) spicy meat stew

pichón pigeon

pichones estofados [peechon-es] stewed pigeon

picoso hot, spicy

pierna [p-yairna] leg

pilón [peelon] sugarloaf

piloncillo [peelonsee-yo] (Mex) unrefined brown sugar

pimentón paprika

pimienta [peem-yenta] black pepper

pimienta blanca white pepper

pimienta de cayena [deh kī-yena] cayenne pepper

pimiento rojo [roHo] red pepper

pimiento verde [bairdeh] green pepper

pimientos rellenos [reh-yenos] stuffed peppers

pinchitos snacks/appetizers served in bars; kebabs

pincho kebab

pino [peeno] (Ch) minced meat/ground beef and onion

pinolillo [peenolee-yo] (CAm) maize flour

piña [peen-ya] pineapple

piña fresca fresh pineapple

piña gratinada pineapple au gratin

piñones [peen-yon-es] pine nuts

pipián [peep-yan] hot chilli sauce with ground nuts, seeds and spices

piré [peereh] (Ven) mashed potato

pitahaya [peetaha-ya] red fruit of a cactus plant with soft, sweet flesh

plantilla [plantee-ya] (Csur, Ven) sponge finger

plátano banana

plátano macho plantain

plátanos flameados [flameh-ados] flambéed bananas

plato central (Ven) main course

plato fuerte [fwairteh] main dish

plato montañero [montan-yairo] beef, sausage, beans, eggs and rice

platos combinados meat and vegetables, hamburgers and eggs etc

poco hecho [echo] rare

pollo [po-yo] chicken

pollo al ajillo [aHee-yo] fried chicken with garlic

pollo a la parrilla [parree-ya] grilled chicken

pollo al vino blanco [beeno] chicken in white wine

pollo asado roast chicken

pollo braseado braised chicken

pollo con verduras [bairdooras] chicken and vegetables

polvorones [polboron-es] sugar-based dessert (eaten at Christmas)

pomelo (CSur) grapefruit

ponqué [ponkeh] (Col, Ven) cake

pop (Urug) popcorn

porotos (CSur) kidney beans

porotos de manteca butter beans

porotos en salsa de tomate baked beans

porotos verdes [bairdes] (Ch) runner beans

posta (CAm, Ch) cut of beef from the back legs of a cow

postre [postreh] dessert

potaje [potaHeh] thick broth

potaje de garbanzos chickpea stew

pozole [posoleh] (Mex) thick broth of vegetables meat and corn

precocinado [prekoseenado] precooked dish

primer plato [preemair] starter, appetizer

puerco [pwairko] pork

puerro [pwairro] leek

pulpitos con cebolla [sebo-ya] baby octopuses with onions

pulpo octopus

pupusa dumpling usually filled with cheese or meat

puré de papas [pooreh deh] mashed potatoes, potato purée

queque [kekeh] cake

quesadilla [kesadee-ya] (Mex) fried corn meal pancake usually filled with cheese

quesillo [kesee-yo] (Andes) curd cheese; (Ven) crème caramel

queso [keso] cheese

queso azul blue cheese

queso crema cream cheese

queso con membrillo [membree-yo] cheese with quince jelly

queso de bola Edam

queso de cabeza (Col) brawn

queso de cerdo brawn

queso de chancho (CSur) brawn

queso de mano (Ven) cheese similar to mozzarella

queso de soja tofu

queso fresco soft white cheese

queso fundido melted cheese; processed cheese

queso graso full fat cheese

queso manchego hard, strong cheese

queso Oaxaca [waHaka] (Mex) soft white cheese used for cooking

queso para untar cheese spread

queso parmesano Parmesan cheese

rábanos radishes

ración [ras-yon] portion

ración pequeña para niños [peken-ya para neen-yos] children's portion

rajas [raHas] (Mex) strips of pickled green chillies; sliced green peppers in cream

ratón (CAm) sinewy cut of meat

ravioles [rab-yol-es] ravioli

raya [ra-ya] skate

raya con manteca negra [neh-gra] skate in butter and vinegar sauce

rebanada slice

receta [reseta] recipe

refritos (Mex) refried beans

relleno [reh-yeno] stuffed; stuffing

remolacha beetroot

repollo [repo-yo] cabbage

requesón [rekeson] cream cheese, cottage cheese

res beef

revoltijo [rebolteeHo] (Mex) traditional dish made with seafood, vegetables and prickly pear

riñones [reen-yon-es] kidneys

riñones a la plancha grilled kidneys

riñones al jerez [Hair-es] kidneys in a sherry sauce

róbalo bass

rocoto hot red pepper

romero [romairo] rosemary

ron rum

ropa vieja [b-yeh-Ha] shredded meat

rosca round sponge made at Christmas

roscas sweet pastries

roseta (Arg) bread roll

rosquillas [roskee-yas] small sweet pastries

sábana (Mex) escalope

saice, saisi [sīseh, sīsee] spicy meat broth

sajta [saHta] chicken in hot sauce

sal salt

sal de ajo [aHo] garlic salt

sal de cocina [koseena] cooking salt

sal de mesa table salt

sal gruesa [grwesa] (CSur) cooking salt

sal marina sea salt

salbute [salbooteh] (Mex) type of filled tortilla typical of Yucatán

salchicha sausage

salchichas de Frankfurt [deh] frankfurters

salchichón salami-type sausage

salmón [sal-mon] salmon

salmón a la parrilla [paree-ya] grilled salmon

salmón ahumado [owmado] smoked salmon

salmón frío [free-o] cold salmon

salmonetes [sal-monet-es] red mullet

salmonetes a la parrilla [parree-ya] grilled red mullet

salmonetes en papillote [papee-yoteh] red mullet cooked in foil

salpicón de mariscos [deh] shellfish with vinaigrette dressing

salsa sauce

salsa allioli/alioli [a-yee-olee/alee olee] garlic mayonnaise

salsa bechamel [bechamel] béchamel sauce, white sauce

salsa de tomate [deh tomateh] tomato sauce

salsa holandesa [olandesa] hollandaise sauce

salsa mexicana/pico de gallo [meHeekana/peeko deh ga-yo] (Mex) hot sauce made with chillies, onions and red tomatoes

salsa romesco sauce made from peppers, tomatoes and garlic

salsa tártara tartare sauce

salsa verde [bairdeh] (Mex) green sauce made from tomatillo and chillies

salsa vinagreta [beenagreta] vinaigrette dressing

salteado [salteh-ado] sautéed

salteño [salten-yo] small pasty usually filled with chicken or other meat and sauce

sancocho vegetable soup with meat or fish

sandía [sandee-a] water melon

sándwich sandwich

sándwich mixto [meesto] cheese and ham sandwich

sánguche [sangoocheh] (Ch) sandwich

sardina sardine

sardinas a la brasa barbecued sardines

sardinas a la parrilla [parree-ya] grilled sardines

sardinas fritas fried sardines

seco (Col) main dish

segundo plato main course

servicio incluido service charge included

servicio no incluido service charge not included

sesos a la romana brains in batter

sesos rebozados [rebosados] brains in batter

silpancho [seelpancho] beef with eggs

sobrebarriga brisket

solomillo [solomee-yo] fillet steak

solomillo con papas fritas fillet steak with chips/French fries

solomillo de cerdo [deh sairdo] fillet of pork

solomillo de ternera [tairnaira] fillet of veal

solomillo de vaca [baka] fillet of beef

solomillo frío [free-o] cold roast beef

sopa soup

sopa de aguacate fría [deh agwakateh] cold avocado soup

sopa de ajo [aHo] garlic soup

sopa de arroz rice soup

sopa de fideos [feedeh-os] noodle soup

sopa de frijoles negros [freeHol-es neh-gros] black bean soup

sopa de gallina [ga-yeena] chicken soup

sopa de mondongo tripe stew

sopa del día soup of the day

sopa de lentejas [lenteHas] lentil soup

sopa de mariscos fish and shellfish soup

sopa de pescado fish soup

sopa de tortilla [tortee-ya] (Mex) soup with corn meal pancakes

sopa de tortuga turtle soup

sopa de verduras [bairdooras] vegetable soup

sopa inglesa trifle

sopaipillas [sopipee-yas] sweet fritters

sopa seca rice or pasta dish served with a sauce on top

sopa tarasca (Mex) creamy bean and tomato soup

sopes [sop-es] (Mex) garnished tortillas

sorbete [sorbeteh] sorbet

soufflé soufflé

soufflé de fresas [deh] strawberry soufflé

soufflé de naranja [naranHa] orange soufflé

soufflé de queso [keso] cheese soufflé

surubí [sooroobee] freshwater fish

taco (Mex) stuffed maize/corn pancake

tacos al pastor (Mex) tacos with grilled meat

tacos de pollo [deh po-yo] (Mex) tacos stuffed with chicken

tajadas [taHadas] fried banana strips

tallarines [ta-yareen-es] noodles

tallarines a la italiana [eetal-yana] tagliatelle with tomato sauce

tamal filled maize/corn dough cooked in banana leaf, tamale

tamarindo tamarind

tapa de ternera rellena [deh tairnaira reh-yena] stuffed veal hock

tapado stew

tapas appetizers

tarta cake

tarta Alaska baked Alaska

tarta de almendra [deh] almond tart or gâteau

tarta de arroz [arros] cake or tart containing rice

tarta de chocolate [chokolateh] chocolate gâteau

tarta de fresas strawberry tart or gâteau

tarta de la casa tart or gâteau baked on the premises

tarta de manzana [mansana] apple tart

tarta helada [elada] ice cream gâteau

tarta mocha/moka [moka] mocha tart

tártar crudo raw minced steak, steak tartare

tequiche [tekeecheh] (Ven) coconut dessert

tejos de queso [teHos deh keso] cheese pastries

tencas tench

tencas con jamón [Hamon] tench with ham

ternera [tairnaira] veal

ternera asada roast veal

tinga [teenga] (Mex) dish made from ground meat, onion, tomato and chili

tocino [toseeno] bacon

todo incluido all inclusive

tomate [tomateh] green tomato

tomates rellenos [tomat-es reh-yenos] stuffed tomatoes

tomatillo [tomatee-yo] green tomato used for sauces

tomillo [tomee-yo] thyme

tordo thrush

tordos braseados [braseh-ados] grilled thrushes

tordos estofados braised thrushes

toronja [toronHa] grapefruit

torrejas [torreHas] French toast

torrijas [torreeHas] sweet pastries

torta filled bread roll with salad, cream and tomato garnish; (Csur, Ven) cake

torta frita (Rpl) fritter

torta pascualina (Urug) spinach and egg pie

tortilla [tortee-ya] maize pancake, (US) corn pancake

tortilla de harina [deh areena] wheat pancake

tortilla de huevo [webo] omelette

tortilla española [espan-yola] Spanish omelette with potato, onion and garlic

tostada fried corn pancake topped with meat, vegetables and salsa; toast

totopo (Mex) thin, fried tortilla

triple [treepleh] (Rpl) double-decker sandwich

trucha [troocha] trout

trucha ahumada [owmada] smoked trout

trucha a la marinera [mareenaira] trout in white wine sauce

trucha con jamón [Hamon] trout with ham

trucha escabechada marinated trout

trutro (Ch) chicken leg

tuco [tooko] (Pe, Rpl) tomato sauce

tuétano [twetano] marrow, squash

tuna [toona] prickly pear

tuntas [toontas] freeze-dried potatoes

turrón nougat

turrón de coco [deh] coconut nougat

turrón de Jijona [HeeHona] hard nougat

turrón de yema [yema] nougat with egg yolk

uchepos (Mex) small sweet tamales

uvas [**oo**bas] grapes

vaho [ba-o] (CAm) dish made of steamed plantains, spicy beef and yam

vainilla [bi**nee**-ya] vanilla

vainitas [bi**nee**tas] (Ven) green beans

venado [be**na**do] venison

verduras [baird**oo**ras] vegetables

verduras capeadas [kapeh-**a**das] courgettes and cauliflower in batter served with hot tomato sauce and cream

vinagre [bee**na**greh] vinegar

vuelvealavida [bwelbeh-a-la**bee**da] (Mex) marinated seafood cocktail with chilli

yema yolk

yerba [**yair**ba] herb

yogur [yo-g**oor**] yoghurt

yuca cassava, manioc

zanahoria [sana-**or**-ya] carrot

zanahorias a la crema carrots à la crème

zapallito [sapa-**yee**to] (Rpl) zucchini, courgette, (US) zucchini

zapallo [sapa-yo] (CSur, Pe) pumpkin, marrow, squash

zapote [sap**o**teh] sweet pumpkin

zarzamoras [sarsam**o**ras] blackberries

zarzuela de mariscos [sarsw**e**la deh] shellfish stew

Menu Reader:
Drink

Essential Terms

beer la cerveza [sairbesa]
bottle la botella [boteh-ya], el frasco
brandy el coñac [kon-yak], el brandy
black coffee el café americano [kafeh amaireekano]
  (strong) el café solo
coffee el café [kafeh]
cup la taza [tasa]
  a cup of ... una taza de ... [deh]
fruit juice el jugo de frutas [Hoogo deh]
gin la ginebra [Heenebra]
  a gin and tonic un gintónic [jeentoneek]
glass (tumbler) el vaso [baso]
  (wine glass) la copa
  a glass of ... un vaso de ... [deh], una copa de ...
milk la leche [lecheh]
milkshake el licuado [leekwado], la merengada
mineral water el agua mineral [agwa meenairal]
red wine el vino tinto [beeno teento]
soda (water) la soda
soft drink el refresco
sugar el azúcar [asookar]
tea el té [teh]
tonic (water) la tónica
vodka el vodka [bodka]
water el agua [agwa]
whisky el whisky
white wine el vino blanco [beeno]
wine el vino
wine list la lista de vinos [leesta deh beenos]

another ... otro/otra ...

agua [**a**gwa] water

agua de fruta fruit drink made from fruit and water

agua de granada [deh] grenadine juice

agua de jamaica [Ham**ī**ka] (Mex) hibiscus blossom drink

agua de melón melon juice

agua de panela drink made from water and sugar

agua mineral [meen**ai**ral] mineral water

agua mineral con gas fizzy mineral water

agua mineral sin gas [seen] still mineral water

aguardiente [agward-y**e**nteh] a clear spirit similar to brandy or white rum

al tiempo [t-y**e**mpo] at room temperature

angostura angostura bitters

anís aniseed-flavoured spirit

añejo [an-y**e**h-Ho] vintage; mellow; mature

aperitivo [apaireet**ee**bo] aperitif

api [**a**pee] thick custard-like drink made from maize and cinnamon

aromáticas herb teas

atole [at**o**leh] (Mex) thick drink made from maize/corn

azúcar [as**oo**kar] sugar

bebida drink

batido [bat**ee**do] milk shake

bebidas alcohólicas alcoholic drinks

borgoña [borg**o**n-ya] (Ch) strawberries in red wine

cacao [kaka-o] cocoa

café [kaf**eh**] coffee

café americano black coffee

café capuchino cappuccino

café con leche [l**e**cheh] coffee with milk (large cup)

café cortado coffee with a dash of milk (small cup)

café de olla [deh **o**-ya] coffee made with cinammon and raw sugar

café descafeinado [deskafay-een**a**do] decaffeinated coffee

café escocés [eskos-**e**s] black coffee, whisky/scotch and vanilla ice cream

café exprés [espr**e**s] strong black coffee

café instantáneo [eenstan-t**a**neh-o] instant coffee

café irlandés [eerland-**e**s] black coffee, whisky, vanilla ice cream and whipped cream

café negro [n**e**h-gro] black coffee, usually strong and often sweet

café perfumado [pairfoom**a**do] coffee with a dash of brandy or other spirit

café perico [pair**ee**ko] (Col) coffee with a dash of milk

café solo black coffee, usually strong and often sweet

café tinto (Col) black coffee

263

calentado (Ven) hot punch made with eau-de-vie, sugar and spices

campurrado (Mex) thick hot drink made with ground corn and chocolate

carajillo [karaHee-yo] coffee with brandy

carato (Ven) drink made from corn or rice flour

carta de vinos [deh beenos] wine list

Cava [kaba] champagne

cebada [sebada] drink made from fermented barley

cerveza [sairbesa] beer, lager

cerveza clara light, lager-style beer

cerveza de barril draught beer

cerveza negra dark beer

cerveza oscura dark beer

champán [champan] champagne

chicha [cheecha] alcoholic drink made from mermented maize

chicha andina alcoholic drink made with corn flour and pineapple juice

chicha de manzana alcoholic drink made from apple juice

chicha de uva alchoholic drink made from grape juice

chocolate caliente [chokolateh kal-yenteh] hot chocolate drink, sometimes sweetened with honey and flavoured with vanilla and spices

chocolate santafereño [santaferen-yo] (Col) hot chocolate and cheese

chop (Ch) beer

clérico apéritif made of wine, fruit and fruit juice

coctel cocktail

cola de mono (Ch) rum punch with milk, coffe and vanilla

con azúcar [asookar] with sugar

con gas fizzy, sparkling

coñac [kon-yak] brandy

cosecha vintage

crema de cacao crème de cacao

crema de menta crème de menthe

cubalibre [koobaleebreh] rum and coke, cubalibre

cubito de hielo [deh yelo] ice cube

cucaracha (Mex) tequila and strong, alcoholic, coffee-flavoured drink

destornillador [destornee-yador] vodka and orange juice, screwdriver

embotellado en ... bottled in ...

espumoso sparkling

fresco (CAm) fruit juice

gaseosa [gaseh-osa] lemonade

ginebra [Heenebra] gin

gintónic [jeentoneek] gin and tonic

gol (Ch) alcoholic drink made from butter, sugar and milk

granizada/granizado [graneesada] crushed ice drink

guarapo [gwarapo] rough liquor made from sugar cane; (Ven) weak filtered coffee

guaro (CAm) [gwaro] sugar-cane liquor

guayayo (Ven) [gwa-ya-yo] rough liquor made from sugar cane

guinda [geenda] alcoholic drink made from black cherries; black cherry

guindada [geendada], guindilla [guindee-ya] cherry brandy

haya (Ch) [a-ya] fermented grape juice

Hidalgo Mexican wine producer

hielo [yelo] ice

horchata [orchata] (Mex) cold drink made from rice and water

horchata de chufas [deh] (Mex) cold almond-flavoured milky drink

huarisnaque [wareesnakeh] (Ch) rough brandy

huevos a la ostra [webos] prairie oysters

infusión [eenfoos-yon] herb tea

jarra de cerveza/vino [Harra deh sairbesa/beeno] jug of beer/wine

jerez [Hair-es] sherry

jerez fino light, dry sherry

jerez oloroso sweet sherry

jora (Andes) [Hora] drink of fermented maize

jugo [Hoogo] juice

jugo de damasco apricot juice

jugo de durazno [doorasno] peach juice

jugo de jitomate [Heetomateh] (Mex) tomato juice

jugo de lima lime juice

jugo de limón lemon juice

jugo de naranja [naranHa] orange juice

jugo de piña [peen-ya] pineapple juice

jugo de tomate tomato juice

jugo de tumbo (Bol) passion fruit juice

leche [lecheh] milk

leche condensada condensed milk

leche de soja [deh soHa] soya milk

leche desnatada skimmed milk

leche en polvo powdered milk

licor liqueur; spirit

licor de avellana [deh abeh-yana] hazelnut-flavoured liqueur

licor de manzana [mansana] apple-flavoured liqueur

licor de durazno [doorasno] peach-flavoured liqueur

licor de melón melon-flavoured liqueur

licor de naranja [naranHa] orange-flavoured liqueur

licores [leekor-es] spirits, liqueurs

licuado [leekwado] milkshake

licuado de fresa [deh] strawberry milkshake

licuado de plátano banana milkshake

limonada fresh lemonade

lista de precios [pres-yos] price list

Málaga sweet wine

malta dark beer

malteada [malteh-ada] milkshake

manzanilla [mansanee-ya] dry sherry-type wine; camomile tea

margarita cocktail of tequila, lime juice and either grenadine, Curaçao or triple sec

mate [mateh] bitter tea made from the dried leaves of the yerba mate bush

mate de coca coca leaf tea

media de agua [med-ya deh ag-wa] half-bottle of mineral water

mediana bottle of beer

merengada fruit juice with ice, milk and sugar

mezcal [meskal] (Mex) spirit distilled from the maguey cactus

mistela (Ch) hot punch

Nescafe® [neskafeh] instant coffee

Oporto port

pinolillo (CAm) [peenolee-yo] drink made with cornstarch and water

piña colada [peen-ya] rum and pineapple cocktail

pisco (Pe) eau-de-vie made from grapes

pisco sour drink made with pisco, lemon juice and egg whites

posh sugar cane liquor

pozol de cacao [posol deh kaka-o] (Mex) cool drink made from ground maize/corn and chocolate

pulque [poolkeh] (Mex) thick alcoholic drink distilled from the pulp of the maguey cactus

puro de caña [deh kan-ya] sugar cane liquor

refresco soft drink, fizzy drink

rompope [rompopeh] (Mex) egg nog, egg flip

ron rum

ron oro matured rum

sangría [sangree-a] mixture of red wine, lemon juice, spirits, sugar and fruit

sangrita orange juice, grenadine and chilli, drunk with tequila

semidulce [semeedoolseh] medium-sweet

sidra cider

sin azúcar [seen asookar] without sugar

sin gas still

sorbete [sorbeteh] (Col) fruit juice with cream

submarino [soobmareeno] (Rpl) hot milk with melted chocolate; (Col) a beer with a shot of eau-de-vie

tafia [taf-ya] (Bol) type of rum

taxallate [taHa-yateh] (Mex) drink from Chiapas made from maize/corn and cocoa

té [teh] tea

té de hierbas [teh deh yairbas] herbal tea

Tehuacán® [teh-wakan] mineral water

tequila [tekeela] spirit distilled from the pulp of the agave cactus

tónica tonic

vino [beeno] wine

vino blanco white wine

vino de casa [deh] house wine

vino de mesa table wine

vino del país [pa-ees] local wine

vino rosado rosé wine

vino tinto red wine

yerbabuena [yairba-bwena] mint tea

yerba mate [yairba mateh] bitter tea made from the dried leaves of the yerba mate bush

How the Language Works

Pronunciation

In this phrasebook, the Spanish has been written in a system of imitated pronunciation so that it can be read as though it were English, bearing in mind the notes on pronunciation given below:

air	as in h**air**	ī	as the 'i' sound in m**i**ght
ay	as in m**ay**	o	as in n**o**t
e, eh	as in g**e**t	ow	as in n**ow**
g	always hard as in **g**oat	s	as in mi**ss**
H	as the Scottish ch in lo**ch**	y	as in **y**es

Letters given in bold type indicate the part of the word to be stressed.

As **i** and **u** are always pronounced 'ee' and 'oo' in Spanish, pronunciation has not been given for all words containing these letters unless they present other problems for the learner. Thus **María** is pronounced 'mar**ee**-a' and **fútbol** is '**foot**bol'.

Latin American Pronunciation

The pronunciation guide given in this book will stand you in good stead wherever you travel in Latin America. But, on your travels, you will encounter a wealth of different forms of pronunciation of Spanish. Here are some instances of this.

Y and **ll** are pronounced in different ways in Latin America. In the Southern Cone (Argentina, Chile, Paraguay and Uruguay), the pronunciation is like the **sh** in the English word **ship**. Generally speaking, the rest of South America (Bolivia, Colombia, Ecuador, Peru and Venezuela) pronounces **y** and **ll** like the **j** in the English word **job**. In Central America (Costa Rica, El Salvador, Guatemala, Honduras, Nicaragua and Panama), Cuba, Mexico and the Dominican Republic, the pronunciation of **y** and **ll** is similar to the **y** in the English word **year**. In this phrasebook we have opted to use this latter pronunciation.

It is also worth mentioning some curiosities about the **s** sound. In Latin America, the letters **s**, **c** and **z** followed by a vowel or coming at the end of the word are all pronounced as **s** in the English word **set**. The **s** sound is sometimes omitted at the end of a word. For example: **hombres** can be pronounced [**o**mbreh].

In Mexico, Central America, Cuba, the Dominican Republic, Colombia and Venezuela, the letter **s** may become an **h**. For example: **pescado** (fish) would be pronounced [pehkado].

In Cuba and the Dominican Republic, you may hear the letter **l** replacing an **r**. For example, **caminar** (to walk) can be pronounced [kaminal].

The **d** sound at the end of a word is very soft or even nonexistent. For example, **usted** is pronounced [oosteh]. It is also possible for **d** to be omitted when it occurs between vowels: **mojado** (wet) becomes [moHa-o].

Abbreviations

adj	adjective	m	masculine	sing	singular
f	feminine	pl	plural		
fam	familiar	pol	polite		

Note

In the Spanish-English section and Menu Reader, the letter **ñ** is treated as a separate letter, as is customary in Spanish. Alphabetically, it comes after **n**.

Abbreviations for Latin American countries and regions

Andes	Andes	Hond	Honduras
Arg	Argentine	Mex	Mexico
Bol	Bolivia	Nic	Nicaragua
CAm	Central America	Pan	Panama
Ch	Chile	Parag	Paraguay
Col	Colombia	Pe	Peru
CR	Costa Rica	PR	Puerto Rico
CSur	Southern Cone (Argentine, Chile, Paraguay and Uruguay)	Rpl	River Plate (Argentine, Uruguay)
Cu	Cuba	Salv	El Salvador
Ec	Ecuador	SAm	South America
Guat	Guatemala	Urug	Uruguay
		Ven	Venezuela

Nouns

All nouns in Spanish have one of two genders: masculine or feminine. Generally speaking, those ending in **-o** are masculine:

> **el zapato**
> el sap**a**to
> the shoe

Those ending in **-a**, **-d**, **-z** or **-ión** are usually feminine:

> **la cama**   **la pensión**
> la k**a**ma   la pens-y**o**n
> the bed   the boarding house,
>   the guesthouse

Nouns ending in **-or** are masculine. To form the feminine, add **-a**:

> **el señor**   **la señora**
> el sen-y**o**r   la sen-y**o**ra
> the man   the woman

> **el profesor**   **la profesora**
> the (male)   the (female)
> teacher   teacher

A small number of nouns ending in **-o** and **-a** (usually professions) can be either masculine or feminine:

> **el/la guía**   **el/la violinista**
> el/la g**ee**-a   el/la bee-oleen**ee**sta
> the guide   the violinist

Plural Nouns

If the noun ends in a vowel, the plural is formed by adding **-s**:

> **el camino**   **los caminos**
> el kam**ee**no   los kam**ee**nos
> the path   the paths

273

la mesera	las meseras
la mes**ai**ra	las mes**ai**ras
the waitress	the waitresses

If the noun ends in a consonant, the plural is formed by adding -es:

el chofer	los choferes
el chof**air**	los chof**air**-es
the driver	the drivers

la recepción	las recepciones
la reseps-y**on**	las reseps-y**on**-es
the reception desk	the reception desks

If the noun ends in a -z, change the -z to -ces to form the plural:

la luz	las luces
la l**oo**s	las l**oo**s-es
the light	the lights

Articles

The different articles ('the' and 'a') in Spanish vary according to the number (singular or plural) and gender of the noun they refer to.

The Definite Article

The definite article 'the' is as follows:

	singular	plural
masculine	el	los
feminine	la	las

el cuchillo/los cuchillos	la mesa/las mesas
el koch**ee**-yo/los koch**ee**-yos	la m**e**sa/las m**e**sas
the knife/the knives	the table/the tables

When the article **el** is used in combination with **a** (to) or **de** (of) it changes as follows:

a + el = al
de + el = del

vamos al museo	**cerca del hotel**
b**a**mos al moos**eh**-o	s**a**irka del ot**e**l
let's go to the museum	near the hotel

The Indefinite Article

The indefinite article (a, an, some), also changes according to the gender and number of the accompanying noun:

	singular	plural
masculine	**un**	**unos**
	oon	**oo**nos
feminine	**una**	**unas**
	oona	**oo**nas

un sello	**unos sellos**
oon s**eh**-yo	**oo**nos s**eh**-yos
a stamp	some stamps
una chica	**unas chicas**
oona ch**ee**ka	**oo**nas ch**ee**kas
a girl	some girls

Adjectives and adverbs

Adjectives must agree in gender and number with the noun they refer to. Unlike English, Spanish adjectives usually follow the noun. In the English-Spanish section of this book, all adjectives are given in the masculine singular. Adjectives ending in **-o** change as follows for the plural:

el precio alto	**los precios altos**
el pr**e**s-yo **a**lto	los pr**e**s-yos **a**ltos
the high price	the high prices

The feminine singular of the adjective is formed by changing the masculine endings as follows:

masculine	feminine
-o	-a
-or	-ora
-és	-esa

un cocinero estupendo
oon koseenairo estoopendo
a wonderful cook

una cocinera estupenda
oona koseenaira estoopenda
a wonderful cook

un señor encantador
oon sen-yor enkantador
a nice man

una señora encantadora
oona sen-yora enkantadora
a nice woman

un chico inglés
oon cheeko eeng-les
an English boy

una chica inglesa
oona cheeka eenglesa
an English girl

For other types of adjective, the feminine forms are the same as the masculine:

un hombre agradable
oon hombreh agradableh
a nice man

una mujer agradable
oona mooHair agradableh
a nice woman

The plurals of adjectives are formed in the same way as the plurals of nouns, by adding an **-s**:

una silla roja
oona see-ya roHa
a red chair

dos sillas rojas
dos see-yas roHas
two red chairs

Comparatives

The comparative is formed by placing **más** (more) or **menos** (less) before the adjective or adverb:

lindo
leendo
beautiful

más lindo
mas leendo
more beautiful

tranquilo	menos tranquilo
trankee**lo**	menos trankee**lo**
quiet	less quiet

este hotel es más/menos caro que el otro
esteh otel es mas/menos karo keh el otro
this hotel is more/less expensive than the other one

¿tiene un cuarto más soleado?
t-yeneh **oo**n kwarto mas soleh-**a**do
do you have a sunnier room?

¿podría ir más de prisa, por favor?
podr**ee**-a **ee**r mas deh pr**ee**sa por fabor
could you go faster please?

Superlatives

Superlatives are formed by placing one of the following before the adjective: **el más, la más, los más** or **las más** (depending on the noun's gender and number):

¿cuál es el más divertido?
kwal es el mas deebairt**ee**do
which is the most entertaining?

el auto más rápido
el **ow**to mas r**a**peedo
the fastest car

la casa más linda
la k**a**sa mas l**ee**nda
the prettiest house

las mujeres más inteligentes
las mooH**ai**r-es mas eenteleeH**e**nt-es
the most intelligent women

The following adjectives have irregular comparatives and superlatives:

bueno	mejor	el mejor
bweno	meHor	el meHor
good	better	the best

grande	mayor	el mayor
grandeh	mī-yor	el mī-yor
big	bigger	the biggest
old	older	the oldest

malo	peor	el peor
malo	peh-or	el peh-or
bad	worse	the worst

pequeño	menor	el menor
peken-yo	menor	el menor
small	smaller	the smallest
	younger	the youngest

'As ... as ...' is translated as follows:

¡Caracas está tan linda como siempre!
karakas esta tan leenda komo s-yempreh
Caracas is as beautiful as ever!

The superlative form ending in **-ísimo** indicates that something is 'very/extremely ...' without actually comparing it to something else:

guapo	guapísimo
gwapo	gwapeeseemo
attractive	very attractive

Adverbs

There are two ways to form an adverb. If the adjective ends in **-o**, take the feminine and add **-mente** to form the corresponding adverb:

exacto	exactamente
eksakto	eksaktamenteh
accurate	accurately, exactly

If the adjective ends in any other letter, add **-mente** to the basic form:

feliz	**felizmente**
felees	feleesmenteh
happy	happily

Possessive Adjectives

Possessive adjectives, like other Spanish adjectives, agree with the noun in gender and number:

	singular		plural	
	masculine	feminine	masculine	feminine
my	**mi**	**mi**	**mis**	**mis**
	mee	mee	mees	mees
your	**tu**	**tu**	**tus**	**tus**
(sing, fam)	too	too	toos	toos
his/her/its/your	**su**	**su**	**sus**	**sus**
(sing, pol)	soo	soo	soos	soos
our	**nuestro**	**nuestra**	**nuestros**	**nuestras**
	nwestro	nwestra	nwestros	nwestras
your (pl)/their	**su**	**su**	**sus**	**sus**
	soo	soo	soos	soos

tu bolsa	**sus pastillas**
too bolsa	soos pastee-yas
your bag	his/her/your tablets
su maleta	**nuestros trajes de baño**
soo maleta	nwestros traHes deh ban-yo
your suitcase	our swimming costumes

If when using **su/sus**, it is unclear whether you mean 'his', 'her', 'your' or 'their', you can use the following after the noun instead:

| | de él | his | de ellos | their (m) |
| deh el | | | deh **eh**-yos | |

de él his   **de ellos** their (m)
deh el   deh **eh**-yos

de ella her   **de ellas** their (f)
deh **eh**-ya   deh **eh**-yas

de usted your (sing, pol)   **de ustedes** your (pl)
deh oost**eh**   deh oosted-es

el dinero de usted   **el dinero de ella**
el deen**ai**ro deh oost**eh**   el deen**ai**ro deh **eh**-ya
your money   her money

el dinero de él
el deen**ai**ro deh el
his money

Possessive pronouns

To translate 'mine', 'yours', 'theirs' etc, use one of the following forms. Like possessive adjectives, possessive pronouns must agree in gender and number with the object or objects referred to:

	singular		plural	
	masculine	feminine	masculine	feminine
mine	**el mío**	**la mía**	**los míos**	**las mías**
	el **mee**-o	la **mee**-a	los **mee**-os	las **mee**-as
yours	**el tuyo**	**la tuya**	**los tuyos**	**las tuyas**
(sing, fam)	el **too**-yo	la **too**-ya	los **too**-yos	las **too**-yas
his/hers/yours	**el suyo**	**la suya**	**los suyos**	**las suyas**
(sing, pol)	el **soo**-yo	la **soo**-ya	los **soo**-yos	las **soo**-yas
ours	**el nuestro**	**la nuestra**	**los nuestros**	**las nuestras**
	el **nwes**tro	la **nwes**tra	los **nwes**tros	las **nwes**tras
yours (pl)/theirs	**el suyo**	**la suya**	**los suyos**	**las suyas**
	el **soo**-yo	la **soo**-ya	los **soo**-yos	las **soo**-yas

ésta es su llave y ésta es la mía
esta es soo **ya**beh ee **e**sta es la **mee**-a
this is your key and this is mine

no es la suya, es de sus amigos

no es la s**oo**-ya es deh soos am**ee**gos

it's not his, it's his friends'

Personal pronouns

Subject Pronouns

yo	I	**nosotros**	we (m)
yo		nos**o**tros	
tú/vos	you (sing, fam)	**nosotras**	we (f)
too/bos		nos**o**tras	
él	he/it	**ellos**	they (m)
el		**eh**-yos	
ella	she/it	**ellas**	they (f)
eh-ya		**eh**-yas	
usted	you (sing, pol)	**ustedes**	you (pl)
oost**eh**		oost**ed**-es	

Tú is used when speaking to one person and is the familiar form generally used when speaking to family, friends and children.

Vos is a familiar form of address which is widely used instead of **tú** mainly in the River Plate area but also in other parts of Central and South America. Although, in certain contexts, it could be used as a formal form of address, it is highly recommended that it is used just in familiar and informal situations.

Usted is the polite form of address to be used when talking to someone you don't know or an older person.

Ustedes is the plural form used in Latin America whoever you are speaking to. The third person of verbs is used with **usted** and **ustedes**: **Usted** takes the same verb form as 'he/she/it'; **ustedes** takes the same verb form as 'they'.

In Spanish the subject pronoun is usually omitted:

no saben	**está cansado**
no saben	esta kansado
they don't know	he is tired

although it may be retained for emphasis or to avoid confusion:

¡soy yo!	**¡somos nosotros!**
soy yo	somos nosotros
it's me!	it's us!

yo pago los tacos, tú pagas las cervezas
yo pago los takos too pagas las sairbesas
I'll pay for the tacos, you pay for the beers

él es inglés y ella es estadounidense
el es eeng-les ee **eh**-ya es estado-ooneedenseh
he's English and she's American

Subject pronouns are also used after prepositions:

para vos	**con él**	**sin ella**
para bos	kon el	seen **eh**-ya
for you	with him	without her

detrás de usted	**después de nosotros**
detras deh oost**eh**	despwes deh nosotros
behind you	after us

The exceptions are **yo**, which is replaced by **mí**, and **tú** which is replaced by **ti**:

eso es para mí/ti
eso es para mee/tee
that's for me/you

After **con** (with), **mí** and **ti** change as follows:

conmigo	**contigo**
konm**ee**go	kont**ee**go
with me	with you

Object pronouns

me	[meh]	me		**nos**	[nos]	us
te	[teh]	you (sing, fam)		**los**	[los]	them (m), you (mpl)
lo	[lo]	him/it, you (sing, pol)		**las**	[las]	them (f), you (fpl)
la	[la]	her/it, you (sing, pol)				

Object pronouns usually precede the verb:

me la dio ayer
meh la dee-o a-yair
she gave it to me yesterday

las compré para ella
las kompreh para eh-ya
I bought them for her

cada viernes la lleva a cenar
kada b-yairn-es la yeba a senar
every Friday he takes her to dinner

los vi ayer
los bee a-yair
I saw them yesterday

When used with infinitives, pronouns are added to the end of the infinitive:

¿puede llevarme al aeropuerto?
pwedeh yebarmeh al a-airopwairto
can you take me to the airport?

intentaré recordarlo
eententareh rekordarlo
I'll try and remember it

When used with commands, pronouns are added to the end of the imperative form. See **Imperatives** page 297.
If you are using an indirect pronoun to mean 'to me', 'to you' etc (although 'to' might not always be necessarily said in English), you generally use the following:

me	[meh]	to me
te	[teh]	to you (sing, fam)
le/lo	[leh/lo]	to him, to you (sing, pol)
le/la	[leh/la]	to her, to you (sing, pol)
nos	[nos]	to us
les/los	[les/los]	to them (m), to you (mpl)
les/las	[les/las]	to them (f), to you (fpl)

me enseñó el camino
meh ensen-yo el kameeno
he showed me the way

le pedí su dirección

leh pedee soo deereks-yon

I asked him/her for his/her address

Reflexive Pronouns

These are used with reflexive verbs like **lavarse** 'to wash (one-self)', that is where the subject and the object are one and the same person:

me	[meh]	myself (used with I)
te	[teh]	yourself (used with singular, familiar 'you')
se	[seh]	him/her/itself (used with singular, polite 'you')
nos	[nos]	ourselves (used with 'we')
se	[seh]	themselves (used with 'they' and plural 'you')

presentarse to introduce oneself

me presento: me llamo Richard

meh presento: meh yamo Richard

may I introduce myself? my name's Richard

divertirse to enjoy oneself

nos divertimos mucho en la fiesta

nos deebairteemos moocho en la f-yesta

we enjoyed ourselves a lot at the party

Demonstratives

The English demonstrative adjective 'this' is translated by the Spanish **este**. 'That' is translated by **ese** or **aquel**. **Ese** refers to something near to the person being spoken to. **Aquel** refers to something further away.

Like other adjectives, they agree with the noun they qualify in gender and number but they are placed in front of the noun. Their forms are:

masculine singular			feminine singular		
este	ese	aquel	esta	esa	aquella
esteh	eseh	akel	esta	esa	akeh-ya

masculine plural			feminine plural		
estos	esos	aquellos	estas	esas	aquellas
estos	esos	ak**eh**-yos	estas	esas	ak**eh**-yas

este restaurante	ese mesero	aquella playa
esteh restowranteh	eseh mesairo	ak**eh**-ya pla-ya
this restaurant	that waiter	that beach (in the distance)

'This one', 'that one', 'those', 'these' etc (as pronouns) are translated by the same words as above only they are spelt with an **é**:

éste	ése	aquél
esteh	eseh	ak**el**
this one	that one	that one (over there)

quisiera éstos/ésos/aquéllos
kees-y**ai**ra estos/esos/ak**eh**-yos
I'd like these/those/those (over there)

The neuter forms **esto/eso/aquello** are used when no particular noun is being referred to:

esto	eso	aquello
esto	eso	ak**eh**-yo

eso no es justo	¿qué es esto?
eso no es Hoosto	keh es esto
that's not fair	what is this?

Verbs

The basic form of the verb given in the **English–Spanish** and **Spanish–English** sections is the infinitive (e.g. to drive, to go etc). There are three verb types in Spanish which can be recognized by their infinitive endings: **-ar**, **-er** or **-ir**. For example:

hablar	[abl**ar**]	to talk
comer	[kom**air**]	to eat
abrir	[abr**eer**]	to open

285

Present Tense

The present tense corresponds to 'I leave' and 'I am leaving' in English. To form the present tense for the three main types of verb in Spanish, remove the -ar, -er or -ir and add the following endings:

hablar to speak

habl-o	[ablo]	I speak
habl-as (tú)	[ablas]	you speak (sing, fam)
habl-ás (vos)	[ablas]	you speak (sing, fam)
habl-a	[abla]	he/she speaks, you speak (sing, pol)
habl-amos	[ablamos]	we speak
habl-an	[ablan]	they speak, you speak (pl)

comer to eat

com-o	[komo]	I eat
com-es (tú)	[kom-es]	you eat (sing, fam)
com-és (vos)	[kom-es]	you eat (sing, fam)
com-e	[komeh]	he/she eats, you eat (sing, pol)
com-emos	[komemos]	we eat
com-en	[komen]	they eat, you eat (pl)

abrir to open

abr-o	[abro]	I open
abr-es (tú)	[ab-res]	you open (sing, fam)
abr-ís (vos)	[ab-rees]	you open (sing, fam)
abr-e	[abreh]	he/she opens, you open (sing, pol)
abr-imos	[abreemos]	we open
abr-en	[abren]	they open, you open (pl)

Some common verbs are irregular:

dar to give

doy	[doy]	I give
das	[das]	you give (sing, fam)
da	[da]	he/she gives, you give (sing, pol)
damos	[damos]	we give
dan	[dan]	they give, you give (pl)

ir to go

voy	[boy]	I go
vas	[bas]	you go (sing, fam)
va	[ba]	he/she goes, you go (sing, pol)
vamos	[bamos]	we go
van	[ban]	they go, you go (pl)

poder can, to be able

puedo	[pwedo]	I can
puedes (tú)	[pwed-es]	you can (sing, fam)
podés (vos)	[pod-es]	you can (sing, fam)
puede	[pwedeh]	he/she can, you can (sing, pol)
podemos	[podemos]	we can
pueden	[pweden]	they can, you can (pl)

querer to want

quiero	[k-yairo]	I want
quieres (tú)	[k-yair-es]	you want (sing, fam)
querés (vos)	[ker-es]	you want (sing, fam)
quiere	[k-yaireh]	he/she wants, you want (sing, pol)
queremos	[kairemos]	we want
quieren	[k-yairen]	they want, you want (pl)

tener to have

tengo	[tengo]	I have
tienes (tú)	[t-yen-es]	you have (sing, fam)
tenés (vos)	[ten-es]	you have (sing, fam)
tiene	[t-yeneh]	he/she has, you have (sing, pol)
tenemos	[tenemos]	we have
tienen	[t-yenen]	they have, you have (pl)

venir to come

vengo	[bengo]	I come
vienes (tú)	[b-yen-es]	you come (sing, fam)
venís (vos)	[ben-ees]	you come (sing, fam)
viene	[b-yeneh]	he/she comes, you come (sing, pol)
venimos	[beneemos]	we come
vienen	[b-yenen]	they come, you come (pl)

287

The first person singular (the 'I' form) of the following verbs is irregular in some verbs:

decir to say	digo	[deego]
hacer to do, to make	hago	[a-go]
poner to put	pongo	[pongo]
saber to know	sé	[seh]
salir to go out	salgo	[salgo]

See page 294 for the present tense of the verbs **ser** and **estar** 'to be'.

Past Tense:

Preterite

The preterite is the tense normally used to talk about the past:

habl-é	[ableh]	I spoke
habl-aste	[ablasteh]	you spoke (sing, fam)
habl-ó	[ablo]	he/she spoke, you spoke (sing, pol)
habl-amos	[ablamos]	we spoke
habl-aron	[ablaron]	they spoke, you spoke (pl)

com-í	[komee]	I ate
com-iste	[komeesteh]	you ate (sing, fam)
com-ió	[kom-yo]	he/she ate, you ate (sing, pol)
com-imos	[komeemos]	we ate
com-ieron	[kom-yairon]	they ate, you ate (pl)

abr-í	[abree]	I opened
abr-iste	[abreesteh]	you opened (sing, fam)
abr-ió	[abr-yo]	he/she opened, you opened (sing, pol)
abr-imos	[abreemos]	we opened
abr-ieron	[abr-yairon]	they opened, you opened (pl)

¿quién te dijo eso?	nos conocimos en Mérida
k-yen teh deeHo eso	nos konoseemos en mereeda
who told you that?	we met each other in Mérida

288

lo compramos el año pasado

lo kompramos el an-yo pasado

we bought it last year

The verbs **ser** (to be) and **ir** (to go) are irregular and have the same form in the preterite:

fui	[fwee]	I was; I went
fuiste	[fweesteh]	you were; you went (sing, fam)
fue	[fweh]	he/she/it was; you were (sing, pol);
		he/she/it went; you went (sing, pol)
fuimos	[fweemos]	we were; we went
fueron	[fwairon]	they were; you were (pl);
		they went; you went (pl)

Perfect Tense

The perfect tense corresponds to the English past tense using 'have' – i.e. 'I have seen', 'he has said' etc. It is formed by combining the appropriate person of the present tense of **haber** with the past participle of the other verb. The present tense of **haber** is as follows:

he	[eh]	I have
has	[as]	you have (sing, fam)
ha	[a]	he/she/it has; you have (sing, pol)
hemos	[emos]	we have
han	[an]	they have; you have (pl)

The past participle is formed by removing the infinitive ending (-**ar**, -**er** or -**ir**) and adding -**ado** or -**ido** as follows:

infinitive	past participle	
hablar	**hablado**	[ablado]
comer	**comido**	[komeedo]
vivir	**vivido**	[beebeedo]

hemos dado una propina

emos dado oona propeena

we have given a tip

hemos comido bien

emos komeedo b-yen

we've eaten well, we've had a good meal

he encendido la luz
eh ensend**ee**do la loos
I (have) put the light on

Some verbs have irregular past participles:

hacer to do, to make	**hecho**	[**ech**o]
abrir to open	**abierto**	[ab-**yair**to]
decir to say	**dicho**	[**dee**cho]
volver to return	**vuelto**	[**bwel**to]
poner to put	**puesto**	[**pwes**to]
ver to see	**visto**	[**bees**to]

Imperfect Tense

This tense is used to describe something or someone in the past, or to describe activities that were habitual in the past. It is also the tense you would use to talk about something that was going on over a period of time. It is formed as follows:

hablar to talk

habl-aba	[**abl**aba]	I was speaking
habl-abas	[**abl**abas]	you were speaking (sing, fam)
habl-aba	[**abl**aba]	he/she was speaking, you were speaking (sing, pol)
habl-ábamos	[**abl**abamos]	we were speaking
habl-aban	[**abl**aban]	they were speaking, you were speaking (pl)

comer to eat

com-ía	[kom**ee**-a]	I was eating
com-ías	[kom**ee**-as]	you were eating (sing, fam)
com-ía	[kom**ee**-a]	he/she/it was eating, you were eating (sing, pol)
com-íamos	[kom**ee**-amos]	we were eating
com-ían	[kom**ee**-an]	they were eating, you were eating (pl)

abrir to open

abr-ía	[abr**ee**-a]	I was opening
abr-ías	[abr**ee**-as]	you were opening (sing, fam)
abr-ía	[abr**ee**-a]	he/she/it was opening, you were opening (sing, pol)
abr-íamos	[abr**ee**-amos]	we were opening
abr-ían	[abr**ee**-an]	they were opening, you were opening (pl)

Other useful verbs in the imperfect tense are:

estar to be

estaba	[est**a**ba]	I was
estabas	[est**a**bas]	you were (sing, fam)
estaba	[est**a**ba]	he/she/it was, you were (sing, pol)
estábamos	[est**a**bamos]	we were
estaban	[est**a**ban]	they were, you were (pl)

tener to have

tenía	[ten**ee**-a]	I had
tenías	[ten**ee**-as]	you had (sing, fam)
tenía	[ten**ee**-a]	he/she/it had, you had (sing, pol)
teníamos	[ten**ee**-amos]	we had
tenían	[ten**ee**-an]	they had, you had (pl)

The following are irregular in the imperfect tense:

ir to go

iba	[**ee**ba]	I was going
ibas	[**ee**bas]	you were going (sing, fam)
iba	[**ee**ba]	he/she/it was going, you were going (sing, pol)
íbamos	[**ee**bamos]	we were going
iban	[**ee**ban]	they were going, you were going (pl)

ser to be (see page 294 for more on this)

era	[**ai**ra]	I was
eras	[**ai**ras]	you were (sing, fam)
era	[**ai**ra]	he/she/it was, you were (sing, pol)
éramos	[**ai**ramos]	we were
eran	[**ai**ran]	they were, you were (pl)

todos los viernes salíamos a dar un paseo
todos los b-**yai**rn-es sal**ee**-amos a dar oon pas**eh**-o
every Friday we used to go for a walk, every Friday we
   went for a walk

era alto y delgado
aira **al**to ee del**ga**do
he was tall and slim

viajaban de Cusco a Machu Picchu
b-ya**Ha**ban deh **koo**sko a **ma**choo **pee**choo
they were travelling from Cusco to Machu Picchu

Future Tense

To form the future tense in Spanish (I will do, you will do etc)
add the following endings to the infinitive. The same endings
are used whether verbs end in **-ar**, **-er** or **-ir**:

hablar-é	[ablar**eh**]	I will speak
hablar-ás	[ablar**as**]	you will speak (sing, fam)
hablar-á	[ablar**a**]	he/she/you will speak (sing, pol)
hablar-emos	[ablar**emos**]	we will speak
hablar-án	[ablar**an**]	they/you will speak (pl)

llamaré más tarde
yamar**eh** mas **ta**rdeh
I'll call later

The immediate future can also be translated by **ir** + **a** + infinitive:

vamos a comprar una botella de vino tinto
bamos a komprar oona boteh-ya deh beeno teento
we're going to buy a bottle of red wine

iré a recogerlo
eereh a rekoHairlo
I'll fetch him, I'll go and fetch him

In Spanish, as in English, the future can sometimes be expressed by the present tense:

tu avión sale a la una
too ab-yon saleh a la oona
your plane takes off at one o'clock

However, Spanish often uses the present tense where the future would be used in English:

le doy ochocientos pesos
leh doy ochos-yentos pesos
I'll give you 800 pesos

The following verbs are irregular in the future tense:

decir	to say	diré	I will say
hacer	to do	haré	I will do
poder	to be able	podré	I will be able
poner	to put	pondré	I will put
querer	to want	querré	I will want
saber	to know	sabré	I will know
salir	to leave	saldré	I will leave
tener	to have	tendré	I will have
venir	to come	vendré	I will come

The Verb 'To Be'

There are two verbs 'to be' in Spanish: **ser** and **estar**. The present tense is as follows:

ser

soy	[soy]	I am
eres (tú)	[**air**-es]	you are (sing, fam)
sos (vos)	[sos]	you are (sing, fam)
es	[es]	he/she/it is, you are (sing, pol)
somos	[**so**mos]	we are
son	[son]	they are, you are (pl)

estar

estoy	[est**oy**]	I am
estás	[est**as**]	you are (sing, fam)
está	[est**a**]	he/she/it is, you are (sing, pol)
estamos	[est**amos**]	we are
están	[est**an**]	they are, you are (pl)

Ser

Ser is generally used to describe a permanent state, for example, what something or someone looks like or what their nature is:

la nieve es blanca
la n-**y**ebeh es bl**a**nka
snow is white

Ser is also used with occupations, nationalities, the time and to indicate possession:

somos escoceses	**mi madre es profesora**
somos eskos**es**-es	mi **ma**dreh es profes**o**ra
we are Scottish	my mother is a teacher

éste es nuestro perro	**son las cinco de la tarde**
esteh es n**we**stro **pe**rro	son las **se**enko deh la **ta**rdeh
this is our dog	it's five o'clock in the afternoon

Estar

Estar, on the other hand, is used above all to answer the question 'where?':

el libro está en la mesa
el **lee**bro esta en la m**e**sa
the book is on the table

San José está en Costa Rica
san hos**eh** esta en k**o**sta r**ee**ka
San José is in Costa Rica

It also describes the temporary or passing qualities of something or someone:

estoy enojado
est**oy** eno**H**ado
I'm angry

estoy cansado
est**oy** kansado
I'm tired

este filete está frío
esteh feel**e**teh esta **free**-o
this steak is cold

Note the difference between the following two phrases:

Isabel es muy guapa
Isabel es mwee gwapa
Isabel is very pretty

Isabel está muy guapa (esta noche)
Isabel esta mwee gwapa **e**sta n**o**cheh
Isabel looks pretty (tonight)

soy inglés
soy eeng-l**es**
I am English

estoy en México
est**oy** en me**H**eeko
I am in Mexico

Negatives

To express a negative in Spanish, to say 'I don't want', 'it's not here' etc, place the word **no** in front of the verb:

entiendo
ent-y**e**ndo
I understand

no entiendo
no ent-y**e**ndo
I don't understand

me gusta este helado
meh g**oo**sta **e**steh elado
I like this ice cream

no me gusta este helado
no meh g**oo**sta **e**steh elado
I don't like this ice cream

lo alquilé aquí	**no lo alquilé aquí**
lo alkeel**eh** ak**ee**	no lo alkeel**eh** ak**ee**
I rented it here	I didn't rent it here

van a cantar	**no van a cantar**
ban a kantar	no ban a kantar
they're going to sing	they're not going to sing

To use negative words like:

nadie	**nada**	**nunca**
nad-yeh	nada	n**oo**nka
no-one, nobody	nothing	never

you can either place them before the verb, or put them after the verb with **no** in front, thus:

no llegó nadie/nadie llegó	**no hay nadie ahí**
no yeg**o** nad-yeh/nad-yeh yeg**o**	no ī nad-yeh a-**ee**
nobody came	there's no-one there

no compramos nada	**no sabemos nada de ella**
no kompramos nada	no sabemos nada deh **eh**-ya
we didn't buy anything	we don't know anything about her

To say 'there's no ...', 'I've no ...' etc, make the accompanying verb negative:

no hay vino	**no tengo cerillas**
no ī b**ee**no	no t**e**ngo sair**ee**-yas
there's no wine	I've no matches

To say 'not him', 'not her' etc just use the personal pronoun followed by **no**:

nosotros, no	**ella, no**	**yo, no**
nos**o**tros no	**eh**-ya no	yo no
not us	not her	not me

Imperatives

When giving a command to people you would normally address with **usted** or **ustedes**, you form the imperative by taking the first person singular of the present tense and changing the endings as follows:

	first person sing.	usted	ustedes
hablar to speak	**hablo**	**habl-e**	**habl-en**
		ableh	**a**blen
comer to eat	**como**	**com-a**	**com-an**
		k**o**ma	k**o**man
abrir to open	**abro**	**abr-a**	**abr-an**
		abra	**a**bran
venir to come	**vengo**	**ven-ga**	**ven-gan**
		b**e**nga	b**e**ngan

coma despacio
k**o**ma desp**a**s-yo
eat slowly

When you are telling someone not to do something, use the forms above and place **no** in front of the verb:

no me moleste, por favor
no meh mol**e**steh por fab**o**r
please don't disturb me

¡no beba alcohol!
no b**e**ba alk**o**l
don't drink alcohol!

¡no venga esta noche!
no b**e**nga **e**sta n**o**cheh
don't come tonight!

To give a command to people you would normally address as **tú** or **vos** remove the endings -ar, -er, and -ir from the verb and add these endings:

	tú		vos	
hablar to speak	**habl-a**	**a**bla	**habl-á**	abl**a**
comer to eat	**com-e**	k**o**meh	**com-é**	kom**eh**
abrir to open	**abr-e**	**a**breh	**abr-í**	abr**ee**

297

To form a negative imperative to people addressed as **tú** or **vos**, **no** is placed in front of the verb and the endings change:

	tú		vos	
habla	no habl-es	no ab-les	no habl-és	no ab-les
come	no com-as	no komas	no com-ás	no komas
abre	no abr-as	no abras	no abr-ás	no abras

por favor, no hables tan rápido (to one person)
por fabor no ab-les tan rapeedo
please don't speak so quickly

Pronouns are added to the end of the imperative form:

despiérteme a las ocho, por favor
desp-yairtemeh a las ocho por fabor
wake me up at eight o'clock, please

bébelo	**ciérralas**	**ayúdeme, por favor**
bebelo	s-yairralas	a-yoodemeh por fabor
drink it	close them	help me please

but when the imperative is negative, they are placed in front of it:

no lo bebas	**no las cierres**
no lo bebas	no las s-yair-res
don't drink it	don't close them

The imperatives of the verb **ir** 'to go' are irregular:

forms	usted	ustedes	tú	vos
	vaya	vayan	ve	ve
	ba-ya	ba-yan	beh	beh

Questions

Often the word order remains the same in a question, but the intonation changes, the voice rising at the end of the question:

¿quieres bailar?   ¿quieres ir al cine?
k-yair-es bīlar   k-yair-es eer al seeneh
do you want to dance?   do you want to go to the cinema?

Dates

Use the numbers on page 301 to express the date, the exception being for the first of the month:

el primero de septiembre [el preemairo deh sept-yembreh] the first of September
el dos de diciembre [dos deh dees-yembreh] the second of December
el treinta de mayo [traynta deh mī-yo] the thirtieth of May
el treinta y uno de mayo [traynti oono deh mī-yo] the thirty-first of May

Days

Sunday domingo
Monday lunes [loon-es]
Tuesday martes [mart-es]
Wednesday miércoles [m-yairkol-es]
Thursday jueves [Hweb-es]
Friday viernes [b-yairn-es]
Saturday sábado

Months

January enero [enairo]
February febrero [febrairo]
March marzo [marso]
April abril
May mayo [ma-yo]
June junio [Hoon-yo]
July julio [Hool-yo]

August agosto
September septiembre [sept-yembreh]
October octubre [oktoobreh]
November noviembre [nob-yembreh]
December diciembre [dees-yembreh]

Time

what time is it? ¿qué hora es? [keh ora]
one o'clock la una
two o'clock las dos
it's one o'clock es la una
it's two o'clock son las dos
it's ten o'clock son las diez [d-yes]
five past one la una y cinco [ee seenko]
ten past two las dos y diez
quarter past one la una y cuarto [ee kwarto]
quarter past two las dos y cuarto
half past ten las diez y media [d-yes ee med-ya]
twenty to ten veinte para las diez [baynteh]
quarter to ten cuarto para las diez
at eight o'clock a las ocho [ocho]
at half past four a las cuatro y media [kwatro ee med-ya]
2 a.m. las dos de la mañana [deh la man-yana]
2 p.m. las dos de la tarde [tardeh]
6 a.m. las seis de la mañana [seh-ees deh la man-yana]
6 p.m. las seis de la tarde
noon mediodía [med-yo-dee-a]
midnight medianoche [med-ya-nocheh]
an hour una hora [ora]
a minute un minuto
two minutes dos minutos
a second un segundo
a quarter of an hour un cuarto de hora [kwarto deh ora]
half an hour media hora [med-ya]
three quarters of an hour tres cuartos de hora [kwartos deh ora]

Numbers

0	cero	[**sai**ro]
1	**u**no, **u**na	
2	dos	
3	tres	
4	cuatro	[**kwa**tro]
5	cinco	[**seen**ko]
6	seis	[says]
7	siete	[s-**ye**teh]
8	ocho	[**o**cho]
9	nueve	[**nwe**beh]
10	diez	[d-yes]
11	once	[**on**seh]
12	doce	[**do**seh]
13	trece	[**tre**seh]
14	catorce	[ka**tor**seh]
15	quince	[**keen**seh]
16	dieciséis	[d-yesees**ays**]
17	diecisiete	[d-yesees-**ye**teh]
18	dieciocho	[d-yesee-**o**cho]
19	diecinueve	[d-yeseen**we**beh]
20	veinte	[**bayn**teh]
21	veintiuno	[bayntee-**oo**no]
22	veintidós	[baynteed**os**]
23	veintitrés	[bayntee**tres**]
30	treinta	[**trayn**ta]
31	treinta y uno	[**trayn**ta ee **oo**no]
40	cuarenta	[kwa**ren**ta]
50	cincuenta	[seen**kwen**ta]
60	sesenta	
70	setenta	
80	ochenta	[o**chen**ta]
90	noventa	[nob**en**ta]
100	cien	[s-yen]

120	ciento veinte [s-yento baynteh]
200	doscientos, doscientas [dos-yentos]
300	trescientos, trescientas [tres-yentos]
400	cuatrocientos, cuatrocientas [kwatros-yentos]
500	quinientos, quinientas [keen-yentos]
600	seiscientos, seiscientas [says-yentos]
700	setecientos, setecientas [setes-yentos]
800	ochocientos, ochocientas [ochos-yentos]
900	novecientos, novecientas [nobes-yentos]
1,000	mil
2,000	dos mil
5,000	cinco mil [seenko]
10,000	diez mil [d-yes]
1,000,000	un millón [meel-yon]

When **uno** is used with a masculine noun, the final -o is dropped:

un auto
oon **ow**to
a/one car

una is used with feminine nouns:

una bicicleta
oona beeseekleta
a/one bike

With multiples of a hundred, the **-as** ending is used with feminine nouns:

trescientos hombres	**quinientas mujeres**
tres-yentos **o**mb-res	keen-**y**entas mooHair-es
300 men	500 women

Ordinals

1st	primero	[preemairo]
2nd	segundo	
3rd	tercero	[tairsairo]
4th	cuarto	[kwarto]
5th	quinto	[keento]
6th	sexto	[sesto]
7th	séptimo	
8th	octavo	[oktabo]
9th	noveno	[nobeno]
10th	décimo	[deseemo]

Conversion Tables

1 centimetre = 0.39 inches

1 inch = 2.54 cm

1 metre = 39.37 inches = 1.09 yards

1 foot = 30.48 cm

1 kilometre = 0.62 miles = 5/8 mile

1 yard = 0.91 m

1 mile = 1.61 km

km	1	2	3	4	5	10	20	30	40	50	100
miles	0.6	1.2	1.9	2.5	3.1	6.2	12.4	18.6	24.8	31.0	62.1

miles	1	2	3	4	5	10	20	30	40	50	100
km	1.6	3.2	4.8	6.4	8.0	16.1	32.2	48.3	64.4	80.5	161

1 gram = 0.035 ounces   1 kilo = 1000 g = 2.2 pounds

g	100	250	500
oz	3.5	8.75	17.5

1 oz = 28.35 g

1 lb = 0.45 kg

kg	0.5	1	2	3	4	5	6	7	8	9	10
lb	1.1	2.2	4.4	6.6	8.8	11.0	13.2	15.4	17.6	19.8	22.0

kg	20	30	40	50	60	70	80	90	100
lb	44	66	88	110	132	154	176	198	220

lb	0.5	1	2	3	4	5	6	7	8	9	10	20
kg	0.2	0.5	0.9	1.4	1.8	2.3	2.7	3.2	3.6	4.1	4.5	9.0

1 litre = 1.75 UK pints / 2.13 US pints

1 UK pint = 0.57 l   1 UK gallon = 4.55 l
1 US pint = 0.47 l   1 US gallon = 3.79 l

centigrade / Celsius   °C = (°F - 32) x 5/9

°C	-5	0	5	10	15	18	20	25	30	36.8	38
°F	23	32	41	50	59	64	68	77	86	98.4	100.4

Fahrenheit   °F = (°C x 9/5) + 32

°F	23	32	40	50	60	65	70	80	85	98.4	101
°C	-5	0	4	10	16	18	21	27	29	36.8	38.3